Also by Sandor Frankel

BEYOND A REASONABLE DOUBT
THE ALEPH SOLUTION

Also by Robert S. Fink

TAX FRAUD: AUDITS, INVESTIGATIONS, PROSECUTIONS

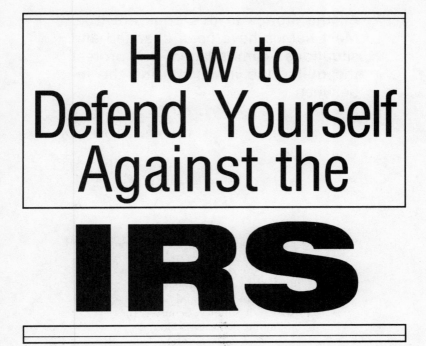

How to
Defend Yourself
Against the

IRS

SANDOR FRANKEL
and
ROBERT S. FINK

SIMON AND SCHUSTER
New York

All the stories in this book are true. Most names have been changed and situations camouflaged to protect the guilty, the innocent, and the in-between.

To Ruth, Jennifer, Annette, Michael, Mom, and Dad
S.F.

To Abby, Juliet, and Robin
R.S.F.

"Taxes are what we pay for civilized society."

—Justice Oliver Wendell Holmes, Jr.

"In this world nothing is certain but death and taxes."

—Benjamin Franklin

"I mow your lawn, hun'erd dollars a month. You pay cash, seven'y-five, know what I mean?"

—Tony, a gardener

"He that is without sin among you, let him first cast a stone at her."

—New Testament, John VIII, 7

CONTENTS

CHAPTER 1

Fail-safe Schemes That Failed—or, Gotcha!

AA, the Advertising Agency, was a dynamic young firm. Walter Main, its owner, president, sole stockholder, and creative genius, had been a Madison Avenue whiz kid with one of the large national agencies before deciding to make his own fortune. Within a few years, he developed his agency from a four-man operation to one of the hottest ad agencies in America.

Main adopted the expensive life-style of an advertising chief executive. He lived in a Park Avenue duplex, traveled by chauffeured limousine, and vacationed in all the "right" resorts.

As business began soaring, Main realized that Uncle Sam had become his partner; and Main figured that if Uncle shared his income, Uncle should share his expenses too.

He therefore began charging more and more of his daily living expenses to the business: trips to Europe and the Caribbean with his family, the annual winter rental of a lodge in Aspen, and a speedboat, which he had once used as a backdrop in a suntan lotion commercial.

On two prior audits, AA's deductions were fully allowed. This year, however, while conducting a routine audit, the revenue agent was struck by the extravagant life-style of Walter Main. The travel and entertainment expenses claimed by AA appeared to him to be extraordinary both in size and nature. The agent doubted the legitimacy or adequacy of much of the data offered by Main's accountant to support the deductions. Indeed, the agency did no business whatsoever in Aspen, and the accountant's rationale that Aspen was an ideal site for product testing and the scouting of shoot locations appeared thin. When asked for substantiation, Main was unable to produce anything but his company's checks; he could prove the money had been spent, but not that it had been spent for any business purpose.

Main finally asked his accountant to explain to the agent that Main had spent a week in Aspen soliciting the advertising business of his old friend Doug Springs, who owned a successful cosmetics firm, and that Main had business discussions with Springs and entertained Springs's entire family for a week to get the account.

But the revenue agent learned that Springs, who owned a condominium in Aspen and often vacationed there, had been out of the country that week. The agent concluded that the write-offs were phonies and the explanations were lies. He called in the Criminal Investigation Division.

WILLIAM SMITH owned a successful restaurant centrally located in midtown Manhattan. He had decided to retire and move to Florida, and advertised his business for sale. Among those answering the ad was John Trilling. He met Smith at the restaurant, and was given a brief tour of the premises.

At their second meeting, Trilling asked for, and Smith showed him, various corporate books and records, including cash receipts and disbursements ledgers, general corporate ledgers, and copies of the restaurant's federal income-tax returns covering the prior five years. After glancing through them, Trilling confided to Smith that he had a partner, and that they were really only interested in acquiring a business with a substantial cash flow susceptible to skimming—that is, siphoning unreported cash out of the business. Smith jokingly asked if Trilling was an IRS agent, and Trilling laughed in response. Smith winked at Trilling and told him not to worry, the restaurant took in a lot of cash.

At their next meeting, Trilling brought along his partner, Porter. Trilling explained that although he was very interested in the business, Porter had only come there reluctantly, as Porter doubted that the business could generate sufficient cash to make the purchase worthwhile. Trilling told Smith that he had been trying to convince Porter to the contrary, but without success, although Trilling emphasized to Smith that Trilling himself believed Smith's statements that large amounts of cash could be skimmed out of the business.

Smith turned to Porter and offered to prove it. He told Trilling and Porter to come with him, and drove them to his suburban home in Great Neck, Long Island. In his den, he opened the top drawer of a filing cabinet and removed a ledger showing dates and numbers covering fourteen years. Smith explained how the ledger reflected daily, monthly, and yearly totals of skimmed income.

Porter expressed doubt about the accuracy of the

ledger, stating that anyone could write up numbers. He requested documentation to corroborate the figures, and selected, at random, the month of April 1983 for a sample examination. Smith thereupon opened the closet door in the den and removed a collection of restaurant bills from one of numerous files on an upper shelf. He handed Porter a calculator and invited him to sit at the desk and satisfy himself as to the accuracy of the secret ledger. With Smith and Trilling watching, Porter reconciled precisely the figure for skimmed income reflected in the ledger for April 1983 with the skimmed bills for that month. Porter turned to Trilling and agreed to go through with the deal.

Before leaving the house, Trilling told Smith that he knew someone who might be interested in purchasing the house when Smith moved to Florida, and Smith walked Trilling and Porter through the house and expressed his thanks for Trilling's personal interest.

In fact, Trilling and Porter were IRS special agents assigned to BOP—the Business Opportunities Project—a special project of the IRS designed to uncover tax fraud by using IRS undercover agents to pose as prospective purchasers of businesses in industries suspected generally of being susceptible to skimming. After leaving Smith's home, the agents returned to their office at the IRS and drafted an affidavit in support of a search warrant for Smith's home. The law requires that a search warrant for a home particularize the place to be searched and the items to be seized. Trilling and Porter described the interior layout of Smith's home punctiliously, based on Smith's gracious tour. Their affidavit described in detail the business records reflecting the skimmed income, and the precise location of those records in Smith's home.

A few days later, Trilling knocked on the front door of Smith's home. When Mrs. Smith opened the door, Trilling, Porter, and seven other IRS agents barged into the house, displaying their badges and announcing they were there to execute a search warrant. They stayed for over an hour, and removed sixteen boxes containing Smith's records. Before leaving, Trilling handed Mrs. Smith an inventory summary for the items taken.

RALPH MEISEL, for reasons of his own, maintained a bank account in the Sterling Bank &Trust Company of the Bahamas. That country's "bank secrecy" laws severely restrict access to bank records, and have made Bahamian banks attractive depositories for people interested in hiding or laundering money which, for reasons of prudence, wisdom, or fear, they would just as soon keep secret. Meisel, an American citizen and taxpayer, was one of those people.

Wholly unrelated to Meisel in particular, the IRS, which has a more than passing interest in Americans using offshore tax havens, initiated Operation Trade Winds, an investigation designed to gather information about American citizens' financial activities in the Bahamas. A narcotics dealer had incautiously deposited a check drawn on the Sterling Bank into a U.S. bank account, and that deposit had focused Trade Winds' attention on Sterling Bank. Special Agent Jack Pickens of the Jacksonville, Florida, office of the IRS, who supervised Operation Trade Winds, conceived a novel idea for piercing the bank secrecy laws of the Bahamas.

Pickens asked an IRS informant named Meddle to obtain the names and addresses of individuals maintaining accounts in Sterling Bank. Meddle, a man of considerable initiative, knew a young lady of comparable intiative named Sybil. Meddle arranged for an introduction of Sybil to one Michael Crostenwol, who happened to be vice president and trust officer of Sterling Bank.

Pickens and Meddle learned that Crostenwol frequently traveled to the United States, carrying a locked briefcase containing bank documents. On one of Crostenwol's trips to the United States, he kept an appointment with Sybil by driving directly from the airport to her apartment. They left her apartment after a short while, and went to a restaurant on Key Biscayne. Because they planned to return to her apartment, Crostenwol did not bother taking his belongings to the restaurant.

Meddle, who had been hiding outside the apartment building, armed only with a key Sybil had given him, entered the apartment as soon as he saw Sybil and Crostenwol drive away, removed Crostenwol's briefcase, took it to a compliant locksmith who had been handsomely rewarded "up front," and photographed by microfilm camera over four hundred documents. The briefcase was relocked and back in Sybil's apartment before Sybil and Crostenwol had finished dessert. Meddle then delivered the microfilm to Special Agent Pickens.

Two weeks later, Pickens told Meddle he needed additional information concerning Sterling Bank's customers. This time, Sybil flew to the Bahamas and visited Crostenwol there. Because she had left her camera behind, she simply stole a Rolodex file from Crostenwol's office, and gave it to Pickens.

The IRS paid Meddle $8,000 in cash for his troubles. Meddle paid Sybil $1,000 for her help.

And one month later, Ralph Meisel received a letter from the IRS advising that four years' worth of his tax returns were being investigated.

AL ROBBINS owned a sporting-goods store in Los Angeles, employing a dozen salesmen and a full-time bookkeeper who had worked for him for over twenty years. He had long ago devised an intricate formula for diverting income. Different percentages of different types of merchandise would be kept "off the books": At the end of each day Robbins would tabulate on a calculator the number of dollars' worth of each category of merchandise to be diverted; remove from the collection of invoices on the bookkeeper's desk the appropriate number of invoices for each type of merchandise sold; remove the corresponding amount of cash from the wall safe in his office, where money was kept before being deposited into the company bank account; and toss each day's calculation into the wastebasket, leaving no record of the diversion. The bookkeeper would enter only the remaining invoices into the cash-receipts book. Thus the invoices and deposits always matched, and Robbins managed to accumulate a substantial amount of unreported cash.

In recent years, his bookkeeper had with increasing frequency demanded considerable raises. Robbins had at first obliged fully, then only partially. She then demanded weekly cash bonuses. Because such payments could not prudently be deducted as salary expenses, and because her salary and bonuses were already excessive, Robbins refused. The bookkeeper quit.

Soon afterward, Robbins received an unpleasant notice from the IRS. He soon learned that his faithful former bookkeeper had been accumulating for many years the daily cash calculations that Robbins had regularly tossed into the wastebasket. He eventually was indicted, but the prosecutors were unable to convince the jury that Robbins had made the calculations—as they were not handwritten —and the jury, after two days of deliberations, acquitted him.

LAURENCE THAYER was executive assistant to the president of High-Class Fashions, a well-known couturier recently acquired by a publicly held conglomerate based in Beverly Hills. His salary and stock options were by most standards substantial, but Thayer perceived no need to spend his own money on what he genteelly considered the "amenities," preferring more inventive sources.

Thayer hired Posh Decorators to decorate his apartment. He told Posh that (a) the apartment was a company apartment, (b) bills were therefore to be sent to Thayer's attention at High-Class Fashions, and (c) for "bookkeeping reasons" the bills should not particularize that the decorating services involved the company apartment. Posh saw no problem with those instructions, and sent a series of bills totaling over $50,000 to High-Class Fashions, all of which Thayer approved for payment.

On most evenings Thayer lived the high life, traveling by limousine charged to High-Class Fashions, dining, dancing, and socializing only in the most luxurious of milieus, always paying with the American Express card High-Class Fashions had provided him for business entertainment, and writing names of nonexistent "potential customers" on his retained copies of the chits. He visited nonexistent customers in various parts of the world, flying first-class and sleeping in only deluxe accommodations.

Thayer left High-Class Fashions for an even more lucrative executive position with a competitor. Two weeks after he left, Posh Decorators delivered the last touch to his apartment, a brass Stiffel lamp, and sent the bill for $600 to Thayer's attention at High-Class Fashions. The bill reached Thayer's successor for approval. He, a lover of good living, thought such a lamp would fit ideally in the office he had inherited, and tried to locate it. When he couldn't, he called Posh to find out who at High-Class Fashions had acknowledged receipt of the lamp.

That call led to discovery of Thayer's having decorated his home at the corporation's expense, and that discovery in turn led to a complete audit of all of Thayer's corporate expenses. When officials at the corporation added up the numbers and learned that Thayer had spent over $200,000 of corporate money to decorate his home and had charged personal expenses to the company, they decided, particularly since High-Class Fashions was publicly owned, that Thayer's transgressions required reporting to the district attorney's office. The DA began an investigation, and obtained copies of Thayer's income-tax returns for the years in question. High-Class Fashions' payments for Thayer's home decorations and personal entertainment were all taxable income to Thayer under both the California revenue laws and the Internal Revenue Code, but had not been reported on any of Thayer's returns. Thayer was now under investigation not only for stealing from High-Class Fashions, but also for income-tax evasion.

ALAN BOGEN owned a computer retail outlet and recorded most sales in his corporation's books and records. He gave thirty-day warranties on all sales. After expiration of the warranty, his charge for repairs was generally reasonable, but he instructed all customers making noncash payments for repairs to make their checks out to him personally rather than to his corporation. He deposited those checks directly into his personal account and never entered them in the corporation's records.

Writing such a check personally to Bogen struck one customer as odd: an accountant for whom the repair was a deductible expense and who did not want any question to be raised later about its deductibility because of a check made out to Bogen personally rather than to the computer store in its corporate name. The accountant protested, but Bogen insisted, and because the price was right the accountant acquiesced. But the repair was defective, and Bogen refused to refund the accountant's money. There was a shouting match; the accountant lost, left the store mad, and was determined to retaliate. When he remembered Bogen's insistence on getting a check made payable to himself personally, the accountant sent in a one-sentence squeal to the IRS.

BERNARD CASS was one of Chicago's most respected attorneys. Others in the profession considered him a lawyer's lawyer: The city's preeminent firms would turn to him for help and would refer substantial litigation matters to him for trial. His legal skills and integrity were above reproach. He was respected as an honored and giving member of the community.

In both his legal practice and his personal life, Cass was financially conservative. His bookkeeper was under strict instructions to keep meticulous records of all of his business and professional affairs. His legal practice, while extremely lucrative, was financially simple and apparently upright. On those occasions when clients offered to pay their fees in cash, Cass would accept only on the condition that the client and he sign a letter of agreement stating the amount of the cash and the client's awareness that Cass would be depositing the money into his business account and would be reporting it as income. Cass maintained only one regular business checking account. His bookkeeper was instructed to deposit all receipts into that account, except for money delivered to him to hold in trust.

Each of Cass's business expenses was also properly recorded and fully documented. Cass followed a simple rule in categorizing his expenses as either business-related or personal: When in doubt, call it personal and don't deduct it. In the long run, it would be cheaper not to have to worry about fighting the IRS. Thus, although others in the profession were deducting country-club dues and the like as business expenses, Cass never did.

That financial conservatism saved Cass a good deal of aggravation. Every three years, he was routinely audited by the IRS for his three prior years' federal income-tax returns. All of his books, records, and financial information would be thoroughly reviewed, and each audit resulted in a "no change" letter being issued by the IRS. That is, until the audit of his 1983 return.

During the audit of that return, the agent asked to see not only Cass's business account but also his escrow account. An "escrow account" is a type of bank account maintained by most lawyers, into which is deposited money that is not income to the lawyer but rather is being held for some fiduciary purpose, later to be disbursed after certain conditions are met. For example, where an attorney has a contingent-fee agreement with a client, the lawyer deposits the gross amount of recovery into his escrow account, out of which he then disburses the client's share to the client and his fee share into his own business account. Cass's escrow account during 1983 contained, on an average day, nearly half a million dollars. Cass assured the agent that all this money belonged to clients or was being held by Cass in escrow for various fiduciary purposes.

Despite these assurances, the agent decided to specifically audit each deposit made into the escrow account during 1983; he then went back to prior years. He learned that most of the money had simply sat in that account, after deposit, for long periods of time. Then he discovered that much of the money in fact represented unreported income to Cass. On many of his sizable contingent-fee cases, Cass had deposited the total recovery into his escrow account, disbursed the client's portion to the client, and simply left his own portion in the escrow account, dormant, without transferring it into his business account. Thus, over the past several years Cass had kept off the books several hundred thousand dollars of income by the simple device of leaving his share of recovery proceeds in his escrow account, without transferring the money into his business account.

The agent referred the matter to the Criminal Investigation Division. Cass was later indicted, but ultimately was acquitted by a jury that bought his testimony that he had only committed an oversight.

GEORGE HERMANN was a manufacturer of electrical appliances. His major customer was a national department-store chain that retailed his appliances under a store-brand label.

Michael Fosterman was the department store's national purchasing agent for electrical goods. The chain's annual sales of such goods totaled millions of dollars. A hefty percentage of those sales—several million dollars per year —were Hermann's appliances. The chain's markup for retail sales averaged approximately 100 percent.

Hermann had the best product for price available on the market. However, it was not merely because of their quality that Fosterman purchased Hermann's electrical appliances. Fosterman played golf with Hermann every few months, and in the middle of the fairway Hermann would drop into Fosterman's golf bag an envelope containing cash equal to exactly 7 percent of the chain's purchases from Hermann since their last golf outing. Fosterman never reported those payments to either his employer or the IRS.

Under the Internal Revenue Code, commissions or pay-offs such as these are not allowable deductions to the payer because they violate various laws, including state commercial-bribery laws. Nevertheless, Hermann wanted and needed some tax benefit to help underwrite these substantial payments that he was making. He therefore entered into an arrangement with his own supplier who supplied him with most of the parts he used to manufacture the electrical appliances.

Hermann explained to his supplier that he needed to generate cash for unspecified cash purchases. He requested his supplier to deliver fictitious invoices to him in various specified amounts for nonexistent parts, which Hermann had never ordered, along with the legitimate invoices for parts actually delivered. Hermann paid his supplier by check for all of the invoices sent, legitimate and fictitious. His supplier maintained an out-of-state bank account in the name of a nonexistent "business." The supplier deposited Hermann's checks for the fictitious invoices into that account, and withdrew 90 percent of that amount in cash, which he delivered to Hermann periodically in envelopes at a different golf game, keeping 10 percent for his troubles. The supplier did not bother reporting that 10 percent on his income-tax returns.

Everyone was happy. The supplier retained Hermann as a customer, as well as 10 percent of the amounts on the fictitious invoices. Hermann generated sufficient cash to pay Fosterman and keep the department store's account. The fictitious invoices were falsely entered as "purchases" in Hermann's books of account, and Hermann thereby managed to deduct on his tax returns the full amount of the payoffs to Fosterman plus the 10 percent cost of the transaction. Fosterman received substantial cash payoffs, unbeknownst to both his employer and the IRS. Pictorially, their satisfaction looked like this:

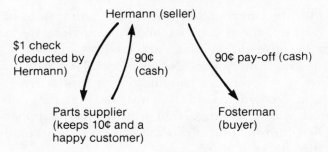

Hermann (seller)

$1 check
(deducted by
Hermann)

90¢
(cash)

90¢ pay-off (cash)

Parts supplier
(keeps 10¢ and a
happy customer)

Fosterman
(buyer)

Transactions such as these are not unique and are subject to unraveling from unexpected loose ends. A completely unrelated department store discovered that one of its purchasing agents was taking kickbacks. His firing was reported by the press, read by the IRS, and resulted in a criminal investigation of that purchasing agent. When the investigative thumbscrews began to tighten, he named the manufacturer who had paid him kickbacks, and that manufacturer, when he in turn felt the pressure, named an obliging supplier of phony invoices. That was Hermann's supplier, who had other customers he had to please besides Hermann. The investigation of the supplier uncovered the existence of his out-of-state bank account. The IRS agents easily obtained, from the bank, microfilms of all checks deposited into that account. Among them were Hermann's. Soon, Hermann's golf games with his supplier stopped, and Hermann was under investigation. When Hermann surrendered to the Service, Michael Fosterman also started looking for a new golfing partner.

LARRY DREW published a small newspaper. He purchased supplies from numerous vendors, and decided that one more vendor wouldn't be noticed. So he invented a fictitious paper-manufacturing company called The Paper

Mill, printed up invoices for that name, and periodically issued those invoices to himself. He paid those invoices by his own company's checks made payable to The Paper Mill, and cashed those checks at a check-cashing service that charged 10 percent and returned 90 percent to Drew in cash. It was well worth the fee: For every $10,000 in checks Drew issued to The Paper Mill, he received a $10,000 deduction—which in his tax bracket saved over $5,000 in after-tax dollars—at a cost of only $1,000, for a net profit of over $4,000.

Then, for reasons wholly unrelated to Drew, the check-cashing service was audited, and its own problems resulted in a full-scale investigation. All federally insured banks are required to retain records, by microfilm or otherwise, of all checks presented for payment. The various banks used by the check-cashing service provided the IRS with thousands of checks, including those drawn by Drew to The Printing Mill. When IRS agents discovered that The Printing Mill did not exist, it did not take long for them to knock on Larry Drew's door.

CECIL DOAKS was chief executive officer of a toy-manufacturing company, in the 50-percent tax bracket, and believed that charity begins at home. Since every dollar's deduction that he could find would save him fifty cents in taxes, he concluded that the business of manufacturing deductions would ideally complement his substantial income.

Doaks generally contributed to about twenty different charities each year. How he sought to maximize his own profit from these contributions is best shown by example. The Boys Club of America was generally the beneficiary of $100 per year of Doaks's largesse. Doaks would contribute that amount by a check written this way:

The canceled check would, of course, be returned to Doaks after deposit by the Boys Club, along with Doaks's monthly bank statement. After receiving the check, Doaks would make two slight alterations:

Doaks believed his scheme was foolproof since he would always alter the check immediately upon clearance, using the same pen with which he had originally written the check, and nothing on the face of the check itself would attract attention.

Doaks's return was never selected for full audit. In some years, however, he received nondescript form requests for substantiation of particular items, and never had any problems with them—until one year when he received the

same type of form request for substantiation of his charitable contributions. He simply photostatted his canceled
checks, which by then bore his alterations, and returned
them to the IRS in the convenient self-addressed
envelope.

Within a few months, Doaks was advised that he was
under investigation by the Criminal Investigation Division
of the IRS. He soon learned that when a check is negoti-
ated through a bank, the bank's computer enters a number in the lower right-hand corner of the check, precisely
reflecting the actual amount of the check when it is presented for clearance. Take another look at the lower right-
hand corner of the altered check; when Doaks did, he was
already too late.

JAMES MORRIS was an entrepreneur who, starting with
nothing, became a real-estate syndicator packaging transactions involving millions of dollars. He ran his business
skillfully and with substantial profits. A considerable portion of his personal net worth, however, resulted from the
fact that he did not file tax returns.

When one of Morris's syndications developed problems,
he commenced a multimillion-dollar litigation against a
partner and pursued it vigorously. In civil litigation, each
party has the right to demand production by the other of
documents relevant to the issues. Morris's adversary coun-
terclaimed and defended by alleging that Morris had improperly siphoned money out of the partnership for two
years, and demanded production of Morris's retained copies of his own income-tax returns for those years. Morris's
claims of irrelevance were rejected by the court, on the
ground that Morris might have disclosed on his returns
the receipt of the sums of money alleged by the defendant,
and production was ordered.

Morris's alternatives at that point were to (a) refuse to

comply, (b) drop the litigation (extracting as a condition the defendant's dropping of the counterclaims), or (c) acknowledge that he had not filed the returns in question. If he refused to comply with the court's order, his case would be dismissed. If he dropped the case himself, he would never recover the substantial damages he sought. If he acknowledged his failure to file the returns, he would be able to continue prosecuting his case, since courts do not require production of nonexistent documents, but he would be providing his adversary with information that, although not relevant to the litigation, could be extremely dangerous.

Morris weighed the alternatives, and concluded that too much money was at stake in the litigation to drop the case. He therefore instructed his attorney to file a "Response to Demand for Production" stating that Morris had not filed tax returns for the years at issue.

Morris's opponent figured that Morris would less vigorously prosecute the case if he was preoccupied with more pressing legal problems, and anonymously forwarded a copy of Morris's "Response to Demand for Production" to the IRS.

All of the stories you have just read are true. Moreover, they are typical. In each instance, the taxpayer believed he would not be caught, or that the odds of getting caught were one in a million. In fact, civil-tax examinations and criminal-tax investigations are generated in many different ways, and each of these taxpayers created a time bomb that exploded in just one of those ways.

But don't think we live in a just world where the guilty are punished while the innocent inherit the wealth. Tax-fraud defense attorneys see many schemes that have worked—so far. Like:

¶**STEVEN LUKAS** owned a fast-food shop. Before locking up every evening, alone, he removed nearly 20 percent of the cash in the register and hid that money in his home. After it began accumulating, he was often tempted to spend the cash and spoil himself: on a new house, a fancy car, diamonds for his wife, or the like. But Steven was cautious by nature and resisted large and luxurious purchases. He was content to spend the siphoned fruits of his labor on moderate day-to-day expenditures: a stylish wardrobe, meals in the city's finer restaurants, and a generally higher—but not knock-your-eyes-out—life-style. While far from modest, Steven's expenditures have never been traced, and he lives quite well, thank you.

¶**NORMAN BELL,** a Florida orange grower, made unreported cash sales of over $50,000 annually to a long-standing and trusted customer. That amounted, of course, to hundreds of thousands of dollars in cash over a period of years. Bell's problem, like that of most taxpayers who accumulate large sums of unreported cash, was how to make use of the cash without exposing his past evasions and causing his own financial house of cards to collapse. He needed a way to launder the money—that is, to allow it to visibly surface—with a credible explanation of how it suddenly appeared. Bell found a way. Through a friend, he learned that the Miami branch of a Latin American bank would lend him money if he brought collateral to one of the bank's European branches. So Bell took a short vacation in Europe, carrying an attaché case stuffed with currency, and deposited $200,000 as collateral in the European bank. When he returned to America, the Miami branch loaned him $200,000: Bell signed the required documentation, and a bank officer handed him a $200,000 check. He deposited the check into his regular business account, and recorded it as a loan in his company's books and records. Thus, $200,000 in dirty money had been laundered through a fully documented bank loan, and Bell was free to use the money.

¶STANLEY BURROUGHS, a fabric manufacturer for more than twenty years, had a simple scheme for evading his tax obligations. In a manufacturing, merchandising, or mining business, a taxpayer's gross income is computed by deducting the taxpayer's cost of goods sold from his total receipts. The cost of goods sold is determined by adding to the inventory on hand at the beginning of the year the cost of all purchases and production during the year, and subtracting from that figure the inventory on hand at the end of the year.* As an accounting matter, larger "closing inventory" means lower cost of goods sold, which in turn

---

* This method of computing gross profit is illustrated by the following chart:

Gross Receipts		$100,000.
less		
Cost of Goods Sold		
Inventory available at beginning of year (opening inventory)	$25,000.	
Purchases and/or production during year	+ 50,000.	
Other costs directly related to purchase or production	+ 10,000.	
Cost of available merchandise	$85,000.	
Inventory available at end of year (closing inventory)	− $30,000.	
Cost of Goods Sold		$ 55,000.
Gross Profit on Sales		$ 45,000.

As this example shows, increasing the closing inventory decreases the cost of goods sold. If you decrease the closing inventory from $30,000 to $20,000, you increase your cost of goods sold from $55,000 to $65,000 and thereby reduce your gross profit from $45,000 to $35,000.

means higher profits. Conversely, lower profits result from lower closing inventory. Stanley knew this. Accordingly, every year, when Stanley's accountants began preparing his corporation's income-tax return, Stanley would provide them with a convenient closing-inventory figure. He would tell them that the figure had been determined by taking a physical inventory of merchandise actually on hand in his warehouse, and that he himself had actually counted the goods. The accountants accepted Stanley's figure and prepared the return. Being an old-timer in the industry, Stanley had a pretty good idea of the correct inventory figure. However, he never actually took a physical inventory, but would arrive at the inventory figure on his tax return only after deciding how much in taxes he wished to pay. For example, if Stanley decided to show a gross profit of $30,000 less than the true figure, he would merely tell his accountants that his year-end inventory was $30,000 less than the true figure. Of course, this practice had a mushrooming effect, because as he undervalued his closing inventory each year, the difference between the inventory on his books and the actual inventory on hand continued to grow. But the problem never bothered him, and for twenty years no one ever noticed.

¶NICK STAROS was a dynamic forty-five-year-old entrepreneur who walked away from a promising career with a public company to build something of his own. People could never quite define precisely what Nick did for a living, except that he was a deal maker, forming real-estate syndications, obtaining financing for cash-hungry companies in exchange for stock, and generally trying to get a piece of various ventures. In one way or another, Nick spent most of his working hours dreaming up schemes. Since practically everything he did was work-related, Nick felt that practically all his expenditures were deductible, and he therefore deducted most of his life: his limousine, New York and California apartments, and food and entertainment costs both at home and while traveling. During the course of a routine audit a revenue agent challenged most of these expenses because of their size and nature, but Nick was able to relate each expense to a specific business project. Although the agent was skeptical, Nick had kept detailed and accurate records that at least attempted to justify every expense, and he never gave the agent a false document or made a provably false statement. As a result, although nearly 30 percent of Nick's deductions were ultimately disallowed, no penalty, civil or criminal, was ever asserted against him.

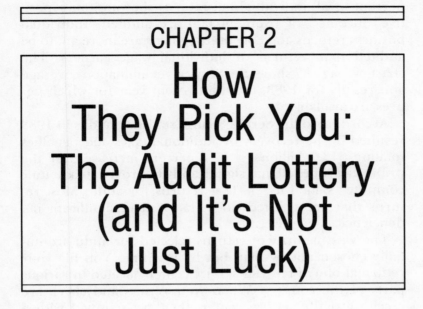

CHAPTER 2

How They Pick You: The Audit Lottery (and It's Not Just Luck)

Computer Selection and How It Works

What are your odds in the audit lottery?

The IRS estimates that taxpayers underreport their income by a total of about $90 billion each year, and that another $3 billion in tax revenues is lost because of people who simply don't file tax returns. Despite this, only a minuscule percentage of tax returns is ever audited. Over 100 million federal tax returns are filed each year. Over 95 million of those are individual income tax returns. Only 1½ percent of all individual tax returns are audited—and many of those are not detailed audits. So the overall odds of your being audited are minimal.

But these statistics are misleading. As a statistical matter, larger income means greater likelihood of audit. Nearly 5 percent of all individual tax returns showing total "positive" income* of over $50,000 are audited. Individual business returns and corporate returns are more apt to be audited than returns of individual wage earners. The chart on page 37 shows the Service's examination coverage and results for 1983, the most recent year for which figures are available.

According to the Service's latest statistics, audits in 1983 resulted in the recovery of additional taxes and penalties totaling $13.7 billion—a 17.1 percent increase over the prior year. The IRS has significantly improved its scientific computer skills for selecting returns for audit. Most returns that are selected do in fact reflect significant tax deficiencies.

The vast majority of returns selected for audit are initially chosen not by man but by machine. You file your return at one of ten IRS service centers located in various parts of the country. When your return and check are received at the service center, they are stamped with a "document locater number," which permits the IRS to identify and locate a specific document. The number, which is unintelligible to you, has meaning to the computer. For example, a canceled check bearing the number 34 11 41 333 001 34 indicates the following: 34 is the district office code for the Cleveland district, 11 is the tax class, 41 is the document code for Form 941, 333 indicates that on the 333rd day of the year the remittance received was deposited, 001 is the block number of the document

---

* "Positive" income is computed by disregarding negative components in your year's financial affairs, such as deductions and tax shelters. Until late 1980, returns were classified according to their adjusted gross income rather than their total positive income. However, that system grouped a $20,000 wage earner with a $200,000 wage earner who had invested in a tax shelter yielding a $180,000 loss. The total positive income system disregards the negative components within the adjusted gross income figure. In the above example, the TPI system will group the $200,000 wage earner with like-size wage earners despite the existence of the $180,000 deductible loss, thus giving him a higher audit profile.

IRS Examination Coverage and Results

	Percent coverage	Average additional tax and penalty per return audited		No-change percent	
		Field audits	Office audits	Field audits	Office audits
Individuals					
Total Positive Income					
$10,000—under $25,000, standard deductions	.64%	$ 3,835	$ 655	11%	20%
$10,000—under $25,000, itemized deductions	2.15	3,821	652	11	15
$25,000—under $50,000	2.61	3,582	758	10	19
$50,000 and over	4.93	14,871	2,822	8	25
Schedule C—Total Gross Receipts					
Under $25,000	1.63	6,144	1,057	12	18
$25,000—under $100,000	3.28	7,462	1,758	10	19
$100,000 and over	6.12	14,930	3,177	13	23
Corporations					
Under $100,000 (balance sheet assets)	1.96	2,481	—	24	—
$100,000—under $1 mil	3.45	5,808	—	22	—
$1 mil—under $10 mil	9.90	24,249	—	15	—
$10 mil—under $100 mil	22.47	79,096	—	9	—
$100 mil and over	57.83	1,609,472	—	3	—
Small business corporations	1.31	10,097	—	32	—

for the date in question, and 34 is the serial number of the specific document-locater number.

Each service center has a Returns Analysis Branch. This consists of real people who look at each return and check it for completeness: to make sure it is signed, that all required schedules and forms have been submitted, and that the enclosed check matches the return. The returns then are sorted into broad categories: individual returns, corporate returns, et cetera.

The information on each return is then fed into a computer, which checks the return for mathematical and clerical errors. The computer highlights such things as mistakes in arithmetic, use of the wrong tax table, inconsistent information on the return, and deductions or credits that exceed the maximum allowable amounts. If your return contains such an error, you receive a written notice to that effect. But that notice does not mean that's all you have to worry about, as the computer's review for technical correctness is only the first computerized taste of your return.

The information on your return is then placed on magnetic tape for further computer processing. All returns and tapes are then sent to the IRS's National Computer Center in Martinsburg, West Virginia. There, the tax-return information is scrutinized by another computer in order to identify those returns with statistically high error potential.

The IRS's computer selection program is called the Discriminate Function System (in bureaucratese, DIF). Over 80 percent of all individual income-tax returns selected for audit are initially chosen by this computer selection program. The goal of this system is to identify those tax returns with a high possibility of either unreported income or improper deductions, based on certain return information and statistically determined relationships.

The complex selection formula used by the Service to select returns for audit potential is its best-kept secret. Several years ago, a couple expended large sums of money and dedicated tremendous time and effort to bringing a federal lawsuit against the United States Government, demanding the release of the Service's computer formulas, pursuant to a statute called the Freedom of Information Act, which gives citizens access to a broad spectrum of the government's records. To the surprise of everyone involved, Goliath appeared to be toppled. The court ruled in favor of the taxpayers and, despite appeals by the government all the way to the Supreme Court of the United States, the courts refused to stop the ordered release of the computer selection information.

Undaunted, the IRS turned its back on the courts and ran to Congress for relief. Congress promptly complied by enacting a statute that specifically exempts the IRS's computer selection formulas from discovery under the Freedom of Information Act.

Although the secrecy of the IRS's computer formula has therefore been hermetically protected, certain valuable statistical information is available to you from the IRS. You can use this information to compare various deductions on your own return with the figures the IRS computes as average, to see whether your deductions are out of line. For example, the IRS has computed that for 1983 (the last year for which the IRS has compiled data), the average taxpayer whose adjusted gross income was between $25,000 and $30,000 reported medical and dental expenses of $1,387, charitable contributions of $797, interest expenses of $3,298, and taxes of $2,195. Comparable figures are also available for taxpayers in higher brackets. Here's what the IRS has computed to be the average amounts of deductions by various taxpayers in various brackets:

Adjusted Gross Income ($1,000s)	Medical and Dental	Taxes	Contributions	Interest
20–25	$ 1,544	$ 1,791	$ 734	$ 3,016
25–30	1,387	2,195	797	3,298
30–40	1,405	2,690	900	3,778
40–50	1,872	3,437	1,113	4,679
50–75	2,741	4,711	1,553	6,259
75–100	5,900	6,833	2,697	9,187
100–200	8,544	10,580	4,860	13,375
200–500	19,696	21,057	12,382	21,192
500–1,000	25,966	47,151	34,055	43,185
Over 1,000	44,957	141,821	128,573	100,395

The above statistics, although useful, do not reflect the complexity of the IRS's computer selection formulas. The fact that your deductions fall within these statistical averages is no guarantee that your return won't trigger a high computer score and therefore be audited, but the odds of an audit increase if your deductions substantially exceed these norms.

The IRS's computer formulas are continually developed and periodically updated on the basis of the latest taxpayer filing and reporting characteristics. The IRS develops those characteristics through a program called the Taxpayer Compliance Measurement Program (TCMP). This program involves the random selection of taxpayers for audit through social security numbers. These audits, which like most audits seek to uncover unreported income and improper deductions, are more detailed and intensive than routine audits, since they are the basis for the IRS's more sharply developing and refining its computer formulas.

The IRS's computers are programmed to classify returns by assigning "weights" to approximately 200 to 300 basic return characteristics. Those weighted variables are then added together to obtain a composite score for each return processed. That score is used to rank the returns in numerical sequence. Statistics have taught the IRS that the higher the score, the greater the possibility of a significant tax change on audit.

Returns selected by the DIF system are forwarded by the service center to the local district offices of the IRS, but not necessarily for audit. At this point, man replaces machine. The local offices receive far more computer-selected returns than they can handle. A manual classification section in the district office makes a further examination of these DIF-selected returns in order to determine which of them are most deserving of audit, and to determine the type and intensity of audit warranted.

At this point the entire return is scrutinized, including the specific item or items that created the high DIF score. In some instances, a high-scoring DIF item may actually have a low audit potential when screened by either an agent or supervisor. For example, the computer may have selected your return because of its unusually high charitable deductions, but the computer is oblivious to supporting documentation that may be attached to the return and which, upon review, may satisfy the screener.

The DIF system is not the computers' only way of catching you. The IRS's computers also match tax returns with various forms, such as W2s, 1099s, and 1087s. Every year, the IRS's computer-matching program discovers hundreds of thousands of discrepancies between such forms and tax returns, and nonfilings of returns. For example, in the Brookhaven Service Center alone (covering New York City, its suburban counties, and New Jersey), the matching program in 1981 generated approximately 495,000 cases, which in turn resulted in 263,000 notices to taxpayers, 32,000 audit referrals, and 1,200 criminal-investigation referrals.

What Returns Are Automatically Picked for a Closer Look?

Certain returns are automatically selected for review by human eyes no matter what the computer says: individual returns showing total positive income of $50,000 or more, corporate returns reporting assets of $1,000,000 or more or total gross receipts of $100,000 or more, partnership returns showing gross receipts or gross income of $500,000 or more, and fiduciary returns showing gross income of $50,000 or more. All of these are sent to the district offices for screening by tax examiners for possible audit selection.

Other types of returns are also automatically reviewed by real people. Amended returns, returns with net operating losses, returns calling for large refunds, returns reflecting foreign business transactions, information returns of foreign corporations controlled by the taxpayer, and returns containing questionable items of substantial amounts (such as returns containing deductions that appear to flow from a tax-shelter investment) are screened manually at the service center for a particularized determination of whether they should be sent to the district office's examination division.

A small number of large-dollar returns are automatically audited under the Coordinated Examination Program (CEP), often called the "large-case program." This program includes all utilities and financial institutions with gross assets exceeding $1,000,000,000 and all other corporations with gross assets of at least $250,000,000. About 1,300 corporations are in this program, and each is audited annually. Each CEP examination has a tax manager and an audit team consisting of revenue agents and technical specialists. CEP audits also involve a review of the individual returns of all key corporate officers to determine whether or not the officers' returns should be audited.

You Can Reduce Your Odds of Being Audited—Here's What the IRS Looks For

A multitude of old wives' tales have suggested ways to reduce your risk of getting audited; many have found their way into published tax-help guides. Most of these are simply false or useless, and as successful as "systems" for winning at dice.

For example, you may have been advised that you will reduce your risk of being audited by typing your return or having it computer-printed instead of handwriting it, to create the appearance of its having been professionally prepared. There is no substance to such advice. There are also two widely held theories about when to file your return: File it on April 15 to get yours buried among tens of millions of others, or get extensions and file it as late as legally possible because by then the IRS has already scheduled, budgeted, and fulfilled its audit requirements. Take your pick of these theories.

In fact, the IRS recently has declassified important gold nuggets revealing how returns preliminarily selected by IRS computers or screeners are ultimately chosen for audit. These secrets are contained in the IRS's Classification Handbook. Until recently, this handbook was printed only in a highly classified government document—the "LEM," the Law Enforcement Manual of the United States Government. Access to a LEM requires special government clearance.

On October 29, 1984, the IRS's Classification Handbook was reclassified from its highly secret LEM status to permit publication in the IRS's own Internal Revenue Manual—the Service's internal soup-to-nuts guide for how-to-do-everything, containing tens of thousands of bureaucratic small-print pages. The secrets of the Classification Handbook are now buried in this morass.

This Classification Handbook is the only authoritative statement of how returns are ultimately picked for audit. Now, if you want to see the most useful portions of the Classification Handbook—the IRS's instructions to its own reviewers telling them what returns to pick for audit—just take a look at pages 259–276 in the Appendix.

Some Things Will Get You Audited— No Matter What

Your audit history can affect the selection for audit of your later returns. A prior failure to keep adequate records, or indications of an intent to cheat on a prior return, are entered into the IRS's computers and will result in the identification of that taxpayer's future returns for audit.

The IRS has not yet developed sufficient statistical data to permit computerized audit selection of all types of returns. Gift, estate, and fiduciary returns are manually selected for audit. Such returns are individually reviewed and selected on the basis of historical experience and limited studies indicating audit potential.

Currently, the IRS is emphasizing the audit of partnership returns and applies a DIF system to such returns. Partnerships that provide tax shelters are being particularly scrutinized. The IRS has announced its intention to audit all abusive tax shelters, and to that end has recently developed a coordinated Tax Shelter Program. The venom of the IRS's campaign against abusive tax shelters was expressed by the Commissioner of Internal Revenue, Roscoe L. Egger, Jr., during an interview in February 1985: "We have pounded hard on the stake, we want to drive it into the vampire's heart."

Examiners with tax-shelter experience analyze all returns reporting shelter-type losses to determine on a return-by-return basis whether each such return should be included in the Tax Shelter Program. These examiners consider the following criteria: (1) a large net loss, (2) low gross income, (3) large amount of investment credit, (4) first-year return (especially of an entity formed late in the year, when large-income taxpayers hunt frantically for deductions), (5) final return, (6) a nonoperating entity, (7) a passive investor, (8) affirmative answers (or omitted answers) to questions asking whether losses are obtainable in amounts greater than the amount that the taxpayer actually has "at risk" (except in real-estate ventures, where losses over amounts "at risk" are permitted), (9) an activity is engaged in in an identified tax-shelter area, and (10) various technical criteria. If a return contains these tax-shelter features, the chance that the return will be pulled for an audit of at least the shelter items is statistically very high.

Audits frequently grow out of other audits. For example, a stockholder will have his individual tax return audited if disallowances resulted from an audit of his closely held corporation's return. Similarly, the audit of an estate tax return showing deductions for executor's commissions or attorney's fees may result in a related audit of the executor or attorney to ensure that such fees were reported as income.

The audit of a business that shows substantial cash deductions often generates a related audit of the recipient of the cash, to determine whether the recipient included those sums in his taxable income. That's what happened to Mark Grant, a New York City cardiologist with a fine Park Avenue practice.

Dr. Grant was respected and loved by his patients, to whom he showed complete dedication. He was one of the old-time breed who did not spend Wednesdays on the golf course and who seemed more concerned with the practice of medicine than with earning medical fees.

Although he employed a receptionist, a nurse, and a bookkeeper, Dr. Grant himself kept careful control over the daily receipts. He would take all checks and cash from his receptionist at day's end. The following morning he would deposit all of those checks, but only small amounts of cash, into a business account; he simply took most of the cash home and kept it in a locked desk drawer, never reporting it on his tax returns. He used the cash for extravagant dinners, vacations, and other luxury items.

All went well for Dr. Grant until a patient of his, Michael Josephson, was audited in connection with a large medical deduction. Josephson was in a cash business and paid for many of his expenses in cash. He explained to the revenue agent examining his return that he had paid Dr. Grant $2,000 in cash in connection with a serious coronary illness. Although Josephson had no proof evidencing that payment of cash, he proved to the agent that (a) he had been hospitalized for his illness, (b) Dr. Grant was his physician, and (c) there existed no check in payment of any medical fees to Dr. Grant. The agent thought that a civil audit of Dr. Grant would be in order for the year being covered in Josephson's audit.

During the course of the doctor's ensuing audit, the revenue agent discovered that Dr. Grant had not made any large deposit of cash anywhere around the time when Josephson had allegedly paid the $2,000 medical fee—or at any other time. The agent did see two checks in substantial amounts representing semiannual payments made by Dr. Grant to an insurance company on a home-owner's policy. When the agent asked for a copy of that policy, he saw that numerous items of jewelry and an expensive fur coat were claimed by Dr. Grant to have been purchased in the year under audit; yet Dr. Grant had no checks for the purchase of any such items, and he had no credit cards or charge accounts to account for their purchase. It was most unlikely that the doctor had chosen to pay insurance premiums on nonexistent highly priced merchandise, so he must have bought them. And if not with checks or on credit, then with cash. The agent considered that to be enough evidence of possible fraud to warrant a criminal tax investigation, and special agents of the Criminal Investigation Division were brought into the case.

Audits are also generated through special audit occupational projects. In recent years, such different callings as tax-return preparers, casino dealers, self-ordained ministers, waiters and waitresses, and private-duty nurses have been specially selected as occupational targets. And many of these targets are quite surprised when the bullet hits:

Nadine was born and raised in Trinidad. The nuns at her parochial school realized she was a gifted child. Although Nadine's family could not afford to send her to high school, the parish assisted the family and Nadine received her high school degree and, ultimately, a college degree in nursing.

After she married and had two children, Nadine continued to work long shifts at an island hospital. But she wanted to give her children opportunities unavailable in Trinidad, and so she emigrated to the United States. Here, she obtained her labor certificate and worked in a leading New York City hospital. She was eventually able to bring her husband and two children to the States. The family was proud of their adopted country and became exemplary citizens.

In order to earn more money, Nadine gave up her regular nursing duties and became a private-duty nurse at the hospital where she had formerly worked. She undertook the most difficult tasks, working twelve-hour shifts for postoperative and critically ill patients.

Although Nadine's husband also worked, the family had

increasing difficulty making ends meet. In addition to her two children, whose needs increased with age, Nadine took responsibility for the son of a friend whose marriage had fallen apart and who had become unable to care either for herself or her seven-year-old boy. Nadine, as always, was prepared to help, and took her friend's son into her home as though he were hers.

Nadine was paid directly by the families of the hospitalized patients, rather than by the hospital, very often in cash. She spent the cash on her substantial day-to-day living expenses. The costs of life were such that as soon as she was paid, the money was spent on food, clothing, and other basic living expenses—nothing extravagant. When April tax-time came, Nadine rarely had money left. Her tax returns were prepared by a local small-time accountant, and when he asked what her gross income was, she estimated it to be about $6,000 per year.

That estimate was incorrect. In fact, Nadine was earning three times that amount. Certainly not a sum large enough to interest the IRS, one might think.

The IRS received information that private-duty nurses were underreporting their income, and so a special short-term project was established by the Service to audit a high percentage of private-duty nurses and create sufficient publicity in order to ensure future compliance. Nadine's return was chosen for audit. The Service was aware that although the hospitals did not employ or pay private-duty nurses, they arranged for their employment and maintained a registry of assignments. Through that registry, the Service was able to establish the number of days Nadine worked and the amount she was paid each day.

The Service wanted publicity. Nadine was indicted for tax evasion.

In addition to special occupational projects such as the one which ensnared Nadine, the IRS has a Return Preparers Program through which it seeks, by routine audits or by undercover work, to identify unethical tax-return preparers. All preparers are required to maintain lists of the clients whose returns they have prepared or copies of the returns themselves. Once the Service has identified an unscrupulous preparer, it carefully reviews all the returns prepared by him and audits those returns suspected to be false.

For example, the returns of Jan Randolph, a journalist, were prepared by an aggressive accountant who nearly always managed to obtain a refund for him. Jan's accountant assured him that his returns, while imaginatively prepared, were legal and completed in a manner that was unlikely to provoke an audit. However, during the course of auditing another client of that accountant, the examining agent discovered that the accountant was involved in padding deductions and claiming fictitious auto expenses. That audit precipitated a review of all the returns prepared by that accountant. Jan, who used his car in business, legitimately deducted auto expenses on his return. But that deduction by that accountant was enough to cause a gruelingly thorough audit of Jan's returns.

What Will Trigger a Fraud Investigation?

The Criminal Investigation Division is the criminal investigative arm of the IRS. Agents of the Criminal Investigation Division are known as special agents. These agents are essentially federal fiscal police.

A special agent is not concerned with the determination or collection of taxes. His sole objective is to develop a criminal case against you. If the special agent is unable to uncover proof of a crime, he will withdraw from a case, no matter how large the tax deficiency. The Internal Revenue Manual specifically directs that if a case has no criminal investigation potential, the special agent must cease all activities and withdraw from the case.

More than half the Criminal Investigation Division's cases are referred by other divisions of the IRS. All referral reports from other divisions are reviewed by supervising personnel within the Criminal Investigation Division in order to evaluate whether sufficient potential exists for criminal prosecution to warrant the acceptance of the case and the assignment of a special agent.

The second major source of criminal investigations is information items, which are tax-related communications received by the IRS suggesting the commission of a tax crime. Such items are regularly screened and evaluated for criminal potential. A special agent may be assigned to make "limited inquiries" to evaluate whether the information item warrants a full criminal investigation of the taxpayer. For example, Criminal Investigation Division personnel regularly review currency-transaction reports (CTRs). These are written reports that the law requires banks and other financial institutions to file with the IRS, disclosing all cash transactions exceeding $10,000.

You can't legally avoid the $10,000 CTR floor by breaking up deposits. Under the law, all "related deposits" are aggregated in determining whether a CTR is required. For example, your bank is required to notify the IRS if you make two or more $9,000 deposits on consecutive days. But defining "related transactions" is itself difficult. If you're selling your house, you should be able to receive and deposit a $9,000 cash down payment and deposit another $9,000 received a month later on closing without generating a CTR.

Similar reporting requirements enacted in 1984 require any person in a trade or business to report the receipt of more than $10,000 in cash in one transaction or in related transactions. So if you're about to buy that Cadillac or diamond bracelet, or pay that hefty legal fee with cash, remember: the person or company you're paying is legally required to send the IRS your name, address, social security number, and information describing the transaction. Many lawyers' groups throughout the country are unhappy with the new law's applicability to attorneys' fees, claiming it violates the confidentiality of attorney-client relations, and are lobbying to try to have it changed.

A CTR can expose you most unexpectedly. Albert Gordon was a roofer. He worked with one assistant and shingled, on the average, one roof a day. His daily net income after expenses was over $400. Since much of that was cash, he thought that reporting it all to the IRS would be gratuitous, and therefore retained a generous percentage.

Gordon computed his taxes from the bottom up rather than vice-versa: that is, he would first decide what amount of tax to pay, and based on that figure, he would compute what income to report. Over the years, he had developed a fairly accurate sense of how much of his income to deposit into his neighborhood bank account, representing the income he would eventually report. He and his family lived in modest comfort in a single-family detached home furnished pleasantly but unostentatiously, and pursued a life-style that did not attract attention.

Gordon would deposit his excess earnings—that is, his income above the to-be-reported amount—into a savings account in a bank located in a city several miles from his home. He had opened that account a number of years ago, in the name of Joseph Green but with his proper home address. When the banking assistant who had opened the account for him asked for his social security number, Gordon/Green said he couldn't remember but that he would mail it to her; he never did, and she never followed up the request. Setting up the account in this manner had been only a little more difficult than Gordon had anticipated;

two other banks had followed up his assurances for his social security number, and he withdrew his applications at those banks. Only at the third bank was his promise to send in the social security number overlooked.*

Every year, Gordon would receive a Form 1099 from the Green account, without a social security number, reflecting the year's interest on the account. Gordon would not report either the amounts deposited into the account, or the interest, on his tax returns. He periodically withdrew cash from the account, but only for nondeductible purchases; deductible items would be bought with checks issued from his regular, neighborhood checking account.

That system worked fine for many years, until Green decided to indulge himself and his family with an in-ground swimming pool. The cost, discounted because a friend of Gordon's was in the business and because Gordon offered to pay cash, was $15,000, payable one fourth before work began and three fourths on completion. When the job was done, Gordon withdrew $11,250 in cash from the Green account. When he made the withdrawal, he did not know that all financial institutions are required by law to file CTRs with the IRS reporting all cash transactions over $10,000. He found out early in the ensuing investigation.

There is practically no privacy for your banking transactions. Although banks are required only to report to the IRS cash transactions of more than $10,000, the law also requires banks to make and maintain photocopies of all checks written on your account and all checks deposited into your account or cashed at your bank. The IRS can obtain this information years later by issuing a summons to your bank.

---

* Presently, if no social security number is furnished, financial institutions are required to withhold on interest earned.

A special agent may discover a new target for investigation during the course of investigating someone else. That's what happened to Michael Heller, a modest man who lived a modest life. He, his wife, and their three children lived in a simple clapboard house in Brooklyn. He owned the neighborhood butcher shop. He had lived and worked in the same neighborhood for over twenty years, and had dotingly watched his children grow there.

Michael was well liked throughout the neighborhood. His butcher shop had become somewhat of a neighborhood institution. It was the kind of old-time shop where the butcher called his customers by their first names and knew their favorite cuts of meat.

Supporting a wife and three children on a butcher shop's profits is no easy task. The older the children grew, the harder the task became. Michael's oldest child was in graduate school, his middle child in college, and his "baby" would soon be there as well. The cost of the children's schooling was now nearly $30,000 a year, with still higher educational costs on the horizon.

Michael loved his children and wanted the best education possible for them. He was proud that all three were excellent students and it was with joy that he felt they would have the tools to surpass him in life. But he realized that he would need a little something extra in order to carry the financial burdens of his children's education, and so Michael had started a private little "scholarship fund" for them. At the close of each day, Michael would remove 10 percent of the cash from the register prior to making his daily bank deposit. He put that cash into a safe-deposit box; nothing large enough to attract attention. But the amount of cash that Michael was able to save this way was not enough. He solved his problem through the King's Manor Nursing Home.

The nursing home was only a short distance from Michael's butcher shop, and each week they purchased a portion of their meats from him. Every two weeks, Michael would receive a check from the nursing home in payment for the meats delivered. These checks ranged between $1,000 and $3,000. Throughout the year, Michael diverted just a few of these checks—not more than a half dozen. Rather than depositing them in his business checking account, he deposited those diverted checks into a savings account that he opened in his wife's name in trust for the children. When it came time to pay for his children's tuition, Michael would take cash from his safe-deposit box, make a withdrawal from the trust account, and then purchase a cashier's check for the amount of the tuition.

Life went well for Michael and his family. On the one occasion when Michael's business was audited by the IRS, his accountant handled matters without difficulty or substantial adjustment—since the books and records of the business tied in perfectly to the business checking account, and that, in turn, tied in perfectly to the tax return.

It wasn't until some years later, when an IRS agent was auditing the King's Manor Nursing Home's deductions, that Michael's financial life began to shatter. The agent, while doing a routine verification of the nursing home's purchases, noticed that certain checks made payable to a local butcher shop were endorsed over and deposited into what appeared to be a family savings account, while other checks made payable to that same shop were deposited into a business checking account. The agent suspected a diversion of income, and, eager to impress his supervisor, made a referral report, recommending a criminal tax investigation of Michael Heller.

The domino effect can also be seen in other common business situations. Often, a taxpayer under investigation will claim that cash sales were not declared as income because the cash was needed for purchases from suppliers who insisted on cash, and the omitted cash sales were off-set by the alleged cash purchases which were not de-ducted. That taxpayer's supplier can soon expect a visit from a special agent to see whether he in turn declared his cash sales.

Similarly, the audit of one person sometimes leads to the discovery of another person's total failure to file any return:

Ed Shane was a free-spirited New Yorker, twenty-six years of age, unmarried, and a dealer in antiques. Al-though he lived in an expensive East Side apartment, he preferred spending his time traveling in his van from one flea market to another.

Shane had no social security number, no savings ac-count, no checking account, no brokerage account, no se-curities. He paid for all things in cash: food, clothing, rental—everything. Ed Shane did not believe that the gov-ernment knew of his existence and he intended to keep it that way.

He had never filed a federal or state income-tax return. At first, he failed to file returns because he really wasn't earning any money—he was more of a trader of antiques as a hobbyist rather than a businessman. Later, he fully realized that he was earning a reasonable living from his dealings in antiques, but most of his profits were rein-vested in new purchases, and anyway, after all these years, the government had never found him and Shane thought there was no reason to believe they ever would. It was certainly cheaper and more convenient that way. And with all of the IRS's sophisticated computers, which matched 1099s and W2s, Shane thought he had nothing to worry about as far as the computers were concerned. He believed in what he called the "NINO" principle: Nothing In, Nothing Out. To the computers, Ed Shane simply did not exist.

Until one day. The IRS was auditing the books and records of Shane's best customer, The Antique Boutique. The agent noticed that numerous checks from The Antique Boutique were made out to cash, endorsed with the name Ed Shane, and apparently cashed at a check-cashing service. The agent immediately suspected that The Antique Boutique was fraudulently issuing these checks to generate false deductions by inventing a fictitious vendor named Ed Shane, forging his "signature" as an endorsement, and simply recovering the proceeds of the checks in cash. However, the owner of The Antique Boutique swore up and down not only that Ed Shane existed but that he sold them merchandise; that the checks were all physically handed to Shane; that none of the cash was kicked back to The Antique Boutique; and that Ed Shane was about five feet ten inches tall, one hundred seventy pounds, brown-haired, and lived on Fifty-second Street near First Avenue.

The agent visited there and confirmed Ed Shane's existence. He then requisitioned Shane's own federal income tax returns from the service center. The service center reported that no such returns existed.

A few weeks later, Shane received a certified letter from a special agent of the Criminal Investigation Division, requesting production of copies of his federal income-tax returns for the past five years.

Another souce of leads for the Criminal Investigation Division is press reports of such diverse activities as crime or settlements of matrimonial lawsuits, or newspaper profiles indicating a recent acquisition of wealth. That's what ensnared Louis O'Rourke, who operated several gas and auto repair stations near Stockbridge, Massachusetts. He kept only one set of books, accurately reporting all sales of gas, but gave bills for repairs only to those customers who requested them. The bills were properly entered into his books of account, and payments of those bills were all reported as income. But payments for repairs for which no bills were requested wound up directly in O'Rourke's pockets, with no record of their receipt or of the repairs.

O'Rourke thus avoided keeping two sets of books, managed to accurately enter all paid invoices into his one set of books, and accurately reported and paid taxes on all customers' payments made pursuant to all paid invoices, while at the same time pocketing tens of thousands of dollars in unreported cash for repairs he never invoiced. He would take the right amount of cash to his home at the end of each day, and kept it in a secure safe built into the concrete floor of his cellar.

One morning, while O'Rourke was at one of his garages, Mrs. O'Rourke heard a knock at the front door of their house. When she opened the door, two strangers barged in, and one jabbed a .38-caliber snub-nosed revolver into her ribs. He kept the gun pointed at her while his colleague went right for the pocketbook lying on a living-room chair. When he emptied it, he found only a few dollars.

The man with the gun jabbed Mrs. O'Rourke with it again and asked where she kept her money. Terrified, Mrs. O'Rourke led the men downstairs and opened the safe. The man with the gun said, "Thanks," and stuffed over $100,000 in cash into a bag. Before leaving, the men hurriedly ransacked the rest of the house, and took a sable coat and assorted diamond jewelry from the O'Rourkes' bedroom. Those items had cost over $75,000. The men then tied up Mrs. O'Rourke, locked her in the bedroom closet, and fled.

Neither the burglary nor Mrs. O'Rourke was discovered until several hours later, when her concerned daughter, unable to reach her by phone, came to the house. After finding and untying her mother, she called the police.

They arrived minutes later. Mrs. O'Rourke, hysterical, gave them a complete inventory of what had been stolen. The culprits were never caught.

The O'Rourkes' robbery made sensational morning reading in the local tabloid. Their misfortune was compounded when that newspaper account was read by an employee of the Criminal Investigation Division who believed that the possession of such a large sum of cash warranted the assignment of a special agent to investigate. O'Rourke did not immediately associate the burglary with a visit he received six months later from agents of the IRS. The interview seemed to be going well until the agents asked to see purchase invoices for furs and jewelry and wanted to know how much cash O'Rourke usually kept around the house.

Taxpayers who underreport their income often feel secure in the knowledge that their records tell no tale of their wrongdoing. But that security is based on ignorance and may be short-lived. For example, the reverse of the facts that caught George Hermann, the manufacturer of electrical appliances whom we met in Chapter 1, who created phony expenses by "paying" fictitious invoices and getting 90 percent of the money back in cash, is also common. A vendor under investigation for improperly attempting to deduct kickbacks to buyers may supply the necessary leads for the opening of investigations of numerous buyers, who often fail to report such largesse on their own tax returns.

The activities of other law-enforcement agencies also lead to referrals to the Criminal Investigation Division. The Securities and Exchange Commission (SEC), for example, recently called for public corporations to come forward and disclose all political contributions, bribes, rebates, kickbacks, or other illegal or "immoral" payments, on the theory that such payments are material to the integrity of the corporation and therefore must be disclosed on the corporation's public reports. As corporations came forth in good faith and supplied the SEC with disclosures of such payments, the SEC routinely forwarded this information to agents of the IRS's Criminal Investigation Division.

In fact, there is a continuous flow of referrals and information to the IRS from such diverse government agencies as the Customs Service, the Drug Enforcement Agency, the Federal Bureau of Investigation, and local police departments, to name only a few. For example, the IRS would have investigated O'Rourke even if his robbery hadn't made headlines: The IRS received a second tip on the same case when local police later notified the Service after receiving the O'Rourkes' complaint.

The receipt and nonreporting of cash by a retail-type business is by far the most difficult tax crime for the IRS to prove. Relatively few are ever uncovered. But the bubble can burst in many different and unexpected ways.

Let's return to O'Rourke and his unreported cash receipts. O'Rourke's plan wasn't really foolproof. He routinely diverted, into his own pockets, cash payments for auto repairs whenever customers did not request a bill. The IRS can learn of such things, and prove them, in a multitude of ways.

Even if O'Rourke had not been burglarized, he could have been caught simply by spending the cash. Suppose, for example, he wanted to use it toward the purchase of an expensive item, such as a down payment for a house. That would have increased his tax exposure severalfold. If a broker was involved in the transaction, the brokerage commission would presumably not be reduced to reflect the cash payment, and an audit of the broker easily could have exposed O'Rourke. Cash skimmers frequently have more difficulty, and get into more trouble, spending their cash than acquiring it.

And if O'Rourke was subjected to a routine civil audit, he might have been exposed on several different flanks. In the first place, his inventory may have been dangerously depleted by unrecorded and unreported repairs. Additionally, the IRS has computed what it considers to be the "normal" profit of most major retail businesses in various geographical areas, and the gross profit recorded on O'Rourke's books may have been completely out of line with this average figure. If, during the course of an audit, an agent believes that the taxpayer's books and records inadequately reflect his income and if there exists both a reliable sales or cost figure and a reliable percentage markup figure, the IRS may reconstruct a taxpayer's income by applying the percentage markup to the gross sales, gross receipts, or cost-of-goods-sold figure. (We'll show you some examples on page 165.)

There is also the constant risk of "the squeal." By skimming cash in his business, O'Rourke had placed himself at the mercy of his own employees who were aware of his actions. Tips from informants, many anonymous, account for roughly 15 percent of all tax investigations. If your dishonest acts are known within your company, you may find it impossible to discharge an incompetent employee, or may find yourself the victim of veiled or outright threats to disclose tax crimes to the IRS if salary or other demands are not met. Because of the nature of a tax crime, an astute bookkeeper either knows or can infer that receipts are being kept "off the books." If O'Rourke had such a bookkeeper, another time bomb was silently ticking. Informants may be jilted spouses, scorned lovers, soured sweethearts, disgruntled (or fired) employees, cutthroat competitors—as numerous a group as the number of human interrelationships. And the law encourages such snitching: The Commissioner of Internal Revenue is authorized to pay snitchers rewards of up to 10 percent of all sums recovered from a taxpayer whom the snitcher's snitch snatches.

CHAPTER 3

If Your Number Gets Picked in the Audit Lottery, Here's How to Handle It

Handling the Audit

If your return has been selected for audit, the Service may conduct one of two types of civil examination: office or field.

There are two types of office examination. The most common is the correspondence examination, which involves noncomplex issues identified either by computer or manually that you can clarify through verification furnished by mail. Examples of items that qualify for a correspondence examination are itemized deductions for interest, taxes, contributions, medical expenses, and simple miscellaneous deductions, such as union dues and expenses for small tools. The second type of office examination is the office interview examination, required if the return raises issues that require individual judgment beyond verification of records. These interview audits take place at the offices of the IRS.

If you receive a notice of office interview but think you can resolve the matter merely by supplying documents, you can try to convert the examination into a correspondence-type by mailing the supporting documentation to the examining agent prior to the scheduled interview. If such documentation is sufficient, an actual physical appearance and interview may become unnecessary. You have nothing to gain by an office audit if you can resolve the matter by mail. The brief satisfaction of saying "so there" to the agent's face is outweighed by the risk of the agent asking questions or looking at other items on the return, which he had not previously been interested in.

There are innumerable issues that are frequently subjects of office interview examinations: dependency exemptions, income from tips, pensions, annuities, rents, fellowships, scholarships, royalties, deductions for business-related expenses, deductions for bad debts, determinations of basis of property, deductions for education expenses, determinations of whether income is capital gains or ordinary income, and complex miscellaneous itemized deductions, such as casualty and theft losses where determination of fair-market value is required. An office interview rather than a correspondence examination is used for any business return that reports income from a business activity involving cash. If your return shows a low income in relation to your financial responsibilities, or if the return itself indicates the possibility of a communications problem, an interview rather than a correspondence examination will be required.

If your tax return is selected for examination and contains complex issues requiring full accounting skills, the return will be assigned to a revenue agent for a field audit.

In addition, all corporate returns are subject to a field rather than office audit.

A revenue agent conducting a field audit of one year's return is instructed to visually inspect the returns of prior and subsequent tax years. This, in turn, may lead to a full audit of those years. On the other hand, if audits of prior years' returns show little or no change as to the same issues under audit, that should be told to the agent and may induce him, with the approval of his group manager, to close the examination. Indeed, prior to selecting a return for audit, screeners at the Service center are instructed to review the results of prior examinations, and a prior "no-change" result is considered in determining whether or not to identify a return for audit.

If your return has been selected for a field audit, you'll first learn the news when contacted orally (occasionally in writing) by the revenue agent and informed that an examination is to begin. In the absence of rare circumstances, the Service is required to conduct its examination at a time and place convenient to you. It is usually sensible to have the audit take place at the office of the return's preparer, since generally this will be less disruptive of your business, will permit a more orderly and controlled examination, and will make you and your employees inaccessible to spontaneous questioning. However, when dealing with larger entities or situations involving voluminous books and records, an examination away from your business premises may be logistically unmanageable.

Audits can be as varied as the underlying facts to be audited. However, prior to initiating the audit, the agent is instructed to review the results of any prior examination, and the results of a prior examination often will affect what subject matters the revenue agent will include within the scope of his current examination.

The Internal Revenue Manual provides audit standards, guidelines, and techniques that are to be followed by all examining agents. The Manual alerts agents on how to detect omitted income and excessive deductions. You can best survive an audit if you know what the agent is looking for. The most widely used portions of the agent's guidelines, which tell him what to look for, are reprinted on pages 277–304 of the Appendix.

The agent is instructed to gather information at the outset of the examination, relating to your financial history and standard of living; the nature of employment to determine your relationship with other entities; the existence of expense allowances, including the possible exchange of merchandise or services (bartering); any money or property received which was determined to be tax exempt and/or nontaxable income; and the potential for moonlighting income. In addition, when warranted by issues on the return or responses to the above questions, the agent is instructed to gather information as to the real and personal property you own, including bank accounts, stocks and bonds, real estate, or automobiles; the amount of your purchases, sales, transfers, contributions, or exchanges of personal assets during the taxable period; and the correctness of exemptions and dependents you claimed.

That's one of the reasons you never want the agent to visit your home: He may see something that will pique his curiosity (your big new car, your small home office, a lifestyle seemingly inconsistent with your modest reported income, or any of dozens of other possibilities). The less the agent learns, the better. An audit is an intelligence war: He's trying to accumulate the most data he can, and to maximize its use. That's one of the reasons that you never give information he hasn't asked for. Volunteer nothing—unless in preparing for the audit you discover your return erroneously overtaxed you in some respect.

Even then, limit your voluntarism to that one issue. Your goal is to end the audit, as inexpensively and painlessly as possible.

The IRS's own auditors' manual requires an examiner looking at an individual's nonbusiness return to verify the following information:

(a) Disproportionate or inadequately explained deductions and exclusions from gross income (sick pay exclusion, for example).

(b) Use of income averaging formula.

(c) Unexplained or apparent unreasonable deductions from gross rents and royalties.

(d) Capital gain and loss schedules indicating capital gain treatment for noncapital assets; sales for nominal consideration; use of capital loss carryovers; installment reporting of gains; and problems of "unstated interest" in installment sales.

(e) Gains and losses from other than capital assets . . . and discounts on obligations of the buyer.

(f) Disproportionate amount of income vs. number of exemptions claimed.

(g) Casualty losses inadequately explained as to method of loss determination.

(h) Deductions for dependents outside immediate family or living apart from taxpayer.

(i) Excessive refunds.

(j) Inadequate or incomplete schedules or responses to questions on return.

(k) Required schedules not furnished.

(l) Business vs. nonbusiness treatment of bad-debt losses claimed.

(m) Separate filing by spouse indicated.

(n) Employee's moving expenses.

(o) Recovered amounts deducted in prior years, such as bad debts, medical expenses, and state income and other taxes, losses, etc., included in income in the year of recovery.

The Internal Revenue Manual instructs agents to review the following on the return of an individual with a business schedule:

(a)   Disproportionate gross profit percentage.
(b)   Inadequately explained business losses.
(c)   Disproportionate bad-debt deductions for indicated volume of sales and bad debts claimed by cash-basis taxpayers.
(d)   Disproportionate repairs to depreciable assets.
(e)   Amortization of emergency facilities.
(f)   Net operating loss deduction.
(g)   Inappropriate or disproportionate travel and entertainment expenses.
(h)   Inadequate description and analysis of any depreciation deduction taken.
(i)   Large acquisition of assets without large deductions for interest expense.
(j)   Other income offset by farm losses.
(k)   Investment income (interest and dividends) disproportionate to other income.
(l)   Recapture of investment credit on disposition of property.
(m)   Treatment of gain on disposition of assets where accelerated depreciation is claimed.

In addition to these business items for an individual, the Manual instructs agents to review the following when auditing a corporation's return:

(a)   The applicable items from examination [of individual returns].
(b)   Type of income and stock ownership as indications of a personal holding company.
(c)   Bad-debt (reserve method) deduction inadequately supported by past experience schedules.
(d)   Credit for foreign taxes not properly supported by required information.

(e) Substantial variations in amounts of balance sheet items at beginning and end of taxable year.

(f) Identification of officers and their stock holding ratios and reasonableness of salaries.

(g) Abnormal or unusual accrued liabilities which remain unpaid at the end of the year.

(h) Improper accumulation of surplus.

(i) High debt-to-capital ratio accompanied by large interest deductions as an indication of thin incorporation.

(j) Surplus reserves for which corresponding deductions may have been taken.

(k) Inadequate description or questionable handling of items appearing in the analysis of earned surplus.

(l) Reductions in capital stock outstanding as an indication of a possible question about dividend income vs. capital gain.

(m) Incomplete or inadequate entries on return and answers to the narrative questions thereon.

(n) Items entered in analysis of earned surplus which are not self-explanatory.

(o) Method of accounting used for book income different from method used for tax income, such as bad-debt deductions on the specific charge-off method vs. the reserve method.

(p) Failure of appropriate officer or officers to sign returns; lack of corporate seal.

(q) Inadequate information for analysis of dividend received credit.

But not every auditor "goes by the book," and many audits entail less onerous examinations than the above lists suggest. On the other hand, the Service provides its auditors with special guidelines for the audit of specific types of taxpayers, such as doctors, lawyers, farmers, and other professionals and specialists. Agents are thereby alerted to the unique tax problems that may exist in each of these occupations, and the guidelines instruct the agent on how he can best discover inaccuracies on such returns.

The handling of an audit by you or your representative cannot be reduced to a scientific formula. Beyond the guidelines and objectively listed criteria is the human factor of the relationship between two parties: the examining agent and you or your representative. No book can teach you how to handle an adversary as formidable as an IRS agent. Experience, negotiating skills, and—perhaps most subtle—human psychology, all play a role in the income-tax audit.

Before meeting with the examining agent, you should take certain basic audit preparation steps. First, the odds are high that you should hire an expert to handle the audit for you. The likeliest expert is the accountant who prepared your return.

He should contact the agent and try to find out the specific items on the return that the agent plans to examine. Even with that information, though, you and your accountant should review the entire return to spot additional problem areas that may arise during the audit.

You should then try to uncover all the facts concerning the areas to be examined. Depending upon the complexity of the issues and the amount of tax at stake, the discovery of facts can involve everything from a single discussion between you and your accountant to the interview of third parties who may have knowledge of the facts—such as employees and business associates—to obtaining and analyzing documents, such as invoices, journals, ledgers, corporate minutes, bank and brokerage house records, and other materials.

Too often, accountants and attorneys identify issues, ascertain the general facts, and then spend the bulk of their preparation researching and analyzing statutes, regulations, and cases as they theoretically apply to the issue in point. However, "the law" results from the application of general principles to specific situations. Different facts often require different legal results. The studious and tedious development of facts helpful to your position often will make the difference between success and failure of either an audit by an Interal Revenue agent or a case at trial.

The entire tenor of an audit may depend on the degree to which you and your accountant have prepared. You can control the audit if your accountant maintains a superior facility with the facts, supporting evidence, and legal principles. Preparation is the key to successfully handling an audit. You and your accountant should not rely on a supposedly keen ability to negotiate and bluff when dealing with an agent. The burden of proof to substantiate the figures on a return lies on your shoulders. If the agent senses that you or your accountant is unprepared, he may more vigorously argue that you have the burden of proof, and claim that you owe lots of money if you can't satisfy that burden.

On the other hand, a well-organized preparation for the audit may cause the agent to be more favorably disposed toward you. If your bills, canceled checks, and other documentation have been organized in such a manner that they can be readily traced to the tax return, the examining agent may give you the benefit of doubt as to borderline items.

While there are no hard-and-fast rules for how to deal with an agent, it generally is not advisable to be too conciliatory. The agent is your adversary, not your friend. You should be willing to fight in order to support a reasonable position that has been taken on the return. If you ultimately concede some issues, the agent will feel as though he has won a "victory" and may be more willing to concede other issues.

Although your objective is for your accountant to conclude the audit as painlessly as possible, don't think that
he's doing you a disservice by arguing long and hard over
a $100 item while you're sitting home worrying about a
$10,000 item that the agent hasn't asked about yet. As long
as they're discussing the $100 item, the agent isn't ques-
tioning the $10,000 item, and that's good for you.

When the examination takes place at your business
premises, you should institute certain procedures to ensure a modicum of control over the audit. Whenever possible, a separate room, away from the business's books and
records and mainstream of activity, should be set aside for
the agent. The agent should not have access to any unnecessary books and records. He shouldn't be given anything
he hasn't asked for.

Either your accountant or a loyal knowledgeable employee should be appointed as the agent's sole contact with
you. All communications, including questions and requests for books and records or other documents, should
be addressed to that one person. When requested, records
should be brought to the agent. When his work on those
records is complete, they should be removed before additional records are given.

The agent should not have free access to photocopying
equipment. Rather, requests for photocopying should be
made to the designated contact, who should maintain a list
of all photocopied items. That list may help you learn the
direction of the audit.

These restrictions should be accomplished with tact. It
is important for you to present a candid and forthright
posture. The agent must not feel that you are hiding information. Although the agent should believe that you are
forthcoming with information, no materials should be
promised until you and your accountant are sure they can
be produced. Unfulfilled promises to produce verification

or other evidence are far more harmful than the mere failure to produce them.

In trying to settle an audit, be careful of any statements you may make, particularly if you're aware of any possible criminal exposure that may lurk somewhere on your return. Although there is a federal rule of evidence which expressly provides that "evidence of conduct or statements made in compromise negotiations is not admissible," the United States Court of Appeals in New York rendered a decision in 1984 holding that the rule does not apply to criminal trials. Rafael Rivera had defrauded two banks out of $9 million. When the banks learned of the fraud and went after Rivera for repayment, Rivera admitted, during the course of settlement negotiations, that he had used forgery to induce one of the banks to part with its money. In the subsequent criminal prosecution the government persuaded the court to reject Rivera's claim that the admission should be excluded from evidence because it was made during settlement negotiations, and the court held that the exclusion of such evidence only applies to civil but not criminal proceedings.

Caution should also be the catchword before any books, records, or other documents are given to an agent. You and your accountant should thoroughly familiarize yourselves with all materials before showing them. And remember: There should be no gratuitous production. All uncalled-for or extraneous materials should be removed before anything is given to the agent.

You should keep memoranda describing all issues discussed, all materials produced, all representations made, and the facts or issues agreed to during the audit. Such record-keeping can be of immeasurable importance at later stages of the audit or at future appellate or court proceedings in which there may be a dispute or uncertainty as to what transpired at the audit.

If you or your representative perceives the possibility of

a fraud investigation, or if the revenue agent's activities suggest that his audit is leading to a fraud investigation, you should immediately consult with an attorney thoroughly familiar with tax-fraud matters. Normally, the revenue agent will not inform you or your representative that he suspects fraud. However, that suspicion may be gleaned from the agent's actions: a circularization of third parties, such as your customers or sources of supply; a direct inquiry to financial institutions you deal with, especially if the inquiry relates to transactions not appearing on your return or to specific large withdrawals or deposits; a request that you furnish a net-worth statement; or the revenue agent's sudden disappearance or inaccessibility. If the revenue agent seems to be dodging or ignoring you, that may be a danger sign. His prolonged absence indicates the possible referral of your case to the Criminal Investigation Division, since the revenue agent is required by his internal regulations to suspend all his activities pending the acceptance or rejection of a referral for criminal prosecution.

Agents Are Fallible—How to Go over Their Heads and Win

While the audit process itself may be a grueling experience, the examining agent does not have the final say. If you're not happy with his determinations, you can obtain review by filing a protest to the Appeal Office of the IRS.

If you do not agree with the examining agent's proposed adjustments, he will give you a written report explaining his adjustments and the tax computation. That report, which is commonly called a "thirty-day letter," informs you that if you do not agree with the proposed adjustments you may file, within thirty days, a "protest" to the IRS's Office of the Regional Director of Appeals.

If the proposed adjustments do not exceed $2,500 in

any single tax period, or if the appeal is from an office audit rather than a field audit, the protest need not be in writing. In all other instances the protest must be in writing and must contain your name and address, the date and reference symbols of the Service's thirty-day letter, the tax periods involved, an itemization of each adjustment that you protest, and a statement setting forth the facts and outlining the law supporting your contentions. The protest must be signed by you or your representative. If by you, you must sign a declaration under the penalties of perjury that the facts set forth are "true, correct, and complete" to the best of your knowledge. If the protest is signed by your representative, he must sign a declaration that he prepared the protest and whether or not he personally knows the truth of the facts within the protest.

In most cases, the protest should include in full detail the factual allegations supporting your position, and a legal brief setting forth the arguments of law in support of that position. However, you may not want to commit yourself to a specific factual position until learning the views of the appellate officer. In such instances, strategy calls for a protest drafted in skeletal form and containing only the bare essentials necessary to furnish the appeals officer with a list of the issues being raised. You will be granted an appellate conference, and after learning the examining agent's facts and positions at that conference, you will be in a better position to assess whether or not to furnish the service with additional evidentiary material or legal arguments.

Many taxpayers and tax practitioners believe that an appeal should be pursued in all cases where the Service has alleged a sizable deficiency at audit, on the assumption that the taxpayer invariably will do better on an appeal. Although the vast majority of cases appealed are settled, the Service will not settle a case merely because of its nuisance value. If the taxpayer is clearly wrong, the Service will spend more money pursuing a "proper result" than the monetary value of that result.

Pursuing an appeal is risky where there is undiscovered vulnerability. While an examining agent may have been unduly harsh to you on one issue, he may have completely overlooked another, or treated it with undue generosity. In such a case you might be well advised to forego an appeal, since the appellate officer is not limited to the issues uncovered and disallowed at audit, and can correct the oversights of the examining agent.

Ray McKenzie, a pharmaceuticals distributor, gambled by appealing, and lost. During a routine audit, McKenzie's only problem was his inability to produce checks to substantiate $67,000 of the $472,000 reported on his corporation's tax return as the cost of goods sold. McKenzie claimed that he had purchased during the year, with currency, that amount of inventory from various manufacturers who offered substantial discounts for cash purchases. His accountant tried valiantly to convince the revenue agent of the validity of the expense, but the revenue agent disallowed the entire $67,000 of alleged cash purchases.

McKenzie's accountant believed he would be able to work out a compromise figure on appeal, and McKenzie followed his advice. The accountant explained to the appellate conferee that all the alleged cash purchases had actually been made and were legitimate. The conferee responded that the revenue agent's analysis of McKenzie's checks showed that the total of his cashed checks was far less than $67,000, and he wondered how McKenzie had obtained sufficient cash to make these large cash purchases. McKenzie's accountant persuasively explained that McKenzie hadn't needed to cash checks to obtain the currency for these cash purchases, as McKenzie had merely used the proceeds of his own cash sales. The conferee sent the case back to the revenue agent for reaudit of McKenzie's income, in particular for investigation of all cash sales McKenzie may have made and not reported on his books and records.

Despite McKenzie's difficulties, cases involving judgment calls, where reasonable people may differ, such as property-evaluation cases, are likely to be settled on appeal if the taxpayer can produce even mildly persuasive evidence.

Upon receipt of your protest, the Appeals Office conferee will contact you or your representative by mailing notification of a conference date. The conference procedure is informal, without oaths or a stenographer. You simply sit in an office with the IRS's appellate conferee and discuss the merits of the case. This negotiating process may entail several meetings during which you make a series of submissions, including relevant documentation.

In most cases the negotiations proceed on an item-by-item basis, with you and the appeals officer analyzing each issue in the examining agent's report and trying to agree on that issue before proceeding to the next. However, some cases lend themselves to settlement on the basis of an overall percentage, where amounts involved in different issues will be considered and resolved for a total settlement sum. The appeals officer later allocates the settlement figure to specific issues when writing up his report.

Most appeals involve give-and-take by both the taxpayer and the appeals officer. If settlement is reached, the appeals officer prepares settlement documents and forwards them to the taxpayer for execution. However, after you work out a settlement with the appeals officer, you've got to sign the proposed settlement before the conferee's boss does. Even when you've signed, all "settlements" are

deemed mere proposals by the taxpayer and are not offi-
cially agreed to by the Service until reviewed and agreed
to by supervising personnel in the appeals office.

If you and the appeals officer cannot reach agreement,
he will prepare an Action Memorandum and Supporting
Statement. The first portion of that document is furnished
to you and contains a statement of the proposed adjustments, mathematical computations, and a brief explanation of each item. The second portion of the document,
which you don't get, contains a detailed analysis of the
Service's positions and of yours, with supporting documentation and a suggested settlement figure.

The tax computations contained in the first portion of
the appeals officer's memorandum and statement are incorporated into a document known as the Statutory Notice
of Deficiency. This notice formally advises you that the
Service is proposing a tax assessment. The notice is sent
by certified or registered mail to your last known address.
By law, the Service may not assess the tax against you for
a period of ninety days (150 days if the notice is addressed
to you outside the United States) from the mailing of the
notice. The ninety-day period gives you an opportunity to
file a petition with the United States Tax Court, seeking a
redetermination by that court of the proposed tax adjustments set forth in the Service's Notice of Deficiency.

By filing such a petition within this ninety-day period,
you obtain independent judicial review of the Service's
proposals without having to pay the tax itself. The form
of the petition is described in the Tax Court Rules. The
petition must set forth the alleged errors in the notice, and
must provide a statement of the facts on which you claim
the Service erred. An issue not raised in the petition's assignment of errors is deemed admitted. The Service must
answer your petition within sixty days from the petition's
service.

Although most taxpayers view themselves as defendants in Tax Court proceedings, defending themselves against the allegations of the IRS's Notice of Deficiency, the taxpayer is actually the plaintiff in such a case. You initiate the lawsuit, you are called the "petitioner" (which is Tax Court parlance for "plaintiff"), and you have the burden of proving your correct tax liability. An important exception to this general rule, however, is that the Service has the burden of proof on the issue of fraud. Therefore, where the Service has alleged that a taxpayer's actions have been fraudulent, the taxpayer has the burden of proving the proper tax, but the Service has the burden of proving that any deficiency resulted from fraudulent intent.

Tax Court cases are tried before a Tax Court judge, without a jury. The proceedings are less rigid than those in federal District Courts. Tax Court judges tend to take an active role in trying to obtain settlements or, if trial cannot be avoided, in narrowing the issues to be tried by requiring the parties to stipulate to undisputed facts. Following the trial, both sides are usually asked by the court to submit written arguments and proposed findings to the judge, and months generally pass before the judge's decision. Either the Service or the taxpayer may obtain appellate review of that decision in the United States Court of Appeals for the circuit in which the taxpayer resides.

Tax Court is not your only forum for obtaining judicial review of the examining agent's proposed adjustments. Instead, you may pay the additional tax, penalties, and interest claimed by the agent and file a Claim for Refund with the IRS. If that claim is denied by the Service or goes unanswered for six months, you may commence a suit for refund in the United States District Court or Court of Claims—both of which are different from the Tax Court. The primary disadvantage of the Claim for Refund procedure available in those courts is that you must fully pay the alleged deficiency before suing.

In many cases, the prepayment requirement renders this procedure impossible. However, if you can afford to pay the alleged deficiency, you should give careful consideration to paying it and suing for a refund in District or Claims Court rather than petitioning the Tax Court. The raw statistics by themselves are illuminating. Approximately 10 percent of all Tax Court cases result in decisions favorable to the taxpayer, as compared with a more favorable rate of approximately 25 percent in the District Court and more than 40 percent in the Claims Court. However, these statistics are somewhat misleading, as the disparity may be explained by the fact that taxpayers tend not to pursue the costly refund procedure unless they have been advised by their representatives that their case has a significant chance of success.

Statistics aside, a refund suit in the District Court does present significant tactical advantages to you. One advantage not available in either the Tax Court or the Claims Court is that a jury trial is available in the District Court, and lay jurors are often unsympathetic to the Service. Other differences between the Tax Court, Claims Court, and District Court are the extent of available discovery, controlling decisional law, and your adversary's and the court's degree of specialization in the area of taxation.

How Deep Can They Reach into Your Pocket?

DEFICIENCIES

Taxpayers often confuse the act of "assessment" with their receipt of items such as the Notice of Deficiency or Notice of Assessment and Demand for Payment. An assessment is the actual bookkeeping entry into the records of the Internal Revenue Service showing an amount receivable from a particular taxpayer. After the assessment is made, the Service is required to send a Notice of Assessment and Demand for Payment to your home or usual place of business, or to your last known address. You have a right, upon request, to be furnished with a copy of the assessment and summary information.

The Service has the right to immediately assess all taxes that you yourself report on your return. (If you failed to file a return, then the amount shown on the return is obviously zero.) Moreover, mathematical errors and certain clerical errors, such as the incorrect use of an IRS table, inconsistent entries on the same return, and certain deductions and credits which, on the face of the return, exceed statutory limits, also may be assessed immediately.

A deficiency is an additional sum alleged by the IRS to be due, over and above the amount of tax shown on your return. Unlike the tax shown on the return or a mathematical error, a "deficiency" may not be assessed or collected until a Notice of Deficiency has been mailed to you and until the expiration of the 90- or 150-day period you have in which to file a petition with the Tax Court—and after you file the petition, assessment continues to be deferred.

There is one important exception to the general rule that a deficiency may not be assessed until after expiration of the period permitting a taxpayer access to the Tax Court. That exception is known as the "jeopardy assessment" and though rarely used, it is the most powerful collection weapon in the Service's formidable arsenal. The jeopardy assessment permits the Service to immediately assess and collect taxes, interest, and penalties whenever the Service deems their future collection to be in jeopardy.

The Internal Revenue Manual states that a jeopardy assessment will be made only when at least one of the following conditions exists:

(1) The taxpayer is or appears to be designing quickly to depart from the United States or to conceal himself/herself.

(2) The taxpayer is or appears to be designing quickly to place his/her or its property beyond the reach of the government either by removing it from the United States, by concealing it, by dissipating it, or by transferring it to other persons.

(3) The taxpayer's financial solvency is or appears to be imperiled. (This does not include cases where the taxpayer becomes insolvent by virtue of the accrual of the proposed assessment tax, penalty, and interest.)

(4) An individual in physical possession of cash or its equivalent in excess of $10,000, who does not claim such cash as his or as belonging to another person whose identity the Service can readily ascertain and who acknowledges ownership of such cash.

In determining whether or not the above factors have been established, the Manual states that the following areas should be explored by the examining agent:

(a) Factors establishing flight

1. Is there any evidence which would indicate that if the taxpayer were free on bond, he/she would flee the United States or conceal himself/herself?

2. What is the taxpayer's citizenship status? A resident alien? A non-resident alien temporarily in the United States? An illegal alien? If the taxpayer is an alien legally in the United States, would his/her conviction on a specific offense result in his/her deportation?

3. Does the taxpayer have a passport? If so, is it in his/her name or the name of an alias?

4. Does the taxpayer have any previous convictions for offenses that would indicate a proclivity toward flight?
5. Is the taxpayer wanted by the police as a fugitive from another jurisdiction?
6. Is there any indication that the taxpayer was about to leave the country, such as airline tickets seized from his/her person at the time of arrest?

(b) Factors establishing concealment or transfer of assets
1. Does the taxpayer own any fixed assets, or does he/she deal solely in cash?
2. If the taxpayer drives a car, is the car registered in his/her name or is he/she using a nominee?
3. What are the circumstances concerning the taxpayer's residence? If he/she lives in leased premises, are they leased to him/her or to someone acting as a nominee? If the taxpayer was residing in a single family house, was the title held in his/her name or the name of a nominee?
4. If the taxpayer was arrested with a large sum of money on his/her person, what are the circumstances concerning this money? Were there indications that the money belonged to him/her?
5. Has the taxpayer ever used an alias to conceal his/her identity?
6. At the time of the taxpayer's arrest, was there an attempt by the taxpayer to destroy evidence?

(c) Factors establishing insolvency
1. Are there any taxpayer delinquency accounts open with respect to the taxpayer under his/her name, or any alias he/she may have used in the past?
2. Did a search of the local Courts reveal any outstanding judgments against the taxpayer?
3. Has the taxpayer ever been adjudicated a bankrupt?

The jeopardy assessment may be made prior to mailing any notice of the assessment to you. However, if it is made prior to the mailing of a Notice of Deficiency, the Service must grant you the opportunity for Tax Court review by mailing such notice within sixty days after making the assessment. Furthermore, in all instances the Service must, within five days after making the assessment, provide you with a written statement detailing the facts on which it relies and justifying both the reason for the immediate assessment and the amount of the assessment. You may then request an administrative review within the Service.

If satisfactory relief is not obtained through the administrative review process, you may sue the United States in the United States District Court in the district where you reside. At the trial of that suit, the burden of proof as to the reasonableness of an immediate assessment is on the IRS. The burden of proof as to the appropriateness of the amount of the assessment is on you. However, to aid you in carrying the burden, the Service must provide the court and you with a written statement containing all the information on which the Service determined the amount of the assessment.

The possibly devastating economic impact of a jeopardy assessment upon a taxpayer is immediately obvious, but there's a remedy if it happens to you.

John and Ellen Randal were in their mid-sixties. On a reported annual income of under $25,000 during the past decade, they had accumulated a net worth of over a million dollars in jointly owned assets. Following an audit, the IRS sent them a statutory notice of alleged tax deficiencies totaling hundreds of thousands of dollars.

One morning shortly after receiving this notice, Mr. Randal told his wife he was going out to visit their club. He never returned. The following day police found his Rolls-Royce parked at the airport.

When the IRS learned of his disappearance, they traced his whereabouts to a bungalow on Cape Cod, but he'd checked out before they got there. Through his credit-card chits, they tracked Mr. Randal's path. He was heading south, possibly by boat, since he made a series of one-day stops in various port cities along the eastern seaboard. They also learned he had run off with another woman. His wife also found out, and promptly transferred all their assets solely to herself.

When the IRS lost track of Mr. Randal in South Carolina, they made a jeopardy assessment against both him and his wife. She retained counsel to seek to remove the jeopardy assessment as far as she was concerned. The IRS opposed. The court ruled that the jeopardy assessment was unreasonable as against Mrs. Randal on the following grounds: she was not planning to leave the United States, she had never attempted to conceal herself, she had never tried to remove her property from the government's reach, and she had never transferred or dissipated her property.

Following the judge's ruling, the IRS tried to get him to change his mind by arguing that under the Internal Revenue Code Mrs. Randal was liable as a transferee for any tax liability that her husband had. The court rejected that argument because irrespective of whether or not she was liable as a transferee, that liability would not jeopardize the government's ability to collect the money. As far as Mrs. Randal's transferring all of the property into her own name, the judge said that was perfectly reasonable after her husband had run away with another woman.

INTEREST AND PENALTIES

In addition to taxes, the Service will assess and collect interest on any tax deficiency. Interest is statutorily required and may not be compromised by the Service during settlement negotiations. The statutory interest rates differ for different time periods:

From	Through	Annual Rate
	June 30, 1975	6%
July 1, 1975	Jan. 31, 1976	9%
Feb. 1, 1976	Jan. 31, 1978	7%
Feb. 1, 1978	Jan. 31, 1980	6%
Feb. 1, 1980	Jan. 31, 1982	12%
Feb. 1, 1982	Dec. 31, 1982	20%
Jan. 1, 1983	June 30, 1983	16%
July 1, 1983	Dec. 31, 1984	11%
Jan. 1, 1985	June 30, 1985	13%
July 1, 1985	present	11%

Interest is compounded daily beginning January 1, 1983, except for individual or corporate estimated taxes. Moreover, for interest accruing after 1984, interest rates are 20 percent higher than shown in the above chart if the underpayment exceeds $1,000 and is attributable to such tax-motivated transactions as over-valuations of 150 percent or more, tax straddles, or other specific transactions designated by regulations.

There is also an array of civil penalties that the Service can assess to punish a truant taxpayer. The most commonly asserted civil penalties are for fraud, negligence, and delinquency.

If any part of an underpayment of tax is found to be due to fraud, the Service may assert a penalty equal to 50 percent of the entire underpayment. In addition, with respect to tax payments due after September 3, 1982, the 50-percent fraud penalty is also applied to the interest payable on that portion of the underpayment that is attributable to fraud.

"Fraud" is defined as the intentional violation of a known legal duty. An error due to an honest mistake, an unsuccessful attempt at legitimate tax avoidance, poor judgment, inefficient or ignorant accounting methods, ignorance of the law, ignorance of the facts, or even gross negligence does not constitute fraud (though it may subject you to other penalties we'll soon describe).

However, such terms of demarcation, while easily stated, are difficult to apply in the real world. The line between fraudulent and careless conduct is often hazy. In many cases the outcome depends upon the discretion of the IRS's examining agent. Mere negligence has been asserted in cases with elements of fraud, while fraud has been asserted in cases at the borderline of negligence.

Negligence has been defined by the courts to mean a lack of due care, or failure to do what a reasonable and ordinary prudent person would do under the circumstances. Thus, the imposition of the negligence penalty does not require a showing of bad faith on the part of the taxpayer, but it does require something more than an honest mistake of law if a complex legal determination is involved. The negligence penalty applies if any part of an understatement in tax is due to negligence or intentional disregard of rules or regulations. The penalty is equal to 5 percent of the total underpayment. For taxes due after December 31, 1981, there is an additional negligence penalty equal to half of the interest due on that portion of the deficiency which is due to negligence.

The Internal Revenue Manual gives the following examples of cases where the negligence penalty will be asserted:

(1) The taxpayer continues to make substantial errors in claiming personal deductions after similar mistakes are called to his attention;
(2) The taxpayer fails to maintain proper records after being advised to do so;
(3) The taxpayer makes exaggerated claims of deductions unsubstantiated by fact; or
(4) The taxpayer fails to offer any explanation for an understatement of income or for the failure to keep books and records.

A well-known and too-clever tax lawyer and his executive wife recently learned the reach of these rules. For many years they were forced, as joint filers, to pay a higher tax under the married-filing-jointly rate table than they would have paid if they both were permitted to use the single person's tax-rate table. To avoid this so-called "marriage penalty," they took annual Christmas trips to Mexico, where they obtained a divorce each year only to remarry after the following New Year's Day. Since they claimed to be single at the close of the year, they filed separate returns on the basis of the single-person tax rates. The Service took a dim view of their ingenuity, refused to recognize the annual divorces, and asserted the negligence penalty for their intentional disregard of rules and regulations. The couple petitioned the Tax Court for review, but the court agreed with the Service and upheld the deficiencies and negligence penalties.

If you fail to timely file a return or to pay a tax, the Service will impose a failure-to-file and/or failure-to-pay penalty unless you prove that such failure is due to "reasonable cause." There are few standards as to what constitutes reasonable cause for the failure to timely file a return or pay a tax, beyond the general requirement that the taxpayer exercise "ordinary business care and prudence." Not having the money is not reasonable cause excusing a failure to file or pay. Moreover, in 1985, the United States Supreme Court unanimously ruled that the failure to file a tax return on time is not excused by a taxpayer's reliance on an attorney to prepare and file the return; where the attorney blows the deadline, his client is liable not only for interest but also for the late-filing penalty.

The failure-to-file penalty is 5 percent of the amount required to be shown as tax on the return for each month past the deadline the return is not filed, but the penalty can't exceed 25 percent. The failure-to-pay penalty is equal to ½ of 1 percent per month for the failure to pay a deficiency after notice and demand, but can't exceed a total of 25 percent. These penalties may not run simultaneously. Therefore, the maximum amount of the failure-to-file and failure-to-pay penalties totals 47½ percent.

In addition to the fraud, negligence, and delinquency penalties, Congress has recently enacted a new series of penalties aimed primarily at tax shelters and tax protesters. These penalties, however, can snare taxpayers who are neither protesters nor investors in tax shelters.

The most important of the new penalty provisions is the "substantial-understatement penalty." This no-fault penalty applies even in the absence of fraud, negligence, or any other type of "bad faith" or fault. The penalty is 10 percent of the underpayment of tax due to a substantial understatement. A substantial understatement is any understatement of tax that exceeds either 10 percent of the tax required to be shown on the return or $5,000 ($10,000 for a corporation), whichever is greater. The amount of the "understatement" can be reduced (except in the case of a "tax-shelter item") by any amount for which the taxpayer's position is supported by "substantial authority" or as to which the "relevant facts" are disclosed on the return.

The "substantial-authority" or "adequate-disclosure" exceptions do not apply to an understatement resulting from a tax-shelter item. A "tax shelter" is defined as an entity whose principal purpose is the "avoidance or evasion of federal income tax."

There is another arrow in the IRS's quiver. Taxpayers who file returns that fail to disclose the information required by the Internal Revenue Code are subject to the "frivolous-return" penalty. This penalty applies to any individual who files a return that does not contain sufficient information from which to determine whether the correct amount of tax is shown, or that contains information indicating on its face that the amount of tax shown is substantially incorrect, if the defect in the return is clearly due either to a frivolous position or to a desire to delay or impede the administration of federal income-tax laws. The amount of the penalty is $500, and may be assessed and collected merely by notice and demand without following the procedures for assessing income-tax deficiencies.

The foregoing are the most common civil penalties asserted by the Service. But beware—there are numerous other penalties available to the Service, although they tend to be more specific in their application and therefore of less interest to the general reader.

THEIR COLLECTION POWERS, AND WHAT TO DO IF YOU OWE THEM MONEY

If taxes are assessed either through the process of self-assessment by the filing of a tax return or as a result of an audit, but are not paid, the matter will generally be referred to the Collection Division of the IRS to obtain payment. Unless the unpaid taxes result from self-assessment through the filing of a return, the Service is required to send you a Notice and Demand for Payment prior to making a physical attempt to collect the assessed deficiency. The notice and demand will state that you have ten days to pay the tax, and that if the payment is not made within that time, your assets may be seized.

These notices were drafted with the obvious intent of striking fear in the heart of anyone unfortunate enough to receive one. What the recipient often doesn't know, however, is that as a general rule these notices are generated by a computer and when payment is not timely received, the computer is programmed to initiate several additional demands. Some of these are marked "final notice" in bold red letters. It is only after all these demands are ignored that the matter is referred to a collection agent

whose job is to contact the taxpayer, with the aim of collecting the tax.

As with any collection agency, public or private, the aim
of these written notices is to obtain payment with the minimal expenditure of time and effort. Therefore, the demand language and description of consequences sound
much more dire and immediate than they are in actual
practice. You should be aware that the collection business
of the IRS is brisk, and there is a long line of delinquent
taxpayers ahead of you, all awaiting the wrath of the Service's collection agents.

If you've ever read about a horror story perpetrated by
the IRS upon a taxpayer, more likely than not it involved
the Collection Division. A collection agent's job is to collect
the assets from delinquent taxpayers. These agents' pro-
ductivity ratings for purposes of promotion are measured
in large part by their success in getting those assets. That
fact, coupled with the fact that the taxpayer who stands
before the collection agent has exhausted his rights to appellate and court review, results in a sorrowfully one-sided
confrontation.

The Internal Revenue Manual contains guidelines in-
structing agents on what collection techniques should be
used, how, and when; the portions most useful to you are
reprinted in the Appendix beginning on page 305.

The collection agent who wishes to flex his muscles has
most impressive powers. First, the Service can file a tax
lien with the county clerk where the taxpayer resides or
has property. With the filing of such a lien, the government acquires an interest in the taxpayer's property to
secure payment of the outstanding tax obligation, and that
interest acts as an encumbrance, dating back to the time
of the assessment of the tax, on all of the taxpayer's property. The lien may also be sent to the taxpayer's bank,
employer, or third parties owing the taxpayer money.

The immediate effect of such notice is to freeze the taxpayer's account and to impede the payment of money to him. The result will be particularly far-reaching for any taxpayer needing credit to conduct his business. As a practical matter, the filing of a tax lien may immediately destroy a taxpayer's credit rating—both currently and as a practical matter even after his taxes have been paid.

The use of the lien is only the first weapon in the Service's powers of collection. If a tax is not paid within 10 days of the receipt of a Notice and Demand for Payment, the IRS has the right to collect the tax by levying on the taxpayer's property. This power permits the Service to seize the taxpayer's property without prior court approval or notice to the taxpayer and to sell that property at a public auction. A taxpayer whose property has been seized but not yet sold does have the right to pay the amount claimed to be due, plus the expenses of the proceedings, and thereupon have his property restored to him. If the seized property is real estate, the taxpayer has the statutory right to reclaim such property within 180 days after its sale, if he pays back-taxes plus expenses.

Before using seizure powers, the collection agent will normally attempt to meet with the taxpayer or his representative in order to amicably obtain full payment or, if full payment is not immediately possible, in order to negotiate an agreement whereby the taxpayer will be permitted to pay his taxes in installments or by means of a payroll deduction plan. But before the collection agent will agree to any deferred payment plan, he will require the taxpayer to furnish both a personal balance sheet and an income-and-expenditures statement. These documents will enable the agent to determine whether assets that can be seized exist, and the appropriate amount of the periodic payment.

By statute, few assets belonging to the taxpayer are beyond the reach of the Service. Exempt property includes wearing apparel, schoolbooks, unemployment benefits, certain annuity and pension payments, workmen's compensation, and the income necessary to comply with judgments in support of minor children. In addition, fuel, provisions, furniture, and personal effects of a head of household are exempt up to $1,500 in value, and books and tools of a trade, business, or profession are exempt up to $1,000 in value. Wages and salary are exempt only to the extent of $75 per week, plus $25 for each dependent of the taxpayer.

Stuart Dunlop learned the meager extent of those exemptions. Dunlop had been a college English professor. A series of personal problems drove him to drink, and he became an alcoholic. For several years his condition deteriorated until he finally entered a detoxification center. He was released after a stay of two months and resumed a normal life and his old job.

In trying to reorganize his life, Dunlop belatedly filed tax returns he hadn't filed during his several years of alcoholism. He fully reported his income, and showed taxes and interest due totaling over $20,000 for those years. He accompanied the returns with a statement explaining that he did not have funds to pay the taxes, and requesting an extension of time to do so.

Soon, a collection agent visited. Dunlop explained his situation, offered to sign a financial statement reciting his bleak financial position, and offered to pay $60 per month until all taxes and interest were fully paid. The collection agent declined the offer, and issued an attachment on Dunlop's salary.

Because of the attachment, Dunlop quit his job, as he would otherwise have been working without being able to receive more than a pittance in salary. He couldn't find another job. As a result, he couldn't pay his rent. His landlord began eviction proceedings. Dunlop had no defense and lost. By the time the final eviction judgment was rendered, Dunlop had drunk himself back into the detoxification center.

Because of cases like Dunlop's, a wise collection agent will not kill the goose that lays the golden egg, though he will occasionally grasp its neck and squeeze a bit. An agent will not generally seize and sell an ongoing business that generates a profit, nor seize for any protracted period of time an employee's wages, when the effect would be merely to place him on the unemployment line. Such dire actions are only used in the most flagrant and aggravated cases where the taxpayer continues to earn money beyond his minimal needs while at the same time making no provision for any payment to the Service—or where the collection agent has lost his sense of perspective.

A question often asked by delinquent taxpayers is whether paying taxes can be avoided through a declaration of bankruptcy. The interplay between the Internal Revenue laws and the bankruptcy laws is an extremely complex subject. Suffice it to say that a bankruptcy will not relieve the debtor from liability for taxes or penalties for any taxable year for a return due within three years from the filing of the bankruptcy petition, or where the taxpayer fails to file a return or files one after its due date and within two years of the filing of the bankruptcy petition. In addition, bankruptcy will not relieve a debtor for liability on any fraudulent return. The bankruptcy laws are thus not generally available as a tax-avoidance device.

However, there are exceptions, and bankruptcy laws can be an attractive alternative for someone who hasn't had income for more than the three-year period. Tom Bennett was an attorney who supplemented his income handsomely during one year by lending his good offices to a profitable cocaine ring. To help prepare his defense, he hired an accountant to thoroughly analyze his financial picture during the year in which he had facilitated large-scale cocaine sales. That analysis showed that Bennett had spent nearly $300,000 in currency while living the profligate high life—for rent in a luxurious penthouse duplex, expensive jewelry for his girlfriend, his-and-hers Jaguars, and similar "necessities" of life.

Bennett's participation in the cocaine conspiracy was documented by various videotapes and tape-recorded conversations provided by a government informer, and Bennett pleaded guilty. Before being sentenced, Bennett was advised by his attorney to file his tax return and to report as income an amount reconstructed from his cash expenditures during the year. So he reported $300,000 in "miscellaneous income" and filed the return without any payment, explaining in an accompanying letter that whatever he'd made he'd spent.

Bennett was sentenced to five years. He was released after four years with good behavior. Shortly after his release, he sought and obtained a discharge in bankruptcy. Because of the passage of those four years, the bankruptcy entirely discharged his tax liability.

The Service has an internal procedure entitled Offers in Compromise that is somewhat similar in concept to the goal of the bankruptcy court. The grounds for a "compromise" may be either doubt as to liability or doubt as to collectibility. In practice, the procedure is most often used where the assessed tax far exceeds the taxpayer's net worth. In such cases, the Service may be willing to accept receipt of all or most of the taxpayer's current assets, and in exchange release him from further tax liability. In most cases, the Service will insist that the compromise contain a collateral agreement whereby the taxpayer agrees to pay an additional specified percentage of future income should he or she earn sizable wages in the future.

Margaret Boyle, sixty-five years old, successfully used this procedure. Her husband was in the midst of a grueling two-year criminal tax investigation when he dropped dead of a heart attack. Mrs. Boyle blamed the IRS for his death. That anger surged when she discovered that her husband left her with a home valued at $125,000, liquid assets of approximately $200,000, and a tax bill of more than $600,000, which with interest was growing by more than $70,000 per year. Mrs. Boyle's defenses to the tax claims had disappeared with her husband's death; she had no other witnesses to dispute most of the government's claims. Despite the fact that there was no real doubt of her liability or the collectability of at least the $325,000 in assets she owned, her attorney was able to negotiate an offer in compromise permitting her to keep her home and $50,000 in cash, thereby permitting her to continue to live in dignity. All of her other assets were turned over to the IRS. This represented a payment of approximately 25¢ on the dollar. Her age, her innocence, and the fact that she'd have otherwise been put on the welfare rolls precipitated that rarest of IRS reactions: pity.

CHAPTER 4

When the IRS Wants Your Hide

Criminal Sanctions

When does a civil tax dispute become criminal?

It is neither immoral nor illegal to arrange your affairs so as to keep your taxes as low as possible. You have the right to reduce, avoid, or minimize your taxes by any legitimate means. But you run into difficulties when you use deceit, camouflage, concealment, or subterfuge in order to obscure events and make things appear to be other than what they are.

Despite the verbal ease of such characterizations, the lines separating mere error from negligence from civil fraud from criminal fraud are often fuzzy. The element of the taxpayer's intent is identical for civil and criminal tax fraud cases. The standards for proving that intent, however, differ. Where the Service seeks to impose the 50-percent civil-fraud penalty, it must prove the taxpayer's fraudulent intent by clear and convincing evidence; in a criminal prosecution the government must prove fraud beyond a reasonable doubt—a heavier burden of proof.

Quite often, the line between civil and criminal fraud is crossed during an attempt to cover up or camouflage a questionable item. One example of this occurred during the Service's recent crackdown on so-called "mail-order ministries." A typical "religious order" whose activities precipitated the crackdown called itself Friends of the Good Church. Its founder, for a fee, sent literature to applicants for admission to the ministry, extolling the virtues of such values as loving kindness. For an additional fee and a vow of poverty, the applicant would become a full-fledged minister. With a handy self-incorporation kit the "minister" would incorporate himself and transfer all of his worldly goods—including his house, personal property, and outside salary (ministering was merely a leisure-time diversion)—to his new wholly owned corporation. In the corporation's hands, because of its religious status, all income would be magically immunized from taxation. Thus, the minister could keep his regular employment, make the same salary, and maintain the same life-style, but do it all tax-free.

Two Wichita firemen, seeing the divine light and tax benefits of finding religion, sent in their money and became ministers of the Friends of the Good Church. They stripped themselves of assets and salary, each man donating all to his private religious corporation. Both firemen took the same vow of poverty, and both continued to live exactly as they had before, except tax-free.

The benefits were enticing. Both firemen completely overhauled and refurnished their homes. One accurately reported on his tax return the true nature of those purchases—new kitchen, new television, new everything—while the other euphemistically labeled similar purchases as "spiritual replenishment devices" and the like. On audit, both men's deductions for these items were disallowed and both were hit with 50-percent fraud penalties. But the fireman who used the euphemisms was also charged with criminal tax evasion.

A criminal investigation will be instituted where the government believes a taxpayer committed fraud. Thereafter, a criminal prosecution will be initiated where the government believes it has obtained admissible evidence proving beyond a reasonable doubt that the taxpayer's actions were in fact fraudulent.

As a matter of policy and in an allocation of its limited resources, the government generally criminally prosecutes only those cases that it believes the government will win at trial. They are particularly interested in prosecuting cases that can serve as a general deterrent against other tax frauds, or that foster a national policy, such as advancing the government's attack against tax shelters, tax protesters, or illicit drugs. Because of the government's limited resources, the more readily accessible the proof, the likelier the prosecution.

An array of criminal statutes exists in the tax area. These criminal sanctions are in addition to—not instead of—civil sanctions. It is usual for the government to first prosecute a taxpayer criminally, and then go after him for additional taxes, interest, and penalties (including the 50-percent civil-fraud penalty on top of the criminal penalty).

The government has three favorite criminal tax statutes. First is the offense you know of as "tax evasion," which the Internal Revenue Code defines as follows:

> Any person who willfully attempts in any manner to evade or defeat any tax imposed by this

> title or the payment thereof shall, in addition to
> other penalties provided by law, be guilty of a
> felony and, upon conviction thereof, shall be
> fined not more than $100,000 ($500,000 in the
> case of a corporation), or imprisoned not more
> than five years, or both, together with the costs
> of prosecution.

The elements of the offense of tax evasion are: (1) an actual and substantial additional amount of tax is due; (2) knowledge on the part of the taxpayer that a substantial additional amount of tax is due; and (3) a willful act of evasion or attempted evasion. The term "willful" has been defined by the courts as the "voluntary, intentional violation of a known legal duty." To obtain a conviction under this statute, the government must prove each of these elements beyond a reasonable doubt.

The act of evasion requires some affirmative wrongdoing, such as preparation of false documents or book entries, destruction of records, concealment of assets, misleading statements, or something similar. Thus, mere failure to file a return or pay a tax, unaccompanied by any of those affirmative acts of wrongdoing, does not amount to tax evasion (though it is subject to another criminal statute we'll get to shortly). The crime of evasion is not limited to income taxes but can cover any tax, and the manner of evasion is as limitless as cheaters' ingenuity.

To be guilty of tax evasion, there must be a tax deficiency. If the taxpayer can offset a claimed deficiency, he cannot be convicted of tax evasion. For example, Marty Gross had a weakness for the ponies. On most sunny afternoons he'd be at the track. One day he was particularly lucky and his triple exacta ticket paid nearly $60,000. Not wishing to share his good fortune with Uncle Sam, Marty gave $500 to Alvin, a down-and-out track regular, for Alvin to cash in the winning ticket under Alvin's name and social security number. As agreed, Alvin also reported the $60,000 on his tax return, but Alvin had no money and therefore paid no taxes. Alvin earned a living by accommodating winners that way.

Alvin was later visited by an IRS agent. Unfortunately for Marty, loyalty was not one of Alvin's stronger traits, and the IRS soon was knocking on Marty's door. Clearly, Marty had tried to evade taxes, but his lawyer was able to establish through track officials, employees, and players that Marty was a known loser who lost between $100,000 and $200,000 at the track each season. With their testimony, and the fact that Marty had saved those losing tickets, an IRS reviewer was convinced that despite Marty's venal intent, he should not be charged with tax evasion, since track losses are properly deductible to the extent of track winnings and, therefore, there was no tax deficiency.

Marty was lucky. In such cases the Service often asserts another charge: filing a false and fraudulent tax return. This is different from tax evasion. The "false statement" statute states:

> Any person who willfully makes and subscribes any return, statement, or other document, which contains or is verified by a written declaration that it is made under the penalties of perjury, and which he does not believe to be true and correct as to every material matter shall be guilty of a felony and, upon conviction thereof, shall be fined not more than $100,000 ($500,000 in the case of a corporation), or imprisoned not more than three years, or both, together with the costs of prosecution.

The elements that the government must prove to obtain a "false statement" conviction are less stringent than those of tax evasion. To obtain a conviction under this section, the government must establish beyond a reasonable doubt: (1) a false statement; (2) the taxpayer's knowledge of the falsity; (3) the materiality of the false statement; and (4) that the taxpayer made and subscribed the document (usually but not necessarily a tax return) under the penalties of perjury. We will explain in Chapter 7 how these required elements of proof can be used by the taxpayer in defending himself against the government's charge.

Unlike tax evasion, in a "false-statement" prosecution the government does not have to prove that the false statement resulted in a tax deficiency or even that the falsification was tax-motivated. As a practical matter, however, in order to establish materiality and willfulness, the government will not bring a false-statement charge without evidence that the false statement on the return was made with an intent to deceive the government. There are exceptions, however, as Ronnie Stella learned.

The government suspected Stella of being a loan shark. He was charged with extortion for having allegedly loaned $3,000 to a hairdresser and charging usurious interest of over 100 percent annually. The government's case was thin, and the jury acquitted Stella.

Unhappy with the acquittal, the government then indicted Stella under the false-statement tax statute. He had reported $3,440 as miscellaneous "other income" on his tax return, but had listed nothing at all in the box for "interest income." The government believed he had deliberately checked the wrong box in order to mislead them as to the true source of that $3,440 in income: they believed it was the usurious interest the hairdresser had paid him. At Stella's tax trial, the judge instructed the jury that if Stella had knowingly entered the right amount of income in the wrong box in order to conceal its true source, he would be guilty. The jury convicted him. Stella appealed, and the Court of Appeals unanimously affirmed.

The third tax crime most commonly charged by the

government is willful failure to file a return or pay a tax. That section provides:

> Any person required under this title to pay any estimated tax or tax or . . . to make a return, keep any records, or supply any information, who willfully fails to pay such estimated tax or tax, make such return, keep such records, or supply such information, at the time or times required by law or regulations, shall, in addition to other penalties provided by law, be guilty of a misdemeanor and, upon conviction thereof, shall be fined not more than $25,000 ($100,000 in the case of a corporation), or imprisoned not more than one year, or both, together with the costs of prosecution.

According to the IRS's most recent figures, there are over six million taxpayers who fail to file returns each year. Sometimes, of course, a failure to file results from a thoroughly thought-out decision made by someone who just doesn't want to pay taxes, period. Frequently, however, a person who fails to file is someone with a life-style filled with similar peculiarities. Dr. Eric Palmer was a typical example.

The Criminal Investigation Division began investigating Dr. Palmer when the IRS's computers tried to match the amount of interest income reported on his 1983 income-tax return with the amounts reported to the IRS by various banks in which he maintained accounts. But the comparison couldn't be made because Dr. Palmer hadn't filed a tax return for over a decade.

The investigating special agent recommended criminal prosecution against Dr. Palmer for willful failure to file his tax returns for all years not time-barred by the statute of limitations. During the administrative review of that recommendation, Dr. Palmer's attorney submitted evidence to try to convince the IRS's district counsel that the failure to file was not criminal because it was not "willful"—that Dr. Palmer's failure to file was simply one manifestation of his psychological inability to fill out or respond to forms.

As evidence of that psychological problem of Dr. Palmer's, and to establish the nonwillfulness of his failures to file, his attorney submitted an affidavit of the doctor's psychiatrist attesting to the doctor's treatment for a variety of psychological problems that, in nontechnical terms, strongly suggested that the doctor was a bit of a "kook." His telephone bills typically remained unpaid for many months at a time, resulting in several disconnect notices; he let utility bills remain unpaid for protracted periods, resulting in several occasions when his electricity was turned off for nonpayment and he suffered through days of no heat during cold winter spells; he often practiced medicine without malpractice insurance because he couldn't bring himself to fill out the application forms; and as persuasive as any of these other factors, Dr. Palmer often failed to collect fees because he didn't fill out the necessary insurance forms. Criminal prosecution was declined.

A second frequent reason for failures to file involves taxpayers who have failed to file one year for some understandable reason—for example, a personal tragedy or major business setback that diverted their thoughts from such mundane concerns as taxes—and then are reluctant to file in subsequent years because of their fear of being caught for the earlier year. Oliver Coogan didn't file his return one year because he'd poured all his money into a failing business and simply didn't have enough left to pay the taxes due with the return. Coogan didn't realize that he could avoid failure-to-file penalties by filing without the accompanying payment. The following year his business improved, but he was frightened about alerting the IRS to his prior year's nonfiling, so once again he didn't file. Four years of nonfiling later, the Criminal Investigation Division began investigating, and after the administrative course had been run, Coogan was indicted for willfully failing to file during the later years. The statute of limitations prevented his prosecution for the first year.

He testified at trial that he hadn't filed in the years at issue because he feared he would incriminate himself for the first year's nonfiling. But on cross-examination, he admitted that despite that fear, he knew the law required him to file the later years' returns. The jury returned a verdict of guilty.

What if Coogan had made a "voluntary disclosure" in the later years of his failure to file in the first year? You'll get the answer in Chapter 5.

You may wonder why filing a false tax return is a felony, while failing completely to file a return is only a misdemeanor. The rationale behind this statutory scheme is that in filing a false return the taxpayer affirmatively misleads the government, in effect throwing sand in the IRS's eyes, whereas a taxpayer who simply does not file isn't affirmatively deceiving the government. However, a failure to file, if coupled with affirmative acts of deception or cover-up, can rise to the level of tax evasion. So if the taxpayer fails to file with the intent to evade taxes, the failure to file the return combined with other acts of evasion (such as, for example, maintaining bank accounts under false names or keeping a second set of records) may constitute the affirmative act of evasion and thereby result in a prosecution under the felony evasion provision.

To be criminally guilty of a failure to file, the taxpayer's failure must be willful: that is, a deliberate and intentional failure to file a return that the taxpayer knew he was required by law to file. That standard of willfulness is what convicted Oliver Coogan. Under this section, willfulness does not require proof that the taxpayer intended to evade the reporting or the payment of his taxes.

Although the failure-to-file statute is most often used in cases of a tax return, the reach of this statute is broader. It can be applied to failure to pay a tax or even failure to keep a required record. The government, however, rarely utilizes the sweeping nature of this statute, and it is primarily applied to failures to file tax returns.

Collateral Consequences

The immediate ramifications of a criminal conviction are obvious: possible imprisonment, criminal fines, and (depending on the community) shame and obloquy. But there are also numerous collateral civil consequences that may be as serious for the taxpayer as the direct punishment itself.

A taxpayer who is criminally convicted of tax evasion is denied the right to contest the 50-percent civil-fraud penalty in any subsequent civil litigation for the tax years involved in the criminal case. What that means is this: Someone convicted of income tax evasion may not, when the IRS goes after him later in a civil tax proceeding for back-taxes and the 50-percent fraud penalty, contest the issue of fraud for any year for which he was convicted. Whatever tax deficiency is ultimately determined, the taxpayer is automatically subjected to the 50-percent fraud penalty on top of that deficiency—he's barred from fighting it. Thus, where the tax deficiency is sizable, the automatic civil fraud penalty can exceed the maximum criminal fine.

Moreover, state laws impose a variety of civil sanctions on people convicted of federal tax crimes, including deprivation of the right to vote, to hold public office, to bear arms, or to obtain or keep a license to practice certain professions or trades. States often apply these collateral disabilities to crimes involving "moral turpitude," and most states have held that tax evasion and the filing of a false tax return, as offenses with an element of fraud, involve moral turpitude. The procedures, licenses, positions affected, and degree of disability vary radically from state to state.

For example, Erik LaTour, a Fifth Avenue coiffeur, was tried and convicted of tax evasion. His battle against the IRS, however, was only the beginning of his problems. Under New York State law, "a license to engage in the practice of hairdressing and cosmetology or to conduct a beauty parlor may be suspended or revoked, or in lieu thereof a fine not exceeding [$500] . . . may be imposed or a reprimand issued . . . for . . . conviction of any crime or offense involving moral turpitude." The courts of New York consider tax evasion such a crime. Erik was permitted to keep his license, but only after convincing the licensing authorities of his high professional skill and moral character and establishing unusual mitigating personal circumstances that had precipitated his fall from grace.

You Can Still Prevail: The Due Process between You and Indictment

An agent's conclusion that a taxpayer has committed tax evasion, willfully filed a fraudulent return, or willfully failed to file any return, does not mean the taxpayer will be charged with a crime. First, the suspect has substantial rights of administrative review.

This review procedure is unique in criminal law. In most criminal cases—murder, for example, or robbery—police investigate the crime, gather evidence, and have the case presented to a grand jury, which then indicts. The defendant usually learns the prosecution's case during pretrial discovery at the earliest, and the first opportunity the defendant has to defend himself is at trial.

Criminal tax cases do not proceed that way. A criminal tax case progresses through several levels of administrative review before a determination is made to seek an indictment. At each level, the reviewing body has full power to determine that criminal prosecution is unwarranted and that the criminal investigation should end. And at each level, the taxpayer is entitled to a conference if he requests one. At these conferences, the government will disclose the essential elements of the proposed criminal prosecution, and the taxpayer has an opportunity to present appropriate arguments of fact and law against prosecution. Taypayers who don't know of their rights to this series of reviews unknowingly waive their rights by not asking for them.

Unlike the civil settlement conferences discussed earlier, the Service will not permit a discussion of financial settlement during the course of these conferences. The Service views criminal and civil tax liabilities as distinct subjects and will not under any circumstances agree to drop a criminal prosecution in exchange for a civil settlement. If you're in criminal trouble and think you can buy your way out by agreeing to pay whatever taxes, civil penalties, and interest may be due, forget it.

After a special agent concludes his investigation, he prepares a report that details the facts of the case. If the agent has concluded that criminal prosecution is warranted, his report is annotated with witnesses' interviews and documentary evidence supporting his conclusion. The agent's report is reviewed by his immediate supervisor.

If the taxpayer requests, he will be granted a "district conference," conducted by the agent's supervisor with the agent present. At this conference the taxpayer is told the nature of the proposed prosecution—though he may already have a pretty good idea of it if he has been following whatever figurative footprints the agent has left during his investigation. The information learned by the taxpayer's representative at this conference may then be further developed through interviews of witnesses and review of documents before responding to the Service's charges. The conference, or a follow-up conference, may be used to provide exculpatory information to the Service if such evidence exists and if, for strategic reasons, it is not advisable at that time to withhold divulging such evidence to the Service.

Almost without exception, no taxpayer should personally attend either this or any later conference in the criminal review procedure. His position should be represented by an attorney, with the taxpayer absent. The risks of the taxpayer himself showing up at these conferences are substantial and the benefits illusory. For example, if the taxpayer were to attend, the agent might simply ask him some questions, in which event he may either answer (and thus waive his right to keep his mouth shut, or say something he shouldn't say), or invoke his privilege not to say anything (which will not be of much use to him at the conference, and may very well hurt him).

The taxpayer's counsel himself is often well advised not to attend the conference alone. Bringing a colleague may avoid a later dispute concerning what transpired or was said at the conference. For example, statements made by an authorized representative of a taxpayer at such a conference are deemed under the law to have been made by the taxpayer himself, and the agent may later claim that the taxpayer's counsel made certain admissions unless counsel has a witness to refute such a claim.

If after the district conference the agent's recommendation to prosecute is approved, the case file is forwarded to the Service's Office of District Counsel. The taxpayer will be notified that his case has been forwarded with a recommendation to prosecute and, if the taxpayer requests, he will be given a conference with the district counsel before a decision is reached on the agent's recommendation.

The district counsel conference differs from the district conference. The district counsel attending the conference sits in a semiadversarial but semijudicial role. You are no longer dealing with a "cop" but rather with an attorney who is divorced from the passions of investigation and has not invested his personal time and effort in developing the case. Moreover, as an attorney, the district counsel is more likely to be receptive to legal arguments against prosecution than were the investigative agents.

As at the district conference, the district counsel conference gives the taxpayer a chance to learn some of the facts and theory of the government's case and to present arguments of fact and law to dissuade the government from prosecuting. The scope of the review will be whether or not a tax crime has been committed and whether or not the Service can prove that crime in court.

The most serious risk to the taxpayer at the district counsel conference is the danger of disclosing a defense that the Service may be able to disprove if given the time to do so. The Service may continue its investigation after the district counsel conference in order to seek additional evidence or simply to refute a disclosed defense. Therefore, the risk of disclosing a particular defense at conference is that the defense, which may have succeeded at trial, could be lost or weakened by the Service's full-scale investigation of the defense after the conference—if the Service is given the time, which it would not have if the defense is disclosed for the first time at trial.

Judgment-calls regarding such disclosures are difficult and vital, as Richard Dwyer learned. Dwyer was a salesman under criminal investigation for tax evasion. He'd alleg-edly underreported his sales commissions one year by over $100,000. The return in question had been prepared by an accountant.

Dwyer planned to defend at trial on the ground that Dwyer had signed his tax return in blank, and that he hadn't even known what numbers his accountant later filled in and forwarded to the IRS without Dwyer seeing them. Dwyer's attorney had a key piece of evidence to prove that Dwyer had in fact signed in blank: a photocopy of Dwyer's signature on the blank Form 1040, clearly showing that Dwyer had signed the return before his ac-countant had plugged in any of the numbers or had signed it as preparer. That would help substantiate Dwyer's claim that he hadn't known that his return was false—he hadn't even known of its contents—and that he therefore was not guilty.

After the special agent recommended criminal prose-cution, Dwyer's attorney had to decide whether to reveal his defense to district counsel in an attempt to persuade him that the case did not warrant criminal prosecution and should be referred for civil audit. The temptation to try to avoid subjecting Dwyer to a criminal trial was great, and Dwyer authorized him to take the risk of disclosing the defense and the evidence in the hope that the criminal investigation would end.

After Dwyer's attorney showed the district counsel the copy of Dwyer's signature on the blank Form 1040, the district counsel referred the case back to the special agent to conduct a further investigation. As a result, the special agent was able, with the luxury of time, to reinterview the accountant who had prepared the return. The accountant now remembered that Dwyer had in fact signed the return in blank because Dwyer hadn't known at the time whether he'd be in town to sign the return after its preparation.

However, one of the accountant's assistants had thoroughly reviewed the return with Dwyer prior to its filing. That assistant had long ago left the accountant's employ. But the special agent had no time pressures in his investigation, and after several weeks managed to track down the assistant, who by then had moved to a small town in Nebraska. He remembered having reviewed the return in detail with Dwyer prior to its filing. As a result, the IRS was able to refute Dwyer's defense, and he was indicted. If Dwyer's attorney had withheld his evidence until trial, the accountant, not remembering the presigned return, would have denied under oath that he prepared the return in such a manner; the government would not have had the time to track down the accountant's assistant, and Dwyer would have had a powerful defense.

As a result of the conference the district counsel will make one of three recommendations: (1) to reject the recommendation to prosecute; (2) to return the case to the Criminal Investigation Division with a request that it conduct further investigation; or (3) to approve the recommendation to prosecute and forward the case to the Tax Division of the United States Department of Justice.

If district counsel recommends prosecution, the case leaves the IRS, which is part of the Department of Treasury, and is forwarded to the Department of Justice. The Criminal Section of the Tax Division of the Department of Justice reviews all recommendations to prosecute that have been made by the district counsel of the IRS. If the taxpayer's representative requests, he will be given yet another conference, this time at the Department of Justice, where the case is evaluated from a somewhat different perspective than in the IRS. At Justice, the case is reviewed primarily to determine simply whether the case will be won at trial.

As a result of its review of the case, the Tax Division will either (1) forward the case to the local United States Attorney's Office with authorization to prosecute; (2) forward the case to the local United States Attorney's Office with a direction to conduct a grand-jury investigation to obtain further information; or (3) decline prosecution. If the Tax Division authorizes prosecution, the taxpayer is notified in writing that the case has been transferred to the United States Attorney's office for the district in which proper venue lies. An Assistant United States Attorney will then begin to present the case to a grand jury, which has the power to indict. Often you can get still another conference at the U.S. Attorney's Office, but by that time, except in the rarest of cases, criminal prosecution is a foregone conclusion.

Even at this stage there can be a slip 'twixt the cup and lip. If the taxpayer has knowledgeably exercised all of his rights during the course of the special agent's investigation and throughout the course of administrative review, several years may have passed between the beginning of the investigation and the case's final arrival in the U.S. Attorney's Office. By that time, the case that is may be radically different from the case that was. Witnesses may have died, recollections may have dimmed, additional evidence may have surfaced, or any number of other circumstances may have changed. The passage of time sometimes heals even tax wounds.

CHAPTER 5

The Battle for Information and Proof: Their Powers and Yours

The American tax system is based primarily on self-reporting. The government expects, or hopes, that you will honestly report and pay your own taxes.

When the government questions your return, an old lawyering maxim comes into play: When you don't have the facts on your side, you pound the law; when you don't have the law, you pound the facts; and when you don't have either the facts or the law, you pound the table. The IRS is unimpressed with table-pounding, and the law often depends on the facts. The fiercest battle is often between you and the investigator, for the facts and for proof of those facts. As in any battle, it is best fought only when you know the extent and limits of their powers and of yours.

The Government's Power to Obtain Information

THE POWER TO AUDIT

The fundamental power of the IRS to gather information derives from its statutory power to "inquire after and concerning all persons who may be liable to pay any internal revenue tax, and all persons owing or having the care and management of any objects with respect to which any tax is imposed." The power is an extremely broad one.

The IRS may audit returns even where the general three-year civil statute of limitations has run if the agent suspects fraud, even in the absence of probable cause for suspicion. The IRS may even conduct more than one audit for the same year, although in order for an agent to inspect your records more than once for any tax year, he is required to provide you with a letter from the Commissioner of Internal Revenue formally notifying you that an additional inspection is necessary. However, if a commissioner's letter is not produced, but you permit the second examination without insisting on prior production of such a letter, you have waived your right to insist on such written authorization.

GENERAL SNOOP-ABOUT POWERS

In conducting audits or investigations, the IRS has available certain powers through which it can force you and others to give up information and provide evidence. But even beyond its power to compel production of evidence, the IRS also has general snoop-about powers that require no compulsion at all. Public records and plainly visible information are as accessible to the IRS as they are to you. The agent may look at court records and at other freely available public records. He may conduct surveillance to see (if you do things visibly enough) whether you are conducting a business or making cash sales. He may knock on people's doors or call them on the phone to ask them questions (although if they say they'd rather not answer, he is limited to the powers of compulsory process, which we will be describing shortly). He may, in sum, gather information so long as he does not violate your rights or someone else's.

FORMS FROM OTHERS

Employers are required by law to report to the IRS the amount of income paid to employees (on W-2 Forms). Banks and other financial institutions are required to report the amount of interest paid to customers, and corporations are required to report the amount of dividends paid to stockholders (on 1099 Forms).

These and similar forms provide a wealth of information to the IRS in tracking down taxpayers who fail to report, or who underreport, such income. The IRS feeds this data into computers that cross-check against information contained (or omitted) on tax returns, using taxpayer social security numbers as the basis for comparison.

In order to catch people who fail to provide social security numbers to payers of dividends or interest, or who provide inaccurate numbers in an attempt to foil the computers, a 1983 amendment to the Internal Revenue Code requires all banks, other financial institutions, and corporations to withhold 20 percent of all interest and dividends otherwise payable to any taxpayer who fails to provide a social security number, and imposes a penalty on anyone who gives the wrong number.

IRS SUMMONSES

Suppose an IRS agent conducting an audit of your tax return wants to obtain documents or testimony from you or from someone with whom you've done business (we'll call that someone Mr. Pway—*potential* *w*itness *a*gainst *y*ou). The agent asks, and you (or Pway) refuse. What can the agent do about it?

The IRS has the power that lawyers call "compulsory process"—the power legally to compel you or Pway to provide information, through documents and testimony. The power is in the form of an IRS summons. It is limited by certain rights you have.

An IRS summons is a piece of paper, signed by an IRS agent and his supervisor, that commands the named recipient to produce designated records and give sworn testimony. If a summoned taxpayer or witness refuses to comply, the government may begin a summons-enforcement proceeding in a United States District Court to obtain a court order requiring compliance.

Ordinarily, the IRS's application to the court will consist simply of an affidavit of the agent who issued the summons, setting forth in brief and conclusory terms compliance with these basic criteria:

1. That the summons is for the purpose of ascertaining the correctness of a return or determining or collecting any tax liability.
2. That the IRS has not recommended criminal prosecution to the Justice Department.
3. That the IRS has followed all required administrative steps and does not already have the information.

If the taxpayer (or the person summoned) is unable to provide the court with any evidence indicating that one or more of these criteria have not been satisfied, the court will order compliance. If he continues to refuse, the court may hold him in contempt of court and impose a fine or imprisonment to compel compliance. However, if the taxpayer is able to provide the court with proof that the summons does not satisfy the above criteria—if, for example, the taxpayer can show that the summons has been issued for the improper purpose of harassment—the court may grant an evidentiary hearing, at which the agent will be forced to testify and be subject to cross-examination, before ruling on whether to order compliance with the summons.

The IRS is required by law to notify you if it issues a summons requiring certain categories of "third-party record-keepers" to produce records involving your affairs: a bank, a broker, a credit card company, an accountant, an attorney, a casino, a telephone company, or a consumer reporting agency. When it issues a summons to any such third party, the IRS must notify you in writing, send you a copy of the summons, and expressly notify you that you have the right to seek a court order quashing the summons on the ground that it has been improperly issued. You then have twenty days to seek a court order preventing disclosure of the information to the IRS, during which time-period the IRS may not obtain the information from the witness.

The IRS is not required to notify you when it issues a summons to other third parties, so you may not even learn of the issuance of such a summons until after the IRS has already obtained the information. But you have the right to forewarn a potential witness that he may receive a summons, and to request that he notify you before complying. If he does notify you, there are circumstances where you can seek a court order barring his compliance. You may be able to seek an injunction against the third party, or if the third party simply refuses to comply with the summons—and thereby requires the government to seek a court order requiring compliance—you may be able to intervene in that action and oppose enforcement.

GRAND-JURY SUBPOENAS

A federal grand jury is a group of citizens, consisting of not less than sixteen nor more than twenty-three, which is authorized by law to investigate suspected criminal activity. In addition to investigating, a grand jury is the body which actually indicts—i.e., formally charges someone with a crime. In theory, the grand jury is an arm of the court, and developed as a buffer between individuals and the government. Today in actual practice that role has been distorted, and grand juries are in fact weapons of prosecution with far-reaching investigatory powers.

Generally, a grand jury is not a tool of the IRS. However, there are times when the law permits the use of grand juries to investigate tax crimes. For example, if an IRS agent is stymied in his investigation, he may be permitted by his superior to turn to the Department of Justice for assistance from a grand jury. Additionally, where a grand jury is investigating general criminal matters with incidental tax ramifications—such as bribery or drug sales, where the alleged recipient of the bribe or seller of the drugs has failed, not surprisingly, to report on his federal income-tax return the money received—a grand jury has the power to issue subpoenas requiring witnesses to testify and produce evidence. Under exigent circumstances, the subpoena may even order the person served to testify or produce documents "forthwith"—which means immediately, without even a day's advance notice.

Noncompliance with a grand-jury subpoena may result in a court order holding the noncomplier in contempt of court, which may in turn result in an order of imprisonment and daily fines until compliance is made. Destruction or alteration of records, or deliberately giving material false testimony to a grand jury (or to an IRS agent), is a felony under federal law, punishable by a substantial term of imprisonment.

Grand-jury proceedings are conducted in secrecy. The only persons present are the grand jurors, the witness giving testimony, a stenographer, and the prosecuting attorneys conducting the investigation. Not even a judge is present.

In 1983, the Supreme Court rendered two decisions that severely limit IRS access to grand-jury materials. Because grand-jury proceedings are nonpublic, the Supreme Court held that attorneys in the Civil (as opposed to Criminal) Division of the Justice Department and IRS personnel may not automatically obtain access to documentary evidence and transcripts of testimony given during grand-jury proceedings. Such materials may not be obtained by the IRS unless in connection with or preliminary to a court proceeding (an audit is not deemed preliminary to a court proceeding), and even then materials may be obtained only upon demonstrating a special need for such evidence —not merely that the evidence would be convenient or useful to the IRS. Prior to these recent decisions, the IRS routinely obtained access to such materials.

The significance of these decisions is not merely their limitation on the IRS's power. If you have been the subject of a grand-jury investigation, you now have the right to seek to determine, in any IRS audit, whether the IRS has improperly obtained grand-jury materials, and if so to prevent the IRS from using any such materials (or evidence derived from those materials) during the civil proceedings.

SEARCH WARRANTS

The Fourth Amendment to the U.S. Constitution states:

> The right of the people to be secure in their persons, houses, papers, and effects, against unreasonable searches and seizures, shall not be violated, and no Warrants shall issue, but upon probable cause, supported by Oath or affirmation, and particularly describing the place to be searched, and the persons or things to be seized.

The government may legally search a home, office, car, or other place, and seize property found there, but only under certain conditions.

A lawful search usually requires a search warrant. A search without a warrant is permissible only in limited circumstances: (a) when the subject of the search has consented, or (b) when the search is incidental to a lawful arrest, or (c) under exigent circumstances such as imminent flight or destruction or removal of the property in question.

In tax investigations, the government usually has difficulty proving the existence of any such circumstances. Therefore, as a practical matter searches pursuant to a search warrant are the more common form of search in tax cases (although not nearly as common as IRS summonses or grand-jury subpoenas).

A search warrant is a written legal authorization, signed by either a judge or magistrate, empowering government agents to search a particular place and to seize materials specified in the warrant. It may authorize the seizure of evidence of the commission of a crime, or fruits of the crime, or property used (or to be used) in the commission of a crime. Thus, for example, banking or brokerage records, a second set of books, or other financial records which you may have in a desk drawer or in a bureau in your bedroom may be seized pursuant to a lawfully issued search warrant.

In order for a warrant to be valid, it must satisfy several conditions: (1) it must be based on probable cause to believe that a crime has been (or is being) committed—although hearsay evidence is sufficient; (2) it must specifically describe the place to be searched and the property to be seized—it can't be a "general" warrant which authorizes the agent to seize whatever strikes his fancy; and (3) it must be executed between the hours of 6 A.M.

and 10 P.M., unless special circumstances exist. If these criteria are not met, then the materials seized may later be suppressed—that is, excluded from evidence at a criminal trial (thus "the exclusionary rule").

There are exceptions, however, which the United States Supreme Court has recently carved out of your right to suppress unlawfully seized evidence. One of these exceptions is the doctrine of "inevitable discovery": where evidence is unlawfully seized but the authorities would inevitably have lawfully obtained it anyway, courts will not suppress the unlawfully seized materials. The second exception is the "good-faith" exception to the exclusionary rule, which holds that where a warrant is defective, evidence seized is nevertheless admissible if the government agents acted in a good-faith belief that the warrant was valid.

The exclusionary rule has been further limited in connection with tax matters. Los Angeles police obtained a search warrant from a municipal court judge and seized bookmaking records and thousands of dollars in currency from Max Tucker. He was charged by the local prosecutor with violating gambling laws. His attorney successfully convinced the judge that the warrant had been improperly granted, and the judge suppressed as evidence everything the police had seized.

By that time, however, the IRS was separately examining Tucker. Tax litigation ensued. Tucker claimed that the illegally obtained evidence that the state court judge had suppressed should also be excluded from evidence in the civil tax litigation. The trial court agreed. The court of appeals agreed. The United States Supreme Court reversed, however, holding that because federal agents did not participate in the illegality and because the state police had relied in good faith on the warrant (which later proved defective), the illegally obtained evidence was admissible against Tucker in the later federal civil tax proceeding.

The Federal Court of Appeals in New York has rendered two related decisions. In one the court held that evidence unlawfully seized by federal agents outside the IRS may be used by the IRS in a civil tax proceeding. But that same court has ruled in another case that evidence unlawfully seized by IRS agents for use in a criminal tax case may not be used by the IRS in a subsequent civil tax proceeding.

ELECTRONIC EAVESDROPPING AND MAIL COVERS

Wiretapping or other forms of electronic eavesdropping by the IRS is extremely rare. In run-of-the-mill tax investigations, agents may not legally place a "bug" on your telephone or use any of the other electronic spying devices that the age has spawned. There are a few exceptions: where agents are participating in strike force investigations of alleged organized crime involving nontax as well as tax crimes; where the IRS's Inspection Division is investigating attempted bribery of an agent; or where there is "consensual" monitoring—for example, agents surreptitiously listening to and recording your phone conversation with your supplier where the supplier consents to the snooping. But even these rare exceptions are closely regulated by internal IRS procedures.

The Service may legally use "mail covers": simply look at information on the outside of mail. Several years ago the IRS used the fruits of a mail cover to target for investigation many American taxpayers with secret Swiss bank accounts. Swiss banks often send mail to American depositors without placing any return address on the envelope, to maintain depositors' secrecy. However, the banks used postage meters instead of stamps, and each meter printed its own distinct meter number. IRS agents monitored all mail entering the United States from Switzerland, and noted the addressees of all envelopes bearing a postage-meter number of a Swiss bank. All of these American tax-payers were audited.

Your Rights and Powers

YOUR RIGHT TO REPRESENTATION

You have the right, in connection with an audit or investigation of your tax return, to be represented. During a routine audit, your representation is often best achieved through a tax accountant knowledgeable about the applicable provisions of the Internal Revenue Code, experienced enough in dealing with auditors to know the bounds of settlement in any particular case, and generally able to persuade an auditor to settle and close out an audit.

When potential problems of fraud exist, you should consult with an attorney knowledgeable in tax-fraud matters. Often, only you and not the agent are initially aware that the potential fraud problem exists. In such instances, it is generally advisable for an attorney not to "surface," but to give behind-the-scenes guidance to you and the accountant handling the audit. If you have a hidden fraud problem, you are under no obligation to let the agent know of it, or to let him know you're concerned or frightened. A taxpayer undergoing a routine audit who suddenly replaces his accountant with an attorney known as a tax-fraud specialist may raise the auditor's eyebrows and create suspicions of fraud where no prior suspicion existed.

When a special agent is already in the case, the IRS *is* investigating fraud, and special tax-fraud counsel definitely should be retained to handle the investigation. There is no need for his rendering only behind-the-scenes advice. The IRS's antennae have already been raised— that's why their criminal investigator is in the case—and you needn't be concerned about the agent thinking you're scared. If the IRS's criminal investigator is examining your return, he already knows you're scared.

YOUR "RIGHT" TO VOLUNTARILY DISCLOSE PAST SINS

Frequently, people who have erred or cheated on their taxes consider whether to voluntarily disclose those sins, but do not know the legal or practical effect of such a cleansing of the fiscal spirit.

Many years ago, the Treasury Department publicly announced that it would not refer for prosecution to the Department of Justice cases of income-tax evasion where the taxpayer had made a clean breast of things to the Treasury before the IRS had begun sniffing about the taxpayer's affairs. But in 1952 the Treasury Department formally abandoned that "voluntary disclosure" policy. Now, the fact that a taxpayer seeks to rectify a false return before being threatened by investigation is considered only as one of many factors in determining whether to prosecute, but is not conclusive.

In practical terms, a taxpayer's voluntarily correcting an erroneous return is very powerful evidence that the error was not committed "willfully" in the first place, and that therefore the error on the return was inadvertent and not criminal. However, instances of *true* voluntary disclosure are far rarer than instances of *claimed* voluntary disclosure. If a taxpayer files an amended return after receiving an audit notice from the IRS, or after a threat from a disgruntled employee or greedy former spouse, then the disclosure is more an act of attempted self-preservation than contrition, and the disclosure is not considered "voluntary" by either the IRS or the Justice Department.

Beware: You need a gambler's fortitude if you are seriously contemplating making a voluntary disclosure. In the first place, it is up to the IRS and the Justice Department to determine whether the disclosure is in fact "voluntary." If they decide that it isn't, there's absolutely nothing you can do about it (except later argue to a jury that the disclosure proves you had not originally intended to commit any tax sins). And even if the IRS and Justice Department consider the disclosure truly voluntary, they have the right to decide to prosecute you anyway, and there's nothing you can do about it except make that same argument to the jury.

While "voluntary disclosure" is considered on a case-by-case basis, the oft-debated concept of "amnesty" carries across-the-board potential. An amnesty program would involve a general forgiveness for a limited time to anyone who reported and paid previously undeclared taxes.

Prospects for enactment of a federal tax amnesty are glum. The IRS has consistently opposed all amnesty proposals, primarily on the arguments that it would breed general disrespect for the law and would impair revenue-gathering ability by encouraging people in the future to cheat on their taxes in the hope that a second amnesty would be enacted. The Justice Department has generally sided with the IRS, although in the last several years various responsible officials in the Tax Division of the Department of Justice have urged that serious consideration by given to enacting an amnesty provision, arguing that such a statute would restore to the tax rolls many taxpayers who have been part of the underground economy for so long that they are afraid to surface, and that the ensuing revenues would go a long way toward erasing the federal deficit.

About half a dozen states have enacted amnesty provisions, which have resulted in substantially enriching the coffers of those states. But many taxpayers who came forward pursuant to those state amnesty statutes were really lambs being led to slaughter. The IRS asked the states to give up the taxpayers' identities. The states complied. Taxpayers who came forward pursuant to the state amnesty statutes received absolutely no protection when the IRS got involved. So if you live in a state that has enacted one of these fiscal life rafts, beware that you may sink if you hop aboard.

YOUR RIGHT TO THE FACTS

A common misconception among taxpayers being examined is that the IRS somehow has a monopoly on the right to learn the facts, or that certain witnesses "belong to" the government. To the contrary, nobody owns either the facts or the witnesses. You are not required to simply sit back and let the government gather the facts and the proof; you can take the initiative and beat the agents to both.

If you believe that a certain Mr. Pway is the key potential witness against you—he's your accountant, or business associate, or customer—you have an absolute right to try to interview him and to ask him for a written statement. We say "try to" because unlike the IRS, you have no power of compulsory process during an investigation (though you do once a case is brought), and if Pway doesn't want to cooperate with you during an investigation, you can't force him to. Very often, however, Pway will be willing to help but isn't asked—the taxpayer is intimidated, or doesn't know his rights, or the thought just doesn't occur to him.

Such an oversight can be devastating. Let's suppose that Pway is the accountant who prepared your return. You recall having provided him with certain information which, you now realize, is not accurately reported on your return—the amount of your interest income, for example, or the cost of the goods that you sold. If your lawyer speaks with Pway before the agents get to him, Pway may be willing to give you an affidavit attesting truthfully to the information you gave him. Also, your lawyer may refresh Pway's recollection with facts helpful to your position, or correct factual errors Pway would otherwise have given to the agent.

Or one of your disgruntled employees may have snitched by telling the IRS that you made unreported cash sales. The agent will try to corroborate that claim by interviewing your other employees and your customers. Your lawyer can get to them first. If your bookkeeper or cashier provides you with a truthful sworn statement that she never saw any customer pay in cash, the agent may have trouble getting her to change her mind or soften her position.

Even where the agent gets to the witness first, that does not make the witness "the government's." The agent has no right to insist or suggest to any witness that he not speak with you or your attorney. Pway's statement to your lawyer may be different from what Pway told the agent, and Pway may give you a written statement that effectively neutralizes what he told the agent—by explaining it, or by additional facts. And even if Pway sticks to his story, knowing what he has told the agent may itself be useful information—it may tell you something about the nature or strength of the agent's case, or it may suggest other witnesses you can use to contradict Pway.

YOUR RIGHT TO BE PRESENT

Although you have no right to learn what the IRS agents have got against you by accompanying them as they seek evidence to build a case against you, there is a way to accomplish much the same result. Suppose the agent summons a witness for a Q-and-A (question-and-answer session) during the investigation, and you and the witness have a friendly relationship—because he is your employee, or your accountant, or anyone else who wants to be helpful to you if legally possible. There are various ways in which you can learn what the agent asks him and what the witness says.

The most obvious is: Ask the witness after he testifies. The sooner the better. He'll forget much of the interview by the following day, and even more a day later.

A second way is for the witness to show up for his Q-and-A with a tape recorder or stenographer. Although the law here is somewhat unclear, at least one court has permitted a witness to bring his own stenographer over the agent's objection. In any event, even if the witness fails to record the interview, he has the right (except in rare instances where the government can prove it would harm their investigation) to be given a copy of his statement as transcribed by the IRS's stenographer if he demands it. He is then free to give it to you.

Another effective way to learn a witness's testimony is to have him demand that your counsel be present as an observer even though that attorney does not represent the witness himself. If the witness stands firm and refuses to be interviewed without the presence of your counsel, the agent has little alternative but to either forego the interview altogether or to proceed in the presence of your counsel. One recent case extended this principle by granting a corporate employee the right to have a corporate executive and corporate counsel present during the employee's interview.

There is one other way to find out what the questions and answers are, which often makes the interviewing agent moderately apoplectic. Any witness being questioned by the IRS has the right to counsel of his choice. The witness can simply use your attorney as his. Obviously, what your lawyer hears when acting as the witness's counsel he needn't forget when acting for you. Special agents generally object to this procedure and suggest to the witness and the lawyer the possibility of the lawyer's conflict of interest. In rare instances, the agent may seek a court order that would prevent such dual representation on the ground of conflict. But frequently no conflict exists. If it does, your lawyer should not represent the witness.

Learning what the agents are learning, while they are learning it, can be extremely useful to you. If witness number one discloses a potential witness number two, you have the chance to interview witness number two and to obtain a written statement from him before the agent gets to him. You may find that witness number two is also interested in having your attorney present during any questioning by the agent. It would not be the first time that an agent sees a taxpayer's lawyer representing witness after witness, and is powerless to prevent it.

Your right to ask "government witnesses" what they've been asked and what they've answered also extends to grand jury proceedings. The law prohibits any grand juror, stenographer, or prosecutor from disclosing during an investigation any matter occurring before a grand jury. But witnesses are not prohibited, and a prosecutor may not instruct a witness not to tell you what went on inside the grand-jury room. So a way to find out what a witness was asked and answered is: ask him.

YOUR RIGHT TO KEEP YOUR MOUTH AND YOUR RECORDS SHUT

The Fifth Amendment to the U.S. Constitution states that no person "shall be compelled in any criminal case to be a witness against himself." If you are being investigated for a possible tax-fraud violation and are afraid of the "stigma" of "taking the Fifth," consider hiring a mortician instead of a lawyer.

Even a routine tax audit may lead to answers to questions by an IRS agent that might tend to incriminate the taypayer. The Fifth Amendment is applicable to such a situation. A taxpayer who wants to "cooperate" will often provide the very proof which the agent might never have otherwise obtained: admissions by the taxpayer that he read and understood the contents of his return before signing it, for example, or that he understood the way his own business records were kept by his bookkeeper, or that he knew that certain items on his return might not be entirely accurate, or that he doesn't remember certain key facts which, at a later stage, he wishes he'd earlier recalled.

Consider the case of Lawrence Payne, who manufactured riding boots in Dallas, Texas. The IRS was investigating an allegation that he had made cash purchases from several of his suppliers. Two special agents visited Payne and explained that their primary interest was in Payne's suppliers, not Payne, as the agents believed that the suppliers had not reported the cash sales. But the agents told Payne that "out of an excess of caution" they wanted to read Payne his rights, and did so—including Payne's right to remain silent and get a lawyer. Payne had seen enough detective movies to know better than to confess, and he fancied himself a sophisticated negotiator, so he figured he'd just talk his way out of the problem. He certainly didn't want to pique the agents' interest in himself by asserting a Fifth Amendment privilege. He figured he could help his suppliers without hurting himself by simply denying that he'd ever made the payments, and so he told the agents he had never done any such thing. After the agents left, Payne, full of self-congratulations, called his suppliers and told them what a pal he'd been to them.

A few months later, Payne learned that the agents had served a barrage of summonses on his customers, suppliers, banks, and others. The face of the summonses stated that they were being issued "In the matter of the tax liability of Lawrence Payne." He decided it was high time to hire a lawyer.

It soon became clear to Payne's lawyer that the agents had uncovered a source of cash income unreported by Payne. The lawyer explored with Payne the defenses available to a tax-evasion charge. One of those was the possibility, if supported by the facts, of Payne's having used the unreported cash to purchase materials from his suppliers —in other words, Payne may have had unreported cash expenses that offset the unreported cash income, thus eliminating any tax deficiency. That struck Payne as a dandy idea. But his euphoria quickly faded. He remembered that earlier interview, when he had happily told the agents that he had made no such cash purchases.

He'd forgotten to tell his lawyer about that interview. When he did, the lawyer told him they'd better look for another defense. Payne had checkmated himself: If his statement to the agents was true, he didn't make the cash purchases; and if his statement was false, he had committed the felony of willfully making a false statement to a government agent.

Because cooperation with a special agent may be placing a noose around your own neck or tightening one already there, the decision of whether or not to cooperate is often an extremely delicate judgment. Where you have not in fact deliberately erred on your return and you have a legitimate explanation for the entry in question, an explanation may persuade the special agent that the matter should be handled noncriminally and without a fraud penalty. It is the agent, however, and not you who decides what questions to ask, and a taxpayer who thinks he can talk his way out of an investigation by answering only those questions he wants to answer is being unrealistic. Speaking where you should have remained silent can inflict incurable wounds on your case by giving the special agent evidence which he may not have had or may not have been able to obtain, or by locking yourself into a position which, on second thought or as events later develop, may be unwise. If waiving your right to remain silent turns out later to have been calamitous, you are not allowed to erase what you've said.

If a special agent wants to interview you during an investigation of your tax return, he is under no court-required obligation to advise you of your rights. The so-called "Miranda" rule, which requires a law enforcement officer to advise an arrested suspect of various rights, including the right to remain silent, does not apply to tax-fraud investigations unless the taxpayer is in custody, which is usually not the case. However, all special agents are under written instructions from the IRS to give taxpayers the same types of warnings as the "Miranda" rule requires—although different courts have reached different conclusions on the issue of whether an agent's failure to give those warnings prevents any later use of a taxpayer's statements.

Whether you're given a warning or not, you should know this: If a special agent knocks at your door and says he'd like to ask you a few questions, you don't have to answer and shouldn't.

A taxpayer occasionally finds himself in the uncomfortable position of having to file a tax return while under investigation or in litigation for a prior year's return. What do you do, for example, if the time has come to file your 1985 return, and in 1985 you engaged in transactions similar to others you engaged in during 1981–1984—and those prior years' transactions are presently being scrutinized by a special agent?

Your first instinct might be to file for an automatic four-month extension, and that instinct will often be correct. Your second instinct might be to seek an additional two-month extension after that—and that instinct will also often be correct. Your next instinct might be to seek another extension beyond those two—but although that instinct may be wise it's useless, since you can't adjourn D day for over six months. What to do?

You have no right to either answer the question falsely (if you do you're committing a felony) or not to file a return (a misdemeanor). You do, however, have a right not to answer particular questions on the return where you actually and reasonably fear self-incrimination, by invoking your Fifth Amendment privilege on the return. Of course, if you do that the red lights on the IRS's computers will have a field day, but if you're already under investigation for fraud those lights are on anyway.

Keeping your mouth shut during an investigation is often an easier and less complicated matter than keeping your records shut. There are special limitations on the Fifth Amendment when the government wants access to your books and records:

A. The privilege is a personal one, applicable only to individual people. That means it is not available to an entity such as a corporation. Therefore, a corporate executive—even if he is the sole stockholder of a small business that functions as if it were an individual person—has no right under the Fifth Amendment to prevent compulsory disclosure of incriminating corporate papers. The reason is that a corporation has a legal existence apart from its stockholders, and an executive's production of a corporation's records compels the corporation, not the executive himself (theoretically), to bear witness against the executive. That is a legal trap of which many unsuspecting entrepreneurs are unaware when they decide to incorporate.

B. Other noncorporate collective entities have no Fifth Amendment privilege. Thus, a labor union, or an impersonal organization such as a three-man partnership, may not resist producing its records under the Fifth Amendment, because such an entity has no privilege against self-incrimination. Nor does any individual member of such an entity have any Fifth Amendment right to resist compulsory production of the entity's records that the individual happens to possess—subject to the following newborn unresolved exception in the law.

C. After the United States Supreme Court established the limitations mentioned above, a hotly debated topic among tax-fraud practitioners was whether the Fifth Amendment applies to business records of a sole proprietor—the corner grocer, for example, or a single-practitioner doctor or lawyer. In 1984, the Court answered that question: No, sort of. The Court rejected the notion that the Fifth Amendment creates a zone of privacy around an individual entrepreneur's business records. The only protection that the privilege gives such a person is this: When the taxpayer's act of production of the records effectively authenticates those records (for example, establishes that they are the records described in a summons), or constitutes an admission that the records exist (by producing, for example, a second set of books), then to that extent the privilege applies. In other words, the Fifth Amendment applies only to the extent that the physical act of producing the records is itself testimonial in nature. Indeed, several courts have suggested that the personal testimonial aspect of the act of producing records exists even where the records are corporate. If this view were ultimately to prevail, the Fifth Amendment privilege, which in the past has been consistently construed as being inapplicable to corporations, may have far-reaching applicability to production of corporate records.

D. Even if the records are within the limited category of privileged documents, the Fifth Amendment does not protect a taxpayer against their compelled production if he does not actually possess them when the IRS serves a summons. Thus, if John Trusting has left his personal records with someone else, such as his accountant, then if an IRS agent serves a summons on the accountant the Fifth Amendment does not permit Trusting to prevent his own accountant from turning over the records. You might therefore expect that if the reverse were true—that is, if Trusting had obtained his accountant's workpapers and were then himself summoned to produce them—Trusting could invoke his own Fifth Amendment privilege against production. Wrong, because the records aren't his. Lesson: You're best off with physical possession of your own records before the agent starts issuing summonses.

E. A further limitation on your Fifth Amendment right to refuse to produce records relates to records that federal or state regulatory laws require you to keep. The courts have held that such "required records" are outside the scope of the privilege. Thus, for example, if you're a doctor under investigation by the IRS for underreporting your fees from patients to whom you gave drug prescriptions, you have no Fifth Amendment right to resist production of your retained copies of prescription forms if state law requires them to be kept as part of the state's general regulatory power over doctors.

The protections of the Fifth Amendment have recently been further eroded by developments in the related area of search-and-seizure. The law concerning the government's right to search and seize property has significantly shifted in favor of the government during the last few years, and this shift is particularly applicable in tax investigations.

Suppose you have certain financial records that, if obtained by the government, would incriminate you. And suppose further that the government can't summons them from you because you still have available the one last thread of the Fifth Amendment applicable to books and records: you can't be forced to authenticate them by the act of production. That would seem to mean that the government may not obtain those records, but seeming isn't so. It was so until several years ago, when the Supreme Court changed the rules of the game in a case involving a lawyer named Peter Anders.

Mr. Anders was suspected by Maryland state investigators of having participated in a fraud. The investigators obtained search warrants for Anders's law office and for the office of a corporation of which he was the sole stockholder, and seized numerous records from both offices. At Anders's later trial, he claimed that those records were seized in violation of his rights under the Fifth Amendment. But the Supreme Court ruled against him (and affirmed his conviction) on the ground that Anders was not compelled to incriminate himself because he was never required to say or to do anything—the government's investigators, not Anders, did the searching and seizing.

These limitations on the Fifth Amendment have marked a radical change in the interpretation of the privilege. Whereas the focus of constitutional scrutiny had previously been the nature of the materials seized, it has now become the manner in which the materials are seized. The only possible exception, which the Supreme Court has not yet ruled on, is that there may be certain records so private—a personal diary, for example—that their production may not be demanded and they may not even be seized by investigators armed with a warrant. But as far as financial and tax records are concerned, you have no Fifth Amendment privilege if the agents properly execute a properly issued warrant.

One restraint that the government has placed upon itself in the area of using search warrants in tax cases is an internal governmental rule that the Department of Justice has adopted, declining to authorize requests for search warrants in tax cases except where the cases are "significant" because of factors such as the amount of taxes due, the nature of the fraud, and the impact of the particular case on voluntary compliance with the revenue laws.

The Fourth Amendment's prohibition against unreasonable searches and seizures grants some protections to a taxpayer that the Fifth Amendment does not. The Fourth Amendment protects not only individuals but corporations. So although a corporation may not resist compulsory production of books and records on the grounds of self-incrimination, it may resist on the grounds of the overbreadth of the demanded production, for example, or on any other unreasonable aspect of an IRS summons.

EVIDENTIARY PRIVILEGES

The law recognizes the importance of certain personal relationships, and the need for people in those relationships to communicate freely without fear that what they say may later be disclosed and used against them. Therefore, the IRS (or any other governmental agency) may not compel disclosure of confidential communications between spouses, or between an attorney and client, or a doctor and patient, or a priest or rabbi and parishioner.

However, other relationships that in everyday affairs are considered confidential are not treated that way by the law. Thus, communications between the taxpayer and his accountant, or a boss and his secretary or employees, or a depositor and his bank are not deemed confidential and may be obtained by the IRS and used against the taxpayer. This means that an agent may summons your accountant and secretary and require them to testify under oath to everything they know about you, your business, and your financial dealings.

In the area of taxes, one of the most significant of these relationships that is not privileged is the relationship between you and your accountant. However, there is a narrow exception to this rule that you can use to overcome this limitation and effectively bring certain communications with your accountant within the attorney-client privilege. Since confidential communications between an attorney and client, made for the purpose of obtaining legal advice (and not to assist the client in perpetrating a fraud), are privileged, such communications between a client and any employees of the attorney are also privileged. For example, what a client tells his lawyer's secretary, or tells his lawyer through a foreign translator, is privileged. The law recognizes that accounting concepts are a foreign language to some lawyers in almost all cases, and to almost all lawyers in some cases. Therefore, if your attorney hires your accountant (or some other accountant) to assist the lawyer in rendering legal advice to you, then communications between you and your accountant made for that purpose are privileged, despite the general absence of a taxpayer-accountant privilege.

VARIOUS FREEDOM OF INFORMATION ACTS

The federal and state governments have enacted various statutes that taxpayers under investigation may use to obtain potentially useful information.

The Freedom of Information Act is a federal statute that requires all federal governmental agencies, including the IRS, to make available to anyone a broad range of documents upon request. Under this statute, you may obtain all records compiled by the IRS in the course of a prior closed investigation, including work papers, memoranda, notes kept by agents, and reports prepared by special agents. However, the statute is rife with exceptions, the most significant being most investigatory records compiled for law-enforcement purposes.

The Internal Revenue Code also contains a provision requiring the IRS to make available, to anyone who asks, the text of any written determination of the IRS in any case, and all background documents relating to any such determination. That section now makes available "private letter rulings," which are written statements issued by the IRS to other taxpayers interpreting specific provisions of the tax law and applying those provisions to specific sets of facts. This can be an extremely useful tool to you where a technical interpretation of the Internal Revenue Code is involved, as you may learn whether the IRS has taken an inconsistent position in any similar case.

In addition, nearly all states have enacted legislation granting public access, in varying degrees, to state governmental records. Occasionally, a state tax (or tax-related) investigation will result in the state declining to prosecute, but the federal government will initiate a similar investigation. Because the state investigation is completed, you may be able to obtain extremely useful documents under a state freedom-of-information act that you could not obtain under the federal act, because of the fact that the state investigation has been closed.

CHAPTER 6

How the Government Proves You Cheated

The government does not always have to prove its case: sometimes you have the burden of proving that the government's allegations are wrong. When does who have to prove what? That depends on the type of legal proceeding involved.

A tax case can be civil or criminal (or both, in which event the civil and criminal cases are separately tried). A criminal case is one where you may be imprisoned or fined or both if you lose. A civil case is one where the IRS seeks a court's determination that you owe an additional tax plus interest, and perhaps a monetary penalty.

In any criminal case, the burden is on the government to prove every element of the offense beyond a reasonable doubt; in a criminal tax prosecution the government's burden of proof is the same as in any other criminal prosecution, from murder on down. In a civil case, the tax-payer, as a general rule (with, of course, a few exceptions that we'll get to in a minute), has the burden of proof. That's right: unless you prove your case, the government does not have to prove anything.

What that means is that in a civil tax case, once the government has issued its statutory notice—discussed ear-lier on pages 77–83—that notice is presumed to be cor-rect, and you have the burden of proving that the government's proposed deficiency is wrong.

Now for the exceptions to the rule that you have the burden of proof in a civil tax proceeding. First of all, the presumption of correctness of the IRS's determination does not apply where that determination is palpably arbi-trary or capricious (terms that are difficult to define, are applied on an *ad hoc* basis, and in the vast majority of cases are found to be inapplicable).

Another important exception relates to the statute of limitations, which is the time period beyond which the government is legally barred from attempting to assert any deficiency. There is normally a three-year statute of limitations on civil tax liability. That means that unless the IRS has mailed you its statutory notice within three years from the due date of your return (or from the date your return was filed, if it was filed late), then the government is legally barred from attempting to assert a tax deficiency against you. There are several exceptions to that general rule; the ones that arise most frequently are these:

1. If your return has omitted 25 percent or more of your true gross income, then the three-year limitations period is extended by an additional three years, to a total of six years from the filing (or due date) of the return. That means, for example, that if your gross income was $40,000, but you reported only $30,000 on your return, then the government can begin chasing you six years later.

(If you're wondering whether the government would bother going after you for only that amount of money, and for tax evasion too if they can prove it, the answer is: you bet they would.)

2. If you committed fraud in filing your return, there is no *civil* statute of limitations. That means the government can seek to impose a tax deficiency against you at *any* time and after the passage of *any* number of years. But where fraud has been committed, the six-year statute of limitations for commencement of *criminal* proceedings charging tax evasion still applies.

When the IRS tries to avoid the legal bar of the three-year statute of limitations in a civil proceeding by asserting that you omitted at least 25 percent of your reported gross income (and that therefore the six-year limitations period applies) or by alleging fraud, then even though the proceeding is civil the IRS has the burden of proving the facts necessary to extend the limitations period. In addition, where the IRS alleges fraud in a civil proceeding and seeks recovery of the 50-percent civil-fraud penalty, then the IRS has the burden of proving fraud—though not the burden of proving the underlying tax deficiency against which the 50-percent fraud penalty would be imposed.

So: In a criminal tax evasion case, the government has the burden of proving the existence of a tax deficiency (and every other element of the crime), while in most, but not all, civil cases, you have the burden of proving the absence of a deficiency.

How does the government prove that your return has underreported your true taxable income and tax? And how do you attempt to defend against the government's proof that you still owe money to the national kitty? There are a number of answers to both questions.

For simplicity's sake, we will provide the answers in the

context of a criminal tax-evasion prosecution, although the same methods (as opposed to burden) of proof also apply in a civil tax proceeding.

Before understanding the government's methods of proof, understand what it is that the government is trying to prove: that your return underreported your true taxable income (and therefore the true tax you owe). In a tax-evasion prosecution, there are other elements that the government must prove: for example, that the understatement was both "willful" and "substantial," and that you committed an affirmative act in connection with the deficiency. Also bear in mind that there are other criminal violations in addition to tax evasion that do *not* require an understatement of taxable income: such as willful failure to file a return, or willfully making a false statement on a return. A false statement violation has been committed even if the false statement does not itself result in a tax deficiency—such as, for example, falsely describing the nature of income (remember the alleged loan shark on page 101) or falsely checking the "no" box after the question, "At any time during the tax year, did you have an interest in or a signature or other authority over a bank account, securities account, or other financial account in a foreign country?" Proof of those offenses is generally more straightforward than what we are here considering: how the government proves an understatement of taxable income on a return which has been filed.

The government uses three basic methods of proving an understatement of taxable income: (1) The "specific items" method, (2) the "bank deposits and expenditures" method, and (3) the "net worth and expenditures" method. The government may also resort to (4) a miscellaneous grab bag of methods. The method the government uses in any particular case depends on the evidence available to it.

The "Specific-Items" Method of Proof

When the government seeks to prove its case through the "specific-items" method, the government offers proof that you omitted some particular item of taxable income from the return, or that some particular deduction or expense you took on the return was improper. It is the least complex of the various methods of proof and, because of its simplicity, the method most favored by the government.

The government has used the specific-items method of proof in innumerable instances. Let's assume the uncomplicated joint federal income-tax return filed by the Johnsons, a typical wage earner and his wife. Johnson is a purchasing agent for a large company and earns a yearly salary of $40,000. He and his wife have two young children (and therefore a total of four exemptions), report interest income of $5,000 per year from a Citibank account, and report no deductions. They file a joint income-tax return showing total income of $45,000 (that is, a W2 Form showing his $40,000 salary and a Form 1099 from Citibank showing $5,000 in interest income); exemptions of $4,000 ($1,000 for each of four exemptions); taxable income of $41,000 ($45,000 minus $4,000); and tax on that amount based on the IRS's tax table. The government would have a specific-items case against them if it could prove any of the following:

1. Johnson had a second job, or Mrs. Johnson had a job, from which either earned income—since that income was not reported on the return.

2. Johnson received kickbacks from vendors to induce purchases from those vendors. Illegal income, like legal income, is reportable and taxable. The Supreme Court held many years ago that the Internal Revenue Code, in defining gross income to include "all income from whatever source derived," imposes a tax on income derived

from illegal activities as well as legal ones. (You ask: "You mean in order not to commit tax evasion I have to confess to a crime on my tax return?" Answer: It is the IRS's position that you are legally required to report the income. However, even the IRS concedes that you may invoke the Fifth Amendment privilege on the return as to the source of the income, but try to guess whether that will or won't raise one or more eyebrows at the IRS.)

3. Johnson earned an additional $5,000 in interest from an account at Chemical Bank, but only reported the interest from Citibank.

4. Johnson maintained a brokerage account, and received stock dividends or capital gains on sales of stock, none of which is reported on the return.

5. And so on.

A specific-items case can be just as simple in the case of a self-employed entrepreneur who is not a W2 wage earner. Take the case of Paul Michaels, a businessman who had five customers we'll call A, B, C, D, and E. The deposits into Michaels's bank account corresponded to the invoices he issued to A, B, C, and D and to the checks issued by A, B, C, and D to Michaels, and there were no other deposits. Those deposits of receipts from A, B, C, and D totaled the gross income reported on his tax return. The government obtained Michaels's invoices to E and E's canceled checks paid to Michaels—none of which were deposited, all of which were cashed by Michaels, and all of which were unreported. E's checks constituted the "specific items" of omitted income that the government charged against Michaels.

Proving a specific-items case does not necessarily require the government to prove the omission of a specific item of income; instead (or in addition) the government may prove the falsity of a specific deduction taken on the return. For examples:

1. Cecil Doaks reported having made charitable contributions of $2,110 during the year. To support the claim, he gave an IRS auditor four canceled checks payable to various charities, in the amounts of $220, $400, $640, and $850. In fact, the agent learned that the checks were originally in the amounts of $20, $100, $40, and $50, and were subsequently altered by Doaks (see the smoking gun on page 28). Although the amounts were small, Doaks was criminally charged for having submitted the falsified checks to the auditor.

2. Robert Hamilton reported having incurred medical expenses of $4,000 during the year. He presented the auditor with checks totaling $4,000, all made payable to Doctors X, Y, and Z. In fact, X was a gardener, Y was a plumber, and Z installed burglar alarms. Hamilton had conferred medical degrees on them by adding "Dr." in front of their names on the checks after the checks had cleared his bank and been returned to him.

3. Richard Horton claimed a casualty loss of $8,643.43, explaining that a tree crashed through his roof in a thunderstorm, and he had to pay a roofer that sum to repair the damage. As proof, he gave the auditor his check made payable to the roofer in that amount. Examination of the roofer's checking account revealed that such a check in fact cleared through the roofer's account, but that ten days later the roofer issued a check to Horton for $7,779.09—exactly 90 percent of Horton's check to the roofer. In reality, the roofer had been paid 10 percent of Horton's original check for his troubles in helping Horton generate a juicy and fictitious deduction.

4. The Tax Reform Act of 1969 radically changed the law regarding the allowable extent of a deduction for gifts to charities of items such as precious manuscripts or other valuable professional papers authored by the taxpayer. Prior to the effective date of the act, a taxpayer donating

such papers to a charitable institution was entitled to deduct their fair-market value—that is, the amount of money that those papers would fetch if offered for sale to the public rather than being donated to charity. Subsequent to the effective date of the act, the taxpayer could deduct only the cost of the paper, irrespective of the item's actual present value. In the case of papers having substantial worth, the act therefore quite literally changed the sublime to the ridiculous. Therefore, if a taxpayer donated such a gift to charity after the effective date of the act, but deducted the fair-market value of the gift (rather than the negligible cost of the paper) by falsely claiming the gift was donated before that date, the government would have a specific-items case against him.

A classic specific-items case involving this change in the law was developed during the presidency of Richard M. Nixon. Various government agencies, including the IRS, gathered evidence showing that President Nixon had contributed pre-presidential papers to the National Archives *in 1970*, but had falsely claimed on his 1969 federal income-tax return (and also as a carry-forward deduction on his 1970, 1971, and 1972 returns) that the gift had been made in 1969, prior to the effective date of the change in the Internal Revenue Code concerning charitable deductions. President Nixon took tax deductions during these years totaling $576,000 based on an appraisal of the fair-market value of those papers. However, even if the papers were worth millions, President Nixon was entitled under the law to deduct only the cost of the paper itself, since the gift was made after the effective date of the new law.

President Nixon was never charged with a crime. The attorney who handled his tax affairs was indicted for making false statements to various investigating agencies, including the IRS, but the charges were ultimately dismissed because of the prosecutor's subsequent misconduct.

A single specific-items case may involve specific items of both omitted income and improper deductions. Take the case of John Highliver, the principal stockholder of a privately held corporation. The corporation paid Highliver's country-club dues and his airfare and travel expenses for several lengthy sojourns to various hithers and yons. Those payments were all entered on the corporation's books as "travel and entertainment expenses." In fact, however, Highliver entertained no business associates at the club and conducted no business on any of his trips. The government charged violations with respect to both the corporation's and Highliver's income-tax returns on those specific items. The payments were charged as dividends to Highliver—"constructive dividends," as lawyers say (in English, that means the law will "construe," or consider, the payments to be dividends). Since dividends are taxable to their recipients and not deductible by the corporation, the corporation thereby had inflated its "T and E" (travel and entertainment) expenses by the amount of these checks, and Highliver's return had understated his income by not reporting, as income to himself, the payments for country clubs, airline tickets, and related expenses.

The "Bank-Deposits-and-Expenditures" Method of Proof

In addition to the direct method of proving a deficiency through proof of specific income items omitted or deductions improperly reported on the return, the government may also use various indirect methods of proving a tax deficiency. The law permits the government to use any method of proving a tax deficiency, as long as the method reasonably proves its conclusion. Over the years, several indirect methods of proof have evolved as the government's favorites. One of the simplest and most frequently used is the "bank-deposits-and-expenditures" method.

The bank-deposits-and-expenditures method of proof combines two different methods: one involving a taxpayer's bank accounts, and one involving a taxpayer's expenditures, each during the same year. Although both methods may be used separately, they are frequently used in tandem.

THE "BANK-DEPOSITS" METHOD OF PROOF

This method of proof "reconstructs" the taxpayer's true gross income for a particular year by analyzing his bank deposits (and his brokerage deposits) for that year. The simplicity or complexity of this method of proof as applied in any case depends on the simplicity or complexity of the particular taxpayer's financial affairs. The principles involved, however, are quite straightforward, and you can understand them by considering a simple example.

DO YOUR BANK DEPOSITS SHOW "UNIDENTIFIED DEPOSITS"?

Assume that John Depositor is a wage earner whose tax return for the year in question reflects only two sources of income: (1) a $40,000 salary, for which Depositor attaches a W2 Form provided by his employer, showing a total of $10,000 withheld out of the $40,000, and (2) interest income of $5,000 from a Chase Manhattan certificate of deposit. Assume also, for simplicity's sake, that Depositor maintained only one bank account in the year in question —a checking account at Citibank.

The IRS obtains Depositor's bank account—from Depositor himself or from Citibank. This consists of copies of the monthly statements, deposit slips, and canceled checks. Those records reflect a total of $120,000 deposited into the account. The bank-deposits method of proof is basically designed to answer the question: Do these deposits mean that Depositor had a substantial amount of unreported income?

The government is not permitted simply to claim that these facts alone prove that Depositor had unreported income of $75,000 (that is, $120,000 in deposits minus the reported total of $40,000 in salary and $5,000 in interest). In legalese, that means that the government has not satisfied its burden of proof if all it can prove is that Depositor's bank deposits exceeded his reported income by $75,000. Such a "burden" would not be burdensome at all to the government, and the law affords taxpayers considerably more protection than that.

Why? Because the law does not permit an inference that all money deposited into a bank account is income.

Why not? Many reasons. Money deposited into a bank account may be a gift, a loan, an inheritance, a dividend from a tax-exempt investment, money previously accummulated, money generated from the sale of an asset previously acquired, a redeposit into the account of funds previously withdrawn from the same account, a transfer from one bank to the other, or some other nonincome source. So the government may not charge unidentified bank deposits as being income unless it has conducted a thorough analysis of the taxpayer's deposits and taken reasonable steps to eliminate all identifiable nonincome items from the amounts deposited (it's got other hurdles to overcome also, which we'll get to).

How does the government satisfy this initial burden? First, it has to analyze the bank accounts themselves. Let's stay for a moment with John Depositor and his one account at Citibank. The government would first have to analyze that account to determine whether, for example, any of the $120,000 deposited merely represents redeposits of money previously withdrawn from that account. For example, if Depositor withdrew $500 in cash, and at a later date deposited $500 in cash (deposit slips generally show whether a particular deposit consists of cash or checks or both), then in a criminal case the deposit of $500 is deemed simply to be a redeposit of the same $500 which Depositor had earlier withdrawn from that account. Thus, that $500 cash deposit is no longer considered an unidentified deposit, but is considered an identified cash redeposit of previously withdrawn funds and is therefore classified as a nonincome item.

Your credits aren't quite so easy in a civil case. There, since the IRS's statutory notice is presumed correct, the burden is on you to establish that the cash you deposited was cash you'd previously withdrawn.

Depositor is similarly entitled to other credits. He may have redeposited a check that had previously been certified. Perhaps he had intended to purchase a $682.95 stereo whose seller demanded a certified check, but changed his mind on the way to the store. The bank would have charged his account in the sum of $682.95 when the check was certified, and credited his account by that same amount when Depositor deposited the check into his own account after changing his mind. The $682.95 deposit— part of the $120,000 in our hypothetical deposits into Depositor's account—would no longer be an unidentified item but a specifically identified nonincome item.

The job of identifying previously unidentified deposits is not always so easy, as you've probably guessed. Let's leave John Depositor for a moment, and consider a person with more complex finances—someone with numerous bank accounts and hundreds (or thousands) of deposits into those accounts. The government is required to fully examine all of those accounts to determine not only whether particular deposits are merely redeposits (for example) of funds into the same account, but also to determine whether any deposits are merely interbank transfers: for instance, a $250 check drawn on Bank A that shows up as a deposit into Bank B, or a $250 check from Bank A and a $125 check from Bank B that show up as a combined $375 deposit into Bank C. You get the point: the more complex a taxpayer's financial affairs, the more complex is the government's job in conducting a full analysis of all his bank accounts. The deposits of a wealthy taxpayer with hundreds or thousands of deposits and withdrawals into and out of numerous accounts require a far more extensive analysis than our John Depositor with his few deposits into one Citibank account. The government generally has a far easier job doing a full bank-deposits analysis on Average-man than on Rich-man.

For example, the IRS worked unsuccessfully for two years trying to develop a bank deposits case against Claude Reynolds. Reynolds had only three bank accounts. But most of his deposits were redeposited into half a dozen brokerage accounts Reynolds maintained. Those accounts also had to be analyzed before a bank-deposits case could be made against him. There were voluminous transfers of funds among those bank and brokerage accounts. Reynolds was an active and expert stock trader, and traded not only for himself but also for several dozen grateful clients. The deeper the agents dug, the more they discovered trades, exchanges, and transfers. Identifying the original sources of deposits and true owners of securities became more muddled and uncertain, until the agents finally gave up the hunt for easier prey.

Now back to John Depositor and his Citibank account. Let's suppose the government has analyzed and found that among the $120,000 in deposits, $4,500 were redeposits of previously withdrawn funds. That is simply the beginning of the IRS's job; it still must attempt to eliminate all other possible identifiable nonincome sources of the deposits. For example, some of the deposits may have been loans to Depositor, or gifts, or a bequest. The government must take all reasonable steps to identify any such items.

There is no clearly articulable standard defining precisely what the government must do in order to determine whether deposits include any such nonincome (and therefore non–income-taxable) items. Because of the government's difficulty in finding out whether a taxpayer received gifts or inheritances or other nonincome items, which may account for some or all of the taxpayer's deposits, and because of the impossibility of defining precisely what steps the government must take to learn of their existence, the "leads" doctrine has developed.

The government must follow leads given by the taxpayer. A lead is an explanation given by the taxpayer that —if true—would effectively negate guilt by providing a nontaxable explanation for the source of deposits. For example, if Depositor claims that a jury awarded him $10,000 for injuries in an auto accident case (under the Internal Revenue Code, personal-injury recoveries are nontaxable) and that he deposited that sum into his account, the IRS would be required to check the court records to verify Depositor's claim before charging that deposit as income to Depositor.

Whether or not to provide an IRS investigator with leads is often a difficult decision to make. The easiest case is where you have not in fact understated income on your tax return. For instance, where your bank accounts reflect a single unidentified deposit and no other significant question has arisen on an audit of the return, and where that deposit represents a documentable nonincome item, the explanation of that item to the agent—giving him a lead he can readily verify—would presumably end the audit.

But where your return presents other questionable

items, and where a substantial possibility exists of a recommendation of criminal prosecution, it may be advisable not to give the agent any leads. That way, you can show at a later stage—such as to a jury in a subsequent criminal trial—that the government's entire method of proof is too tenuous and speculative to support a conviction. An effective way of doing that is by using a particular item that you can explain as illustrative proof of the frailty of the method that the government is using. As a general rule, you're better off being charged in a bank-deposits prosecution with an omission of $100,000 in unidentified deposits if you can explain $50,000 of those deposits (thus leaving $50,000 unexplained), than being charged with $50,000 in unidentified deposits if you can't explain any of them.

The leads doctrine is related to and directly affects your Fifth Amendment privilege against self-incrimination, and frequently presents a substantial dilemma. Any citizen has a constitutional right not to incriminate himself. As applied to a bank-deposits case, the privilege means that you are not required to inform an IRS agent of any leads. If you provide certain leads, you expose yourself either to a claim by the government that you have waived the privilege, or that no other leads than the one(s) suggested actually exist. Moreover, you give up the later advantage of surprising the prosecution as to that item. But if you do not provide any leads, you are hard-pressed to argue later that the government should have followed leads that the government never knew existed—though you may do so if the government in fact knew or should have known of such leads through other available sources.

The bank-deposits method of proof also limits to a degree the government's traditional burden of proof in any criminal case, and the presumption of any defendant's innocence. In proving a bank-deposits case, the government is not required to negate all possible nonincome sources of a taxpayer's deposits; the rationale for this principle is that the source of the deposits is uniquely within the taxpayer's knowledge. The government is required only to perform a sufficiently thorough investigation, including an analysis of the accounts themselves and leads that are reasonably susceptible of being checked, to justify the conclusion that the unexplained excess is in fact currently taxable income. What is a "sufficiently thorough" investigation depends upon the facts and circumstances of each case. But where the government's investigation is sufficient, then the taxpayer remains silent at the risk of being convicted. And though that sounds somewhat inconsistent with a defendant's right not to testify in any criminal case, the courts have nevertheless upheld that principle for many years.

The thought may have occurred to you, "How can I possibly be expected to remember the sources of all my deposits?" In reality, few people can. Nevertheless, this method of proving a tax deficiency has been sanctioned by the law. But because it is a circumstantial method of proof, and the courts have recognized that it is only an approximation, there are additional requirements imposed on the government in allowing this type of proof of a deficiency; merely analyzing the deposits, pursuing leads, and proving unidentified bank deposits is not enough.

CASH-ON-HAND: THE TRICK QUESTION

Too often, a taxpayer has exactly the wrong instinct when asked by an IRS agent: "How much cash do you usually have available?" or "How much cash did you have at the beginning of the tax year?" Most taxpayers instinctively say something like: "Who me? Hardly any," thinking that the agent is trying to trick them into admitting possession of a lot of cash—and therefore, they fear, the commission of tax fraud. The trap, however, may be exactly the opposite.

To understand why, let's turn to John Depositor and his total deposits of $120,000 during a year when he received only a net income (after withholding) of $30,000 from his employer plus $5,000 in interest. Suppose his deposit slips show that those deposits consisted of $90,000 in checks and $30,000 in cash. Suppose further that during the course of the year he has not cashed anything close to $30,000 in checks. If he has self-defensively told an agent "Who me? I only had $100 in cash at the start of the year," then where did the $30,000 in cash deposits during the year come from? It couldn't have come from cash accumulated in prior years—the "cash hoard" or "money in my pillow" defense—because his claim to the agent that he only had $100 in cash at the beginning of the year would make any later contrary claim inconsistent, and would paint Depositor as a liar. Thus, in trying to protect himself by minimizing the amount of his cash on hand at the beginning of the year, Depositor has checkmated himself.

In fact, the taxpayer with something to worry about is often best advised not only *not* to give the "I only had a few bucks" answer to the trap question, but not to give any answer at all. The reason for this is that an essential element of the government's proof in a bank-deposits case requires the government to establish an "opening cash-on-hand" figure for the beginning of the tax year. If the taxpayer's deposits during the year came from a safety-deposit box or from a cash hoard in his pillow or under a floorboard, and if that cash was in the taxpayer's possession at the beginning of the tax year, then the money does not become taxable income when transferred from its storage place to a bank account.

The government is therefore required to prove with

"reasonable certainty" the amount of the taxpayer's cash at the beginning of the year so that a corresponding amount may be subtracted from the total of deposits made during the taxable year. Establishing this opening cash-on-hand figure is often a very difficult job for the government, and without it there is no bank-deposits case. The government has tried in many cases to avoid this requirement where it is unable to establish an opening cash-on-hand figure, by giving the taxpayer credit for all cash deposits, thereby not charging him with unreported income for any cash deposits. Although many courts have permitted this lessening of the government's burden, there is a split of judicial authority on the issue.

How does the government establish an opening cash-on-hand figure? Frequently, from the taxpayer's own mouth or pen: either he answers when they ask him, or the figure appears in the taxpayer's own books and records, or he has filled out an application for a loan of some kind (such as a mortgage application or a new-car loan). Otherwise, the government's job in proving the opening cash-on-hand figure is a difficult one, usually requiring detailed investigation and analysis. If you are ever the subject of a bank-deposits investigation and want to help the IRS make a case against you, tell them what your opening cash-on-hand was, and make it a low figure.

The concept of cash-on-hand at the beginning of the year has a partner: cash-on-hand at the end of the year. If you had $10,000 in cash at the beginning of the year and $10,000 in cash at the end of the year, then you had an effective cash availability (to explain deposits into your bank accounts) of zero from your opening cash-on-hand figure. In other words, your opening cash balance presumably remained in your pillow during the year, and does not provide an explanation for deposits made during the year.

In a tax prosecution, the government frequently introduces into evidence a chart—large, clear, and impressive —to summarize its case. The chart is not additional evidence, but merely a summary of the government's evidence. At the end of the bank-deposits case against John Depositor, the government's chart might look like this for the year in question (the government usually charges multi-year offenses, rather than just one year, in a bank-deposits case):

Total Bank Deposits		$120,000
Less:		
Income:		
Salary checks	$30,000.	
Interest checks on CD	5,000.	
	$35,000.	
Nonincome deposits:		
Gifts	$ 500.	
Insurance recovery	1,200.	
Checks redeposited	500.	
Cash redeposited	4,500.	
	$ 6,700.	
Cash-on-hand:		
January 1	$10,000.	
− December 31	−2,000.	
	$ 8,000.	
		$ 49,700.
Unidentified deposits		$ 70,300.

(The chart assumes, for purposes of simplicity, that Depositor deposited all of his salary and interest checks. As far as the cash redeposits of $4,500 are concerned, that figure assumes that Depositor wrote out checks to cash in excess of that amount during the year, and he is entitled to the presumption that the cash deposits are simply redeposits of some of that cash.) The government has thus established a prima facie case of unreported income—sufficient evidence for the law to permit the jury to conclude as a matter of fact, if the jury wants to, that Depositor had unreported income of $70,300.

Except for one last requirement: the government may have to prove that Depositor was engaged in a business capable of producing additional taxable income ("may" because the government has no such obligation where its investigation has been sufficiently thorough to eliminate verifiable nontaxable sources). In many cases this is the easiest element for the government to establish in proving a deficiency in a bank-deposits case. However, in the case of a wage earner—such as our John Depositor—that is not the case: a salaried employee generally has only his salary. And if the government is unable to establish that he was in fact engaged in some business that could possibly have been the source of the alleged unreported income— either legal (such as moonlighting) or illegal (such as moonshining)—then it has failed to prove its case unless it has effectively eliminated all verifiable nontaxable sources. If the government could establish that a salaried employee who reported only his salary as income had another job, the government would be able to prosecute a specific-items case rather than a bank-deposits case, although the government is allowed to prove its case through both methods of proof, or use one method to corroborate the other, which the government frequently does.

Bank-deposits analyses are also used by the government to prove cases against taxpayers in whom the government has an interest beyond just taxes. For example, it is common knowledge that when the federal government could not convict the notorious Al Capone for any of his alleged basic criminal activity, "they got him for taxes." Less well known is that key evidence used against Capone was that during a period of time when Capone claimed to have sustained financial setbacks that allegedly rendered him unable to pay his taxes, $1,851,840.08 had been deposited into various bank accounts under Capone's control (those are 1920s dollars, when a million-eight was a million-eight).

THE "EXPENDITURES" METHOD OF PROOF

This method of proof, which is frequently used in conjunction with either the bank-deposits method just discussed or the net-worth method (which we will be discussing shortly), is based on a very simple theory: When a taxpayer spends during a particular year more than his reported income and the source of those expenditures is otherwise unexplained, the government is permitted to claim that those excess expenditures represent unreported income.

The IRS frequently uses this method of proof in combination with a bank-deposits case. The reason can easily be understood by returning for a moment to the bank-deposits method.

A bank deposit is merely one way you place a sum of money somewhere. It is, in effect, a transfer of money in exchange for a credit at a bank in an equal amount. Similarly, your purchase of a car, or of stock, or of any other item is the exchange of money for an asset. When the IRS uses the expenditures method of proof, it is simply adding up the number of dollars you paid out in a given year, whether spent for pleasure or for the acquisition of any assets (a car, shares of stock, weekly groceries, or money deposited into a bank); comparing it to your reported income for that year; seeking an innocent explanation for the source of the money spent (such as funds previously available or nontaxable receipts acquired during the year); and if the amount spent exceeds the amount reported, and if the difference is unexplained, charging you with unreported income in an amount equal to the difference. Put another way, the IRS adds up your total expenditures (including deposits to bank accounts, brokerage accounts, purchases, and other such items), subtracts funds available to you during that year, and assumes that the difference between the two figures represents your actual income for that year. And if that amount exceeds the amount of income reported on your return, the IRS treats the difference as unreported income.

As in a bank-deposits case, however, the government is required to establish certain other elements before the law will permit it to reach that nifty conclusion. The government must establish with "reasonable" accuracy a financial "starting point" for you at the beginning of the year. If during the year you spent $50,000 more than your reported gross income but had $50,000 available to you at the beginning of the year, then that $50,000 availability provides an explanation for the $50,000 differential. The government also has the same burden regarding proof of a "likely source" for the allegedly unreported income as it has in a bank-deposits case.

Several other principles applicable to a bank-deposits case also provide additional protection to you in an expenditures case. The IRS is required to investigate your financial affairs sufficiently intensively to eliminate the possibility that the difference between expenditures and reported income may in fact have been attributable to nontaxable items acquired during the year—such as, for example, a loan or a gift or other nontaxable acquisition of assets that you may have converted into money during the year and that may account for all or part of the excess of expenditures over reported income. Similarly, where the government uses a combined bank-deposits and expenditures method, the amount of cash—greenbacks—

you spent during the year must be reduced by the amount of cash withdrawn from your own bank accounts during the year. This is because you are entitled, at least in a criminal case, to the presumption that the cash withdrawn is the same cash as the cash expended (assuming that the cash is withdrawn before it is spent).

The expenditures method of proof is used frequently not only in conjunction with a bank-deposits case, but also with another commonly used method by which the IRS seeks to prove a tax deficiency: the "net-worth-and-expenditures" method.

The "Net-Worth-and-Expenditures" Method of Proof

The "net-worth-and-expenditures" method of proof—for short, a "net-worth" case, but in actuality very much a net-worth-*and-expenditures* case—is often the most complex and difficult for the government to use. Nevertheless, its basis is quite simple to understand.

Your net worth as of a particular date is merely your assets minus your liabilities on that date. To use a simple example, suppose your assets total $20,000 (for instance, $10,000 in a bank and a new car that cost $10,000) and your liabilities are $5,000 (a loan on the new car). Then your net worth is $15,000. That is, as of a particular date you are "worth" $15,000.

The essential starting point for the IRS in proving a net-worth case is establishing your net worth on January 1 and on December 31 of the year in question. The IRS must determine all of your assets and liabilities at the beginning of the year to arrive at a net figure as of January 1 of that year (the "opening net worth"), and do the same for December 31 ("closing net worth"). Assets are generally valued at cost, and any increase in actual value of those assets during the year is not considered unless the assets were sold during the year.

The required starting point for the government is far easier to state than to satisfy. Proving a "firm" (that is, reasonably certain) opening net-worth figure, without which no net-worth case is possible, is a substantial undertaking. Your opening net worth is the starting point in any net-worth prosecution—much like the opening cash-on-hand figure in a bank-deposits case—and if the government cannot establish it, the government hasn't got a net-worth case. So if an IRS agent ever asks you for a net-worth statement, be careful: He's asking you to make his hard job easy.

Establishing your opening net worth is only the beginning of the government's burden. Assume you had a net worth of $15,000 on January 1 of a particular year, a net worth of $115,000 on December 31, and reported income during the year of $30,000. That does not mean the IRS may charge you with unreported income of $70,000 (i.e., $115,000 minus $45,000 [$15,000 plus $30,000]). Your true financial picture may be worse, or better, depending on the following factors.

Your situation is worse (or better, from the IRS investigator's standpoint) to the extent of your nondeductible expenditures during the year—such as payments for food and other normal living expenses, payments of tuition, payments of federal income taxes, and similar items. The IRS is permitted to add the total of these expenditures to the increase in your net worth, since items such as these obviously cost money and that cost must be explained—the money must have come from somewhere. Thus, if your net worth increased over the year by $100,000 and you also spent $30,000 on additional items not reflected in your "closing" December 31 assets figure, then the IRS would be entitled to "charge" you with this additional

$30,000 in expenditures. In short, the IRS charges that the total increase in your wealth from the first to the last day of the year, plus your total nondeductible expenditures made during the year that do not show up as part of your year-end wealth, represent your true income for the year.

Almost, but not quite. You also are entitled to some credit. Suppose, for example, you acquired funds or assets during the year from such nontaxable sources as we have previously discussed: gifts, loans, inheritances, and so on. You are entitled to have all such items subtracted from the increase in your net worth, and to have only the difference charged against you as income. Thus, the leads doctrine is also applicable in net-worth cases, and in fact first developed in net-worth cases and only later was held applicable to bank-deposits cases.

The IRS determines your increase in net worth from the beginning to the end of the year, adds your nondeductible expenditures, and subtracts nontaxable assets you received during the course of the year. If that net figure is equal to or lower than your reported income, there is no net-worth-and-expenditures proof of a deficiency. But if the figure is higher than your reported income, then the IRS is entitled to claim that there is a deficiency. The difference could not have come from assets you owned at the beginning of the year (because you have already been credited with that figure as part of your opening net worth) or from nontaxable sources acquired during the year (because you have already been credited with those). Since the excess came from somewhere, the government is permitted to claim that it must have come from taxable sources.

Other Indirect Methods of Proof

While the bank-deposits, net-worth, and expenditures methods of proof, alone or in conjunction with one another, are by far the most frequently used "indirect" methods (as opposed to the "direct" or specific-items method) used by the IRS in attempting to prove a tax deficiency, the IRS is also permitted to use any other method of proof reasonably designed to provide a fair and rational measure of any taxpayer's true taxable income during a particular year. A few examples of different methods which the IRS has successfully used (almost exclusively in civil cases) illustrate the scope of the IRS's permitted inventiveness:

¶ The "percentage markup method." The IRS has analyzed many major types of businesses in different geographical areas to determine the "normal" net profit of each such business. Where the taxpayer's reported net profit on sales is significantly less than the norm, the IRS may use this method of proof to reconstruct his taxable income. In essence, the IRS applies a predetermined "reliable" percentage of presumed profit to the taxpayer's gross sales, gross receipts, or cost of goods sold. To obtain a reliable markup figure, the IRS may use against the taxpayer the very same markup percentage used by the taxpayer himself in other years. For example, the IRS has applied a percentage markup based on a store's current shelf price of liquor to that liquor store's prior year's purchases in order to determine the store's prior year's income. Even more far-reaching, the IRS has determined a percentage markup of gasoline by various neighborhood gas stations and determined another gas station's income by applying the others' markup percentage to that station's purchases.

¶ The "percentage-of-error" method. An understatement of taxable income for a particular time period is specifically computed, and the percentage of the understatement is applied against taxable income reported for other time periods in order to approximate the amount of assumed deficiency for those other periods. Similarly, where police raided an illegal numbers operation and seized one week's worth of receipts, the IRS multiplied those receipts by fifty-two to determine the operation's total annual gross receipts. Although the taxpayers protested, the court upheld the IRS's method.

Other methods approved by the courts in light of the circumstances of the particular situation include these examples:

¶ A motel's gross income has been reconstructed based on the number of fresh sheets rented by the motel during each taxable year (with adjustments for personal use and estimated nonpaying guests). A massage parlor's income has been reconstructed on the basis of the number of towels laundered.

¶ A tavern's gross sales have been reconstructed by assuming the sale of twenty-eight shots of whiskey per bottle purchased, at an acknowledged price per shot; 198 measured mugs of beer per keg purchased, multiplied by the per-mug price; and comparable figures for other drinks.

¶ A bagel bakery's gross sales have been reconstructed by ascertaining the number of pounds of flour purchased by the bakery during the year, and computing the number of bagels physically producible from each hundred pounds of flour, with appropriate adjustments for other ingredients, personal consumption, waste, and similar factors.

¶ The gross income of a doctor who specialized in abortions has been reconstructed by multiplying the doctor's average fee per abortion by the number of morphine tablets he purchased during the year, after determining that the doctor generally prescribed one tablet per operation.

¶ The IRS reconstructed the income of a taxpayer involved in assorted crimes by calculating the cash expenditures of his equal partner in crime and charging that amount as income not only to the partner but also—since they were equals—to the taxpayer.

CHAPTER 7

Your Defenses to the Government's Proof that You Cheated

When the IRS is seeking merely to assert a deficiency in a civil tax proceeding, the issue of your intent is irrelevant: if your return understates your true taxable income, then an additional tax is due and owing irrespective of whether the understatement was inadvertent or deliberate—only the number of dollars is important. However, the government may be seeking to impose sanctions beyond simply the deficiency, and in those cases the issue of your intent is highly significant. That happens where the IRS seeks to impose a 50-percent fraud penalty in a civil proceeding, or where it seeks the penal sanctions of the criminal law. In such cases, the defense generally fits into two broad categories: dollars and intent. You may claim that (a) my return accurately states my true taxable income, (b) any error on my return was unintentional, or (c) both.

In a tax-evasion prosecution, the government is required to prove that the defendant willfully attempted to evade or defeat any tax or the payment of any tax. Where the government seeks in a civil litigation to establish "fraud" in order to impose the 50-percent fraud penalty, the government must similarly prove that the taxpayer willfully paid less tax than he knew was due. While the respective burdens of proof in a tax-evasion prosecution and in a civil tax-fraud litigation are different, the nature of the government's proof generally is similar in both types of cases, and the various defenses available to the taxpayer are also similar.

We will explain these defenses in the context of a criminal prosecution for tax evasion. However, bear in mind that the first set of defenses discussed—based on "the dollars," i.e., the claim that there is no tax deficiency—are available not only in a tax-evasion prosecution or fraud case, but also in an ordinary civil tax proceeding. The second set of defenses—those based on the taxpayer's intent—apply only in those more serious cases where the government has alleged fraud, either in an indictment or in an attempt to assert the 50-percent civil-fraud penalty.

Defenses Based on the Dollars

The manner of defending against the government's claim that a tax return understates taxable income depends upon the method of proof used by the government. Defenses against a specific-items prosecution differ from defenses against a bank-deposits or a net-worth prosecution.

For this reason, the first thing the taxpayer seeks to obtain in a tax-evasion case is a bill of particulars requiring the government to state its method of proof and the financial particulars of the government's claim of a deficiency.

The taxpayer's motion for a bill of particulars will frequently look like this:

1. For each year state whether the alleged deficiency of taxable income and tax is based upon each of the following methods of proof:
   (a) Omission of specific items;
   (b) Overstatement of deductions, exemptions, or exclusions;
   (c) Net worth and expenditures;
   (d) Bank deposits and expenditures;
   (e) Expenditures;
   (f) Any other circumstantial method of calculation, identifying such method;
   (g) Any combination of the above, identifying each.
2. Set forth an itemized statement of the gross income, deductions, and credits which it is claimed made up the defendant's taxable income for each year charged.
3. As to each of the items specified as gross income in response to ¶2 hereinabove, state:
   (a) The nature of each item claimed by the government to be included in the total gross income;
   (b) The amount and date it is claimed the same was received by the defendant;
   (c) The name of each person or entity from whom it is claimed the same was received by the defendant;
   (d) The manner in which it is claimed the payments referred to in the preceding subparagraph were made, whether by cash, by check, by goods, services, or other means; if any of said items were not received by or paid to the defendant, state to whom they were paid, and if the defendant's constructive receipt of said items is relied upon, state the basis therefor.
4. Provide an itemized statement of each and every deduction, credit, exemption, and exclusion, and the nature and amount thereof, it is claimed should be allowed for each year to the defendant.

5. If it is claimed the defendant omitted specific items of income, identify such items and set forth the particulars requested in ¶3 hereinabove as to each such item.

6. If it is claimed the defendant overstated deductions, exemptions, or exclusions, itemize each such alleged overstatement, specifying the nature, amount, date, payer, and recipient, if any, and the alleged basis for disallowance.

7. As to each year in which the government relies in whole or in part upon the net-worth and expenditures theory, set forth the net worth of the defendant at the beginning and end of each year and any prior years used in calculating said net worth, specifying each item claimed to constitute the defendant's assets and liabilities at each such time, and the additions and subtractions claimed to have occurred during each such year; and set forth an itemized list of each expenditure claimed to have been made by the defendant, including the date, amount, payee, payer, and manner of payment of each such expenditure.

8. As to each year in which the government relies in whole or in part upon the bank-deposits and expenditures theory, set forth the alleged cash-on-hand figure for the beginning of each taxable year; set forth an itemized list of each and every deposit including, if by cash, the date, amount, and depositary, and if by check, the date, amount, payee, depositary, maker, and endorsements thereon; and set forth an itemized list of each expenditure claimed to have been made by the defendant, including the date, amount, payee, payer, and manner of payment of each such expenditure. As to the deposits, set forth each item of deposit which has been eliminated from the defendant's alleged gross income and the reason therefor.

9. As to each year in which it is claimed that the alleged income is based in whole or in part on the expenditures theory, set forth an itemized list of the assets attributed to the defendant at the beginning and close of each such year, the date, consideration for, and source or disposition of each asset added or disposed of during each such year,

and an itemization of the expenditures claimed to have been made by the defendant, including the date, amount, payee, payer, and manner of payment of each such expenditure.

Only after the taxpayer learns these particulars of the government's method of proof is he in any position to prepare intelligently to meet the claim of a deficiency.

"DOLLARS" DEFENSES TO A SPECIFIC-ITEMS CASE

Let's assume that the government responds that its method of proof is based upon specific items, either specific items of income omitted from the return or specific items of deductions improperly taken on the return. The defenses to such a claim of deficiency are often straightforward. Remember, we are here considering only one of the required elements of the government's proof—that a deficiency exists; a defense to a second element, willfulness, is very often available even where a deficiency does in fact exist, and we will be considering that defense a little later.

How do you prove you didn't receive the specific items of income charged against you? Sometimes, of course, you cannot. And in those instances where you cannot, it is often strategically wise not to try to, and to defend instead only on the issue of willfulness—because if you have an arguable defense against the claim of willfulness but a weak claim of nonreceipt of the alleged omitted income, then raising the weak claim can taint, in a jury's or judge's eyes, the arguable defense.

Sometimes, however, you can defend against the charge that you received the income in question. That defense frequently arises where the government charges that the income arose out of other criminal conduct—such as a taxpayer's receipt of a bribe, or embezzlement, or sales of illegal drugs. In fact, where the federal government obtains indictments charging such offenses, tax-evasion counts are frequently included, charging the defendant with having willfully failed to report the ill-gotten gains on his tax return. In such cases, the defense to the tax-evasion charge is substantially the same as the defense to the charge of the underlying criminal conduct. After all, if the defendant prevails on his claim that he didn't receive the kickback, embezzle the money, or sell the drugs, then he wasn't required to report the same money as income on his tax return. Thus, the defense mechanisms in such cases are similar to those used in garden-variety criminal trials: disproving contentions of witnesses who claim that the defendant received money and attacking the government's corroborative evidence.

The defense that you never received the money is not unique to cases involving nontax crimes. For example, a physician who is accused of receiving and failing to report cash fees from patients may defend against that charge by challenging the claims of the patients testifying against him, countering that their false testimony is motivated by the fact that they overstated medical deductions on their own tax returns and are therefore now claiming they paid the doctor in cash.

A second defense sometimes used against the government's claim that alleged specific items of income were not reported by the taxpayer is to acknowledge the receipt of the money but contest the charge that the money was income to the taxpayer. For example, a taxpayer's employer may have wanted to make a questionable payment to some third party in a secretive manner, and may have delivered that money to the taxpayer for him to redeliver to the third party. In such a case the taxpayer would be merely a conduit for the money, a go-between linking the giver to the receiver, and the money that passed hands did not become taxable income to the taxpayer merely because he possessed it at one point in the money's travels. Or a friend of the taxpayer may have needed a favor and requested the taxpayer to receive funds payable to the friend, with the understanding that those funds would later be transmitted to their real intended recipient; possession of those funds as a mere custodian does not render them taxable income to the taxpayer.

A specific-items case may also be defensible on technical interpretations of the Internal Revenue Code. For example, the taxpayer may concede having received and not reported the money in question, but claim that the money was not "income." One taxpayer argued successfully that payments received for sale of her own blood plasma (the particular blood had high commercial value due to the presence of an extremely rare antibody) were not included within the Internal Revenue Code's definition of income.

A similar technical defense is one where the taxpayer concedes the receipt of the money but claims that it is not yet income because his right to the money is conditional— for example, additional services are yet to be rendered and until rendered the money does not belong to him and must be held separately for possible return. Or where the government charges that an item was improperly taken as an expense, the taxpayer may defend on the theory that the IRS's interpretation of the applicable provision of the tax law is incorrect, and admit having deducted the expense but attempt to defend the propriety of the tax treatment of that specific item. For example, where the government claims that a portion of a retailer's reported expenses resulted from a sham year-end transaction designed solely to increase expenses for the year, thus decreasing taxes, the retailer may attempt to support the bona fides of the year-end transaction.

In cases such as this, the distinction between a defense

based on "dollars" and one based on "intent" often blurs. You may assert a two-pronged defense: your return treated the item correctly as a matter of tax law, but even if it was not correct you believed it to be, perhaps relying on expert (albeit erroneous) advice, and you should therefore be found to have erred not deliberately but only inadvertently and in good faith, if at all.

A further defense to the "dollars" aspect of a direct or specific-items prosecution is also applicable to a prosecution based on any of the indirect methods of proof. It is essential to a tax-evasion prosecution that a tax deficiency in fact exist. To the extent that a taxpayer's return has failed to credit him with all allowable deductions or expenses, the taxpayer may have an offset sufficient to eradicate the omitted income. Thus, for example, as a retailer you may have purchased goods for less than wholesale price by paying cash to a wholesaler, and generated that cash by not depositing (and not reporting) cash sales of your own in an equal amount. Or you may have diverted cash from your books (and from your tax return) to pay your own employees who insisted on being paid in cash. Or you may have omitted income for a particular year without any justification, but failed to claim the benefit of deductions totaling the same amount to which you were entitled (for example, overlooking your own charitable contribution carryover from a prior year, or an accelerated depreciation deduction or an accounting or other professional tax-deductible fee paid), as a result of your oversight or that of a careless or harried accountant.

In such a case, the omitted income would be offset by the deductions not taken, and there would be no deficiency. For reasons such as these, where there is an omission of income, deliberate or otherwise, it is often extremely helpful to review the entire return and to analyze your entire financial year in order to determine whether items of expense or deductions that were available to you were not claimed; odd as it sounds, there are many such cases. You have not committed tax evasion, even if you tried to, where there is simply no deficiency. A sloppy would-be tax cheat may be innocent of evasion because of his own slovenliness. In this respect, the word *attempt* in the tax-evasion statute does not have its ordinary meaning of "try." If you try to cheat the IRS but your return does not in fact understate your taxable income, then you have not committed tax evasion.

This is not a wholly foolproof defense, however. Although a tax-evasion charge requires proof of an actual deficiency, the government may alternatively charge a defendant with a false-statement violation. As we have earlier explained, a false-statement charge requires only the willful making of a material false statement on the return, even in the absence of a tax deficiency (as contrasted with a tax-evasion charge, which does require a deficiency). However, the maximum penalty for a false-statement violation is somewhat milder than for tax evasion (although both are felonies). Moreover, as a practical matter the government has difficulty obtaining even a false-statement conviction under these circumstances, since a conviction requires proof that the false statement was made willfully (rather than accidentally), and a taxpayer's failure to claim expenses or deductions that would have actually offset the omitted income (an error which in the normal course of human nature would be inadvertent) is persuasive evidence that the understatement of gross income was itself inadvertent. In short, you were sloppy but not a tax cheat.

"DOLLARS" DEFENSES TO AN "INDIRECT" CASE

Because of the greater complexities that are often involved in bank-deposits and net-worth cases (both of which also generally include expenditures, as you recall), the taxpayer in such cases often has additional defenses available to him on the issue of the existence of a deficiency. Several of those defenses apply to both bank-deposits and net-worth cases, while some apply to only one or the other.

THE "CASH-HOARD" DEFENSE

The "I had cash under my mattress" defense—or in a pillow or vault or under a floorboard—can be a legally valid defense to either a bank-deposits or net-worth case. The defense that you possessed prior accumulated cash is really the other side of the coin of the government's obligation in a bank-deposits case to establish the taxpayer's opening cash-on-hand figure; it is also the other side of the coin of the government's obligation in a net-worth case to establish the taxpayer's opening net worth (including his total assets on January 1 of the year in question).

The cash-hoard defense attacks the accuracy of the government's opening-year figures.

Such an attack can be effectively made even where you neither testify at trial nor introduce any actual evidence of a cash hoard. How? By putting the government to its proof, punching holes in that proof, and convincing the judge or jury that the government simply has failed to establish with reasonable certainty—or even reasonable probability—your opening assets figure, or your opening cash-on-hand.

Because the government's obligation to establish a reasonably firm opening cash figure is so crucial an element, the frailty of the government's opening cash figure—the amount of cash that the government credits the taxpayer with having had at the opening of the year—may win the case for you. Weakness in the government's opening cash figure may convince a judge or jury that the government has totally failed to disprove the high probability (your attorney's words) that a person who has worked for so many years would have accumulated more cash over the years than the government has credited you with.

The cash-hoard defense is more effective where you offer some affirmative evidence—even if only through your own self-serving testimony—that you in fact had a significant cash hoard at the beginning of the tax year in question. Of course, convincing a jury that you possessed sufficient cash to explain away the asserted deficiency is not easy, since your claim may be difficult to document, and since the ease with which the claim may be asserted, and the frequency with which it is asserted, often render the claim inherently suspect.

Despite the difficulties that may exist in establishing the existence of a cash hoard, its effectiveness as a defense to indirect methods of proof should not be underestimated. Particularly where a jury is involved, it is usually impossible to predict with confidence what will or won't be believed. Thus, a jury may very well accept your completely undocumented assertion that rich Uncle Albert years ago gave you a deathbed bequest of a briefcase full of cash in an amount that, quite coincidentally, is sufficient to offset the claimed deficiency. And if Uncle Albert gave it to you, Uncle Sam can't charge it as income to you. Your cash-hoard defense may even contain a confession (of sorts), as you explain to the jury how you won the money gambling in Las Vegas many years ago, didn't report it to Uncle Sam, and squirreled it away until now, because you knew the statute of limitations had expired and you could no longer be convicted of tax evasion (a gutsy defense, but the only one you may have).

There are also ways of corroborating your claim of a cash hoard and thus increasing the possibility of the jury accepting the claim. For example, prior to the IRS's becoming interested in your affairs you may have signed a financial statement asserting your ownership of substantial cash—perhaps on a mortgage application. Or you may be able to document a financial history that supports the contention of a cash hoard, such as large cash purchases in years long before the ones under attack by the IRS. Therefore, in defending against a bank-deposits or net-worth case, it is often advisable to do a thorough accounting analysis of your financial history, going back many years, in order to support the contention of a cash hoard and make its assertion more credible.

Such an analysis may take many forms. The simplest involves reviewing only the most significant financial transactions of your life. For example, you may have sold a particularly valuable asset—a painting, a home, a boat, a car—for cash, or for a check plus cash. Financial transactions have at least two sides, and a prior purchaser of your asset may himself have had a financial life-style that put a lot of unreported cash under his own mattress. You can sometimes document such transactions. Payment of cash may be reflected in a contract, in a side-letter signed simultaneously with a contract, or in a purchaser's doodled note. Such evidence may be sufficient to establish the existence of a cash hoard equal to the amount of the alleged deficiency.

Kim Dong, a fifty-year-old Korean immigrant, owned a fruit and vegetable store. The IRS began a fraud investigation following its receipt of a Currency Transaction Report from the Irving Trust Company reporting Kim's deposit of $15,000 in currency. The special agent, after learning that Kim had also paid $70,000 in cash toward the purchase of a home in the same year and had also bought a new car that year for over $12,000 in currency, concluded that there was no explanation for the currency except unreported income, and recommended criminal prosecution.

During administrative review of that criminal recommendation, Kim's lawyer produced documents demonstrating that Kim had in fact maintained a sizable cash hoard. He submitted old records written in Korean, accompanied by translations, showing that Kim had sold a home and boat in Seoul for cash, and copies of promissory notes Kim had signed for cash loans shortly before emigrating. The IRS's district counsel declined criminal prosecution and referred the case back for civil disposition. The reasons: He thought Kim might be innocent, and he concluded the government would lose the case if it prosecuted.

The financial analyses used to corroborate the claim of a cash hoard may also be more complex. For example, an accountant, usually working under the direction and supervision of your attorney, may perform a complete review of your life-style over the course of past years in an attempt to reconstruct the approximate amount of cash that you accumulated or could have accumulated by such transactions as checks drawn to cash, cashing of salary checks, cashing of dividend or interest checks, and other legitimate means of generating cash. Or detailed net-worth analyses of you for prior years may be undertaken, in order to demonstrate that in those early years you earned (and reported, otherwise your troubles may multiply) more than you spent, and therefore had a net balance over the years sufficient to account for the alleged deficiency.

THE "NONTAXABLE SOURCES" DEFENSE

Loans received, repayments of loans previously given, returns of capital, gifts, inheritances, insurance proceeds, and similar items are nontaxable receipts that a taxpayer may use to rebut the prosecution's claim of a deficiency in either a bank-deposits or net-worth case. Other types of nonincome transactions are also applicable to one but not both types of cases: for example, interbank transfers or redeposits in a bank-deposits case, and assets acquired but held in trust in a net-worth case.

If the "unidentified" deposits into a bank account, or the "unexplained" increase in net worth, represent in reality your acquisition of nonincome money or other nonincome assets acquired during the year, then to that extent you can rebut the government's claim of a deficiency. In fact, you may get even greater mileage out of such items than the mere dollar value of any particular nonincome item, particularly in a criminal trial where a jury is involved, for the following reason.

One method of attacking the government's proof in a bank-deposits or net-worth case is to attack the very methodology upon which the entire prosecution is based—in other words, attacking the government by claiming it can't prove any specific item of omitted income and is unfairly trying to avoid its traditional burden of proof in a criminal case by requiring you to explain numerous bank accounts involving events many years old. A juror may be persuaded that such a task would present problems for him if he were in your predicament. If you can demonstrate that the government's proof has wrongfully charged one or more nonincome items as income against you, you may be able to convince a jury that those particular errors merely illustrate the great dangers and inherent unreliability of the government's entire method of proof, even though you are unable to similarly account for all (or even any) of the other unexplained sums charged against you.

INADEQUACY OF THE GOVERNMENT'S INVESTIGATION

Although the courts have sanctioned both the bank-deposits and net-worth methods of proof as permissible means for the IRS to use in reconstructing a taxpayer's alleged true taxable income, the courts have also recognized that because both methods are really only indirect approximations, the government must perform a full and adequate investigation of the taxpayer's financial affairs before either method may constitute sufficient proof against a taxpayer in any particular case. One means of defense is to take the offensive by attacking the adequacy of the government's investigation. For example, if you or your representative has furnished the government with an explanation of certain unidentified bank deposits or an explanation for your increase in net worth, and where that explanation is reasonably susceptible of being investigated but the government has failed to do so, then the government has failed to satisfy its obligation under the leads doctrine and either its case should fall entirely (if the lead involves an amount large enough to offset the entire deficiency) or be severely damaged (by not only reducing the alleged deficiency but also demonstrating the tenuous nature of the case against you).

However, often you may be well advised not to furnish leads during an investigation, in order to preserve for trial a specific explanation for part of the alleged deficiency and to use that example as a battering ram to attack the entire theory on which the government's case is built. You probably know more than the government does about your own affairs, especially where you wisely have resisted the often suicidal temptation of "cooperating" during the government's investigation, and thus may be able to surprise the prosecution in mid-trial by explaining portions of the claimed deficiency much to the detriment of the government's position.

An attack on the government's investigation may take other forms as well. For example, if neither you nor your attorney furnished any leads to the government, various governmental agencies—including courts—are obvious sources of information concerning your acquisition of assets through such means as gifts, inheritances, or transfers. Moreover, records pertaining to you that the government has obtained from other sources may also contain leads that the government should have tracked down.

Certain attacks on the government's investigation are particularly applicable in cases involving different types of indirect methods of proof. For example, the government in a bank-deposits case may have failed to conduct a sufficiently thorough analysis of your bank accounts and may have failed to credit you with certain interbank transfers or redeposits, or may have charged you with ownership of an account held formally in your name but actually used as a conduit for other funds—for example, a trust account (such as an account in your name which really belongs to your elderly parents), an account used by you to cash your employees' checks, or some other type of accommodation account. Another error that the government occasionally makes in bank-deposits cases involves misallocating as income for a particular year a deposit that really represents income in another year; for example, a deposit made on January 2 of the year in question may represent a check received during December of the previous year, and thus is income for the prior year but not for the year in question.

So too in a net-worth case, the government may have charged you with having acquired during the year assets that you hold only nominally. Or the government may have overlooked certain of your year-end liabilities—for example, the $10,000 new-car loan not reflected as a year-end liability used to purchase the $15,000 car reflected as a year-end asset acquired during the year—and thus artificially increased the spread between your opening and closing net worths. Or the government may have overlooked or undervalued an asset owned by you on January 1 and sold during the year, or may have overstated the amount of your yearly nondeductible expenditures for such items as normal household costs, such as when you are able to show that your live-in girlfriend was employed and used her salary for your joint day-to-day living expenses.

The defenses we have been discussing may often be combined. Take for example a bank-deposits case in which the government charges you with $46,000 in unreported income during the year. That may represent too large a cash hoard for you to convince a jury of, and too large a gift, and too large a loan, but you may be in a position to introduce sufficient testimony and other evidence from a variety of sources to whittle it away. That evidence would be summarized by a chart, large and clear enough to match the government's:

Calculation of Absence
of Additional Income

Alleged Omitted Income		$46,000.
Less:		
Prior cash accumulation through taxpayer's 15 years of labor	$15,000.	
Gift from Uncle Albert	5,000.	
Loan from friend #1	6,000.	
Repayment by friend #2 of prior loan	4,000.	
Insurance recovery	2,500.	
Reallocation of January 2 deposit of check received in prior year	3,500.	
Interbank transfers [supported by accountant's testimony]	10,000.	
		−$46,000.
Actual Omitted Income		$ 0

The government is not required to prove the exact amount of your underpayment of tax, but must prove that the underpayment is substantial. The courts have not clearly defined what the word "substantial" means in this context. However, one federal appellate court has upheld a two-count tax-evasion conviction based upon the taxpayer's return falsely claiming his own two minor children (who in fact lived with his ex-wife pursuant to a divorce decree) as dependents and claiming exemptions for them, even though the resultant tax deficiencies were only $134 and $264 for the two years in question. But where an indirect method of proof is used, the substantiality requirement is itself more substantial, since such a method of proof is only an approximation. For example, in one recently tried bank-deposits case, the judge dismissed, on grounds of lack of substantiality, one count of an indictment that had alleged an enormous deficiency, after the government's proof established an omission of only $1,000.

ACCURACY OF YOUR BOOKS AND RECORDS

Another aggressive way of attacking the government's attempted proof of a deficiency is through your own books and records. Your attorney may be able to demonstrate that you maintained a complete and apparently honest set of records during the year, and if the government is unable to establish any specific items omitted on your return, or any particular pattern of omitting income (such as diverting all or a set percentage of receipts from a particular customer), then a jury in a criminal case, or a Tax Court, Claims Court, or District Court judge or jury in a civil case, may be persuaded not to accept the government's conclusion of a deficiency based on an indirect method of proof. Such proof may be offered not only by your own testimony but also your employees who handle or oversee your receipts, such as cashiers or bookkeepers. After all, the mere presence of unidentified bank deposits or an unexplained increase in net worth, even though it may permit an inference of a deficiency, does not compel that inference, and the trier of facts is free to reject the inference being urged by the government.

A defense based on your own books and records can be an especially useful defense where the defense next discussed also applies to you.

NO "LIKELY SOURCE"

You may be able to establish that you had no likely source for earning the additional income with which the government is charging you. For example, your only known business may have been incapable of generating the additional income charged by the government; or illness or absence for other reasons may have prevented you from working the number of hours that would have been required for you to have earned the additional income charged.

In a specific-items case the government is always able to prove a likely source of the alleged additional income: the source is identified by the very item in question. In a bank-deposits or net-worth case, however, a jury may be persuaded to acquit if the government is unable to prove a likely source from which the alleged additional income materialized—particularly if the jury is convinced the tax-payer shouldn't bear the burden of explaining unidentified deposits or an unexplained increase in net worth during past years long since forgotten. Thus, although the government is not legally required to prove a likely source if it has conducted a sufficiently thorough investigation to eliminate verifiable nontaxable sources, you may nevertheless win as a practical matter by demonstrating to the jury the absence of a likely source of the alleged additional income, particularly where your own books and records themselves have the appearance of accuracy.

THE PROTECTIVE PRESUMPTIONS

If you find yourself in the unhappy position of being criminally prosecuted, you have at least the protections that safeguard all defendants in any criminal prosecution. And in a criminal tax case, these can sometimes be effectively exploited even where you have in fact sinned.

Assume that the government has established a prima facie case of tax evasion (that is, the government has produced sufficient evidence for the law to permit the jury, if the jury so chooses, to conclude you are guilty). Take, for example, either a bank-deposits case or a net-worth case, and assume that the taxpayer, out of either fear or prudence or a good sense of reality, does not testify or introduce any evidence whatsoever. Nevertheless, the taxpayer or his attorney is still allowed to argue to the jury that there are certain principles of law upon which this country is built, and these are stronger than the steel girders that support the courthouse; primary among those principles is that a defendant, even one accused of tax evasion, is presumed innocent. That presumption may not be overcome merely by the government proving that the taxpayer *may have* omitted income, or even *probably* omitted income, on his return. Instead, only where the government has proved each essential element of its case, including the existence of a substantial deficiency, beyond a reasonable doubt—beyond *any* reasonable doubt—may a jury convict. And where the government has failed to show a single specific item of omitted income, but has merely ("merely," the prosecutor harrumphs to himself) relied on circumstantial evidence of unidentified bank deposits made years ago and long since forgotten, or an unexplained increase in net worth too long ago for anyone to be able to explain, the presumption of innocence itself requires a verdict of not guilty. And remember: The verdict in this criminal trial will not itself result in the taxpayer having to pay one penny in tax. After the criminal case is over, the taxpayer will be involved in civil tax litigation, and the government there—not here—will seek to collect whatever tax, plus penalties and interest, may be owed to the IRS. Don't convict. Let this victimized man go home with his wife and children.

But wait: the play to the jury's heartstrings may be premature. We have only dealt so far with defenses based on the dollars. There may be hope yet on the issue of intent —your state of mind when you filed the return. A great many tax prosecutions—probably most—are defended on this very issue: there may be a tax deficiency, but you didn't mean it.

Defenses Based on Intent

If your return has understated your tax liability, then you owe a tax if they catch you, whether or not you knew of the understatement when you filed the return. Furthermore, if the government can prove additionally that you did know of the deficiency when you filed the return, you may be liable for the 50-percent civil-fraud penalty, or for criminal punishment for tax evasion, or both. These latter sanctions apply only if you acted with the requisite state of mind—or, more precisely, only if the government can prove that you acted with the requisite state of mind. The intent to cheat—in the words of the Internal Revenue Code, "willfulness" or "fraud"—means something more than mere ignorance, oversight, or negligence.

To impose the 50-percent civil-fraud penalty, the government must prove that an understatement of tax was due to the taxpayer's "fraud." To impose criminal sanctions, the government is required to prove that the taxpayer acted "willfully." The Internal Revenue Code does not define either term, but legal meanings have evolved for both terms. Generally, "willfulness" and "fraud" mean the same thing: a voluntary and intentional violation of a known legal duty.

Tax evasion (or tax fraud) and tax avoidance are two different concepts. You are entitled to take advantage of all benefits available to you under the law, through legal "loopholes" or whatever "technicalities" the law permits. In the words of Judge Learned Hand,

> There is nothing sinister in so arranging one's affairs as to keep taxes as low as possible. Everybody does so, rich or poor; and all do right, for nobody owes any public duty to pay more than the law demands; taxes are enforced exactions, not voluntary contributions. To demand more in the name of morals is mere cant.

Where you owe a deficiency because you made an inadvertent or honest mistake, you simply pay the tax (plus interest and, if you made the mistake negligently, a 5-percent negligence penalty). But if you knew you were violating the law in understating your true taxable income, and if the government can prove you knew it, then the more serious 50-percent fraud penalty and/or criminal sanctions come into play.

The defense most frequently raised by taxpayers in tax-evasion prosecutions or civil fraud cases is: I didn't act willfully. Since the concept of willfulness involves a person's state of mind, how does the government prove it, and how do you prove it isn't so?

At least as of today, the IRS does not have equipment capable of scientifically probing the inner workings of your mind, particularly retroactively (the relevant state of mind is the one that existed when the return was filed or not filed). How then does the government establish that you acted willfully in understating your taxable income? Or in layman's language, how does the government prove that you tried to cheat on your taxes?

You may have made it easy for them. Perhaps you confessed to the agent, or you confided your true intent to a trusted employee whose loyalty has been withered by time or insufficient salary. In most cases, however, the IRS has to prove your fraudulent intent without having it served on so silver a platter. The IRS has a checklist of factors that indicate willfulness. These factors are set forth in a written set of audit guidelines given to all IRS agents conducting any civil tax audit, and are referred to by the IRS as the "badges of fraud." The more common badges include:

- Understatements of income accompanied by concealing bank or brokerage accounts, concealing unexplained currency, diverting receipts into nonbusiness accounts, or covering up sources of income.
- Claiming fictitious or improper deductions, such as deducting personal expenses as business expenses, inventing nonexistent deductions, grossly overstating deductions, or claiming exemptions for nonexistent or deceased "dependents."
- Accounting irregularities such as keeping two sets of books, altering records, backdating or postdating documents, intentionally under- or over-footing columns in journals or ledgers, or posting erroneous figures from source records onto ledger accounts.
- Misallocating income by distributing profits to fictitious partners or improperly shifting income or deductions to a return of a related taxpayer in a different tax bracket.
- Taxpayer's misconduct, such as making false statements

to an agent, destroying records, or transferring assets for purposes of concealment.

The IRS Manual's complete listing of illustrative "badges of fraud" is reprinted verbatim on pages 299–301 of the Appendix.

If the IRS can prove a deficiency and can pin one or more badges of fraud on you, there is a realistic risk that the Service may conclude that you acted willfully in connection with the particular return involved. That does not mean, however, that you cannot rebut the charge. In fact, in most tax-evasion and fraud cases the issue of willfulness is hotly disputed. How do you dispute it?

Let's assume that the government has proved, through one or more of the methods of proof previously discussed or through your own confession (for which you may be graced with a gold star by either heaven or the sentencing judge, but not by the IRS), that your return understates your true taxable income. Your only defense is that you did not act willfully. In such a case, you will be reminding the jury whenever possible that the issue before it is not (or not only) whether a deficiency exists—the government will eventually determine and collect in a later proceeding whatever tax may be due—but only whether you deliberately tried to cheat your country—which, of course, was the furthest thing from your mind when you filed your return. The government relies upon the circumstantial evidence of whatever badges of fraud it can pin on you, in an attempt to convince the jury (in most criminal cases) or the judge (in most civil tax-fraud cases) that you acted willfully. You claim the badge is undeserved, and base your defense of lack of willfulness on one or a combination of the following factors.

INADVERTENCE

Neither the criminal nor the civil fraud provisions of the Internal Revenue Code punish good-faith mistakes. Nor do they punish honest but stupid errors (although they do impose a negligence penalty on such errors, which is quite tolerable compared to the penalties for fraud). If you can prove that you simply made a mistake, pure and simple, even a big mistake, you have not committed tax evasion or fraud.

But, you say, a defendant in a criminal case is not required to prove anything. That is true in theory, but not wise in practicality. In fact, once the government has introduced sufficient evidence of willfulness to permit a jury to infer the existence of fraud, your practical job is to prove the opposite. If you attack the issue of willfulness in that way, then even though you may ultimately fail to convince the jury of your lack of willfulness, you still may have at least created sufficient doubt to prevail on the ground that the government has failed to carry its burden of proof.

What kind of honest mistake will suffice? Any kind, as long as it relates to the issue in question and is sufficiently credible either to be believed or to create reasonable doubt about the government's proof of willfulness. You may have believed that the profitable resale of your home was not a taxable event; or you may have forgotten about that long-dormant bank account that generated substantial interest, and about the IRS form that the bank had sent to remind you; or you may even have believed that setting up your son-in-law in business was a charitable contribution—ignorance, negligence, even gross negligence. If that's all the government can prove about your intent, it hasn't proved you acted willfully. Of course, the grosser the negligence, the greater your difficulty in convincing anyone of its inadvertence.

An inadvertence defense succeeded at the tax-fraud trial of Joe Conte. Joe, a recent immigrant without formal education, was a landscape gardener, charged by the government with having omitted from his reported income $30,000 a year in gross receipts. At trial, Joe testified that he prepared his tax returns from his retained copies of bills to his customers. He kept those bills in a dresser drawer at home, with all his other important papers and his socks. That drawer was in a constant state of disarray. Throughout the year he would dump the contents of the drawer onto his bed in order to search for some missing record or to match an old sock. When the time came to prepare the prior year's tax return, he went through the same dumping ritual. He should have found everything; he could have sworn that he did; he just didn't realize how sloppy the system was. The IRS had not believed him, but the jury did.

GOOD-FAITH RELIANCE ON OTHERS

Since willfulness depends on your own state of mind, if you can establish that you relied on someone else who committed the error that caused the understatement you may be able to defeat the claim of willfulness. For example, you may have entrusted your bookkeeper with properly entering financial transactions in your books and records, and she failed to make an entry or erred in making another; or you may have relied on your accountant to prepare your return, and the accountant made a mistake. A wife's claim that she signed a return without even reading it may remind a juror of his own wife's practice.

The availability of this defense depends on the good faith of your reliance. If you diverted money without telling the bookkeeper—so that the transactions in question never reached the bookkeeper's attention—or if you failed to disclose to the accountant material facts that resulted in the return's understatement, then your "reliance" has not been made in good faith and the defense will fail. To succeed with a reliance defense, you must have adequately disclosed all relevant facts to the person upon whom you claim to have relied. You aren't allowed to cheat the IRS by misleading others.

The defense of reliance can be successful where, for example, you disclosed all relevant facts to your tax-return preparer and signed the completed return without checking (or even reading) it; or where you can prove that you signed the return in blank and the preparer thereafter filled in the information (assuming again that you gave or thought you gave the preparer all the necessary information). But even proving that you signed it in blank will not defeat a charge of willfulness if the government can show that you knew that the preparer would later be filling in the blanks based upon inaccurate information.

When the defense of reliance is raised or anticipated, a previously friendly accountant-taxpayer relationship may be magically transformed into hostility. Your tax preparer, whom you claim to have relied upon, will claim that you did not disclose to him the material facts in question —for example, the off-the-books customer or the cash receipts. The IRS often tries to pit you against your accountant, in order to undercut your claim of reliance and to induce the accountant to self-protectively claim that the error on the return (for instance, the unreported income) was also concealed from him. Sometimes the inducement will take the form of an implied, or even explicit, threat that the accountant may find himself co-boiling in the taxpayer's soup unless the accountant "cooperates." In fact, however, where an accountant has erred despite your full disclosure to him of all revelant facts, a stand-up accountant may be able to help both himself and you escape unscathed from a criminal investigation.

MISTAKE OF LAW

Despite the expression that everyone "is presumed to know the law," the falsity of that fiction is often useful in defending against a charge of tax evasion. If, for example, your return understates taxable income because you omitted an item of income or erroneously included a deduction as a result of your belief that you were acting correctly, then that belief—if you can prove it or create a reasonable doubt out of it—will defeat the government's claim of willfulness. This type of defense is most often used if a complex issue of tax law is involved, or at least an issue that does not have a self-evident answer. A salesman, for instance, would be hard-pressed to convince anybody that he actually believed that sales receipts from customers whose first names were Larry were excludable from gross income under the Internal Revenue Code. However, one might believe that he honestly (though incorrectly) thought that sales made overseas were not taxable in the United States until the money was repatriated, and that's why he kept it in Switzerland.

The mistake-of-law defense sometimes arises in combination with the defense of reliance on others in a specific-items case, where the item in question involves a legal interpretation of one or more sections of the Internal Revenue Code. For example, if you have invested in a tax shelter and taken substantial deductions based upon an attorney's opinion of the propriety of both the shelter and the deduction, you may defend against a charge of tax evasion, even where the deduction was improper, if you relied on supposedly expert (but actually incorrect) legal advice.

OTHER ASPECTS OF THE RETURN

Let's assume that the government is able to prove convincingly that your return omitted a substantial amount of income, and that you are unable to defend against the deficiency. You defend instead on the issue of willfulness, claiming you made an innocent mistake. A reanalysis of your financial affairs during the year may uncover other inadvertent errors made on the return that worked *against* you—an overlooked deduction or expense, for example. In such a case, even where the overlooked item is not sufficient to eliminate or substantially reduce the deficiency, it may nevertheless be a valuable weapon for attacking the government's claim of willfulness: "Some tax cheat—he forgot to even take the deductions he was entitled to!"

The government may respond to such an argument by contrasting the small amount of the overlooked deduction against the large amount of the omitted income, and perhaps suggesting that you did not inadvertently overlook the deduction but intentionally ignored it in order to use it as an escape hatch if your omitted income was later detected—precisely what you're now doing. A jury may not be willing to believe, however, that a greedy tax cheat would have engaged in such overly cautious and far-sighted preventive self-sacrifice, and may find the overlooked deduction persuasive evidence of lack of willfulness.

Your tax return may contain other information useful to refute an allegation of willfulness. Your return may have in some way "red-flagged" either the item being questioned or some other item on the return—for example, where the propriety of the tax treatment of an item is questionable, not attempting to "bury" the item among other items in the return, but highlighting it by an attempted explanation of its claimed propriety. In most such cases, the very disclosure of the questionable nature of the item would be sufficient to refute a claim of willfulness directed toward that item itself. Moreover, even if the alleged fraud does not relate to that item itself, your having highlighted that item on your return, and thereby directing the IRS's particular attention to the question of its propriety, can be convincing evidence that any other error on the return was not deliberately made.

YOUR COOPERATION

If you have cooperated with the IRS during its investigation of you—answered their questions and produced whatever records or other materials the IRS requested—then at a subsequent trial you may be able to argue effectively that your cooperation demonstrates that you had nothing to hide, since such forthrightness is inconsistent with the government's claim of willful misconduct. Just as "the guilty flee where no man pursueth," so too the innocent don't flee when the IRS pursueth. Such evidence has been persuasive at trial, such as in the case of our landscape gardener, who told the IRS investigative agents during their first visit the full story of his dresser-drawer method of accounting.

More often, by cooperating you may purchase a jury argument at the cost of having placed your neck on the jury's chopping block. A taxpayer's cooperation frequently gives the government a case that without cooperation the government could not prove.

One further aspect of cooperation frequently arises in tax investigations: whether to close the barn door after the horse is out. In a tax-evasion case, that means whether to file an amended return correcting an original return's alleged error(s); in a failure-to-file case, it means whether to file a delinquent return.

In both situations there is one common caveat: Forget about getting any benefit from the IRS for a "voluntary disclosure." We have already explained that even under the best of circumstances a voluntary disclosure cannot be banked on; but once an investigation has begun or has become likely (for example, where you have learned that a snitch has reported you to the IRS), an attempted voluntary disclosure is simply not voluntary.

In attempting to prove that you did not commit your tax sin willfully, attempting to correct the sin may be helpful—but may also be damaging. Different considerations apply to tax-evasion cases and failure-to-file cases.

The decision of whether to file an amended return when you are under investigation for tax evasion often presents more complex considerations than in failure-to-file investigations. It is most important to remember that the filing of an amended (or delinquent) return is an act that cannot be undone. The return itself constitutes a written statement by you and may be used against you in a subsequent criminal or civil trial. Therefore, before deciding whether to file an amended return, you must make a final determination (at a time when final determinations are usually not yet made) as to what position you will be taking on the issue of whether or not to fight the government's claim that your return understates taxable income.

For example, if you have filed a return reporting $50,000 in gross income and the government claims that you willfully omitted twice that amount, your filing an amended return increasing your gross income figure from $50,000 to $150,000 would be evidence admissible against you as proof that your original return (which will be the return whose fraudulent nature is charged) understated your true income by $100,000. Where you do in fact have a defense or partial defense against the claim of a deficiency, or where the government may have its own problems in proving the existence of a deficiency, the filing of an amended return may furnish the missing proof to the government. You will have given up a substantial no-deficiency defense while trying to buttress your lack-of-willfulness defense through the filing of the amended return.

Suppose in a bank-deposits case the government has a problem establishing your opening cash-on-hand figure; or in a net-worth case establishing your opening net worth; or in a specific-items case, the government can prove that you failed to report income from a particular aspect of your business (such as a failure by a coffee shop owner to report the income from all take-out sales), but cannot prove the amount of the omission. Where the government has such problems of proof, filing an amended return narrows the range of your tenable defenses by effectively conceding the "dollars" aspect of the government's case, leaving you with no defense but lack of willfulness.

Although filing an amended return is evidence against you on the issue of the understatement of taxable income, it is also evidence in your favor on the issue of willfulness: When you learned of your inadvertent omission of income you corrected the error (there are some conflicting judicial decisions on the admissibility of such evidence). A jury may very well accept this defense, despite the prosecution's expected argument that you filed the amended return only because you were caught and knew you had no practical choice but to amend.

The issue of whether to "cooperate" by filing a delinquent return in a failure-to-file case often presents less complex considerations. The government's burden in proving that a failer failed to file is considerably easier than proving that an evader evaded. The government can easily prove the failure to file in a failure-to-file case, merely by proving receipt of sufficient income to trigger the obligation to file and the Service's own records of filings. The only defense available is usually that of willfulness. Therefore, your cooperating by filing a delinquent return after the investigation has begun in a failure-to-file case is usually not much of a concession and may strengthen your defense of lack of willfulness.

Furthermore, a continued failure to file after its discovery by the IRS lends credence to the government's claim that the failure to file was willful (the interest also mounts). It is difficult, to say the least, for a defendant in a failure-to-file case to demonstrate lack of willfulness in having failed to file his return, when he hasn't even filed it by the time he's on trial for that very offense. Moreover, a failer's continuing failure to file, even after being discovered, can undercut a personal or psychiatric defense specifically geared toward proving lack of willfulness, to which we now turn.

PERSONAL ATTRIBUTES

Because a defense based on lack of willfulness involves a most personal attribute of the taxpayer at the time of his commission of the alleged offense—his state of mind— you may be able to exploit your own personal characteristics in your own defense, either alone or in conjunction with one or more of the defenses previously discussed.

YOUR BACKGROUND

A jury is generally more likely to believe a claim of lack of willfulness in connection with a tax-reducing error contained in a plumber's return than in a tax attorney's return. Whether you knew you were falsely understating your taxable income often depends on your own personal background: education, business experience, knowledge of tax law, accounting expertise, and similar factors. Of course, even an illiterate can be fully aware that he is cheating on his taxes. If the plumber reports only $10,000 in income on his return when he in fact received $40,000, his lack of an accounting degree may not convince a jury that he did not act willfully. Nevertheless, many cases are not so clear-cut, and a jury may accept the claim of inadvertent error, or reliance on advice of others, or ignorance of the law, where the taxpayer lacks an educational background or is inexperienced and unsophisticated in either accounting or the law.

CHARACTER WITNESSES

A defendant in a tax-evasion prosecution is permitted to call witnesses to testify as to his integrity. Indeed, you are entitled to have the judge instruct the jury at the conclusion of the case that such testimony may itself be sufficient to create a reasonable doubt about guilt. While the trial judge has the discretion to limit the number of character witnesses, you are entitled to call a sufficient number reasonably necessary to establish your integrity—and the right character witnesses can help win your case.

PSYCHOLOGICAL PROFILE

In most criminal trials where the defendant's psychological makeup is contested, the inquiry normally focuses on either or both of only two issues: (a) the defendant's claim that because of his mental condition at the time of trial he is incompetent to stand trial because he is unable to understand the nature and consequences of the proceedings against him or mentally unable to assist properly in his own defense, and/or (b) the defendant's claim that he lacked criminal responsibility at the time of his alleged commission of the offense because, as a result of a severe mental disease or defect, he was unable to appreciate the nature and quality or the wrongfulness of his acts. The defendant has the burden of proving this defense by clear and convincing evidence. In a tax-evasion case, however, a defendant's mental condition may be asserted as a defense in a third respect: your mental condition was such that you did not act willfully in doing or failing to do your allegedly criminal act or omission.

An accused is permitted to offer evidence of a pertinent trait of his character for the purpose of proving that he acted in conformity with that trait on the occasion in question—here, that trait may be integrity, or carelessness, or unmercenariness. Such evidence relevant to the willfulness element in a criminal tax charge may be both technical and nontechnical. You may have undergone a period of extreme pressures and stresses in your personal life during the period of time you filed (or failed to file) your tax return, as a result of domestic problems, illness, financial or business reverses, or similar problems. Or you may manifest extreme negligence in the conduct of your affairs generally, or your financial affairs specifically, as illustrated by your careless work habits, your permitting funds to accumulate in a non-interest-bearing checking account, your constantly overdrawn checking account, or your needless accumulation of unopened mail or unpaid bills. While proof of these characteristics may be offered by lay witnesses, psychiatric testimony also may be offered to attempt to establish through a supposed expert's opinion that you lacked the mental capacity at the time of your alleged offense to form a willful intent or to exercise it, or that you did not do so in connection with your filing (or nonfiling) of the tax returns in question.

CHAPTER 8
Preparing for Your Preparer

Before your taxable income has hit $20,000, you're in the 25-percent bracket. That means the IRS takes 25¢ out of the next dollar you earn. If you're single, you've reached the 50-percent bracket when your taxable income is $81,800 (you reach that peak several thousands of dollars later if you're married and file a joint return or if you're the head of a household).

Look at that percentage against the background of your average workday. If you're in the office at 9:00 A.M. and out at 6:00 P.M.—eight working hours and a one-hour lunch—you're working four of those hours for Uncle Sam. When you've reached the 50-percent bracket, you work thirty minutes of every hour for your federal income tax partner. That's *over* thirty minutes of each hour when you add on the state tax bite.

When you consider that you work more than half your day for the tax man, you should understand the importance of knowing how big a chunk he's biting out of you, and the importance of making the chunk as small as legally possible.

Just as most of your day is spent working for the tax man, much of your day is tax-related, in ways you may not realize. Recognizing the tax-related aspects of your day—of every day, and many hours of every day—is the first step in keeping the tax dragon under control.

The next step is making sure that when you finally meet with the one who separates you from the dragon—your tax preparer, prior to his preparing your return—you are thoroughly prepared and armed.

Rather than just dumping on his desk a pile of miscellaneous receipts and canceled checks for him to wade through and maybe exaggerate here and there, you should be presenting him with a complete picture of your tax year. That picture begins on the first day of the year, and it's not at all hard to paint.

Here's how.

Consider a day in the life of the typical 1985 tax person: you. You're a professional, or businessman, or salesman, or teacher, or anybody else; it doesn't matter. The Internal Revenue Code is interwoven into your life.

Let's say you're in business—you sell garments, or medical services, or cars. You have the average 2.3 children, a home, and the usual 1980s life-style. Your day starts, continues, and ends with tax consequences.

If you take a business associate or client out for breakfast, you deduct the cost of yours and his. You also deduct the cost of the garage you park in near the restaurant, and tips you give in the garage and the restaurant. If you drove straight to your office every day, commutation costs —depreciation on the car, cost of garage, tolls, gas —

would not be deductible. So you regularly make interim stops before going to the office—to see a client, or to buy goods, or something similar—and presto, your travel costs become partially deductible.

During the morning, you visit your broker and your attorney. You jot down in your diary the costs of taxis to each; they're deductible. You visit your broker to discuss stocks you're thinking of buying and selling, but your decisions depend not merely on the economic strength of the companies under consideration but also on the tax consequences of each possible transaction: whether a gain or loss will be long- or short-term, whether holding the stock a few days longer will lessen the tax bite, and what offsetting transactions are available to reap the full tax advantages of the transaction. Other investment decisions depend not simply on the rate of return but the after-tax yield: if your highest tax bracket is 30 percent, a tax-free municipal bond paying 8½ percent produces a considerably higher after-tax yield than a taxable investment paying 10 percent.

At your attorney's office you discuss the financial alternatives available in connection with your pending divorce case, and the tax ramifications of alimony versus lump-sum payment versus support for your average 2.3 children. Part of the attorney's fee is deductible if it includes advice on the preservation of income-producing property or on the tax consequences of the divorce, and you make sure your attorney gives you a letter maximizing the amount of his time (and your money) spent on those parts of your case. Then your attorney suggests you reschedule your upcoming second marriage for late December instead of early January, so that on December 31—the only date that matters for this purpose under the tax laws—you will be married and therefore eligible to file a joint return next April at the lower tax rate available for marrieds. If he's a truly devoted professional and totally devoid of romanticism, he may also suggest that you and your wife try to conceive the child you're planning in the first quarter of the year, so the birth will take place before year-end and you will qualify for another exemption.

Later in the day, you meet an old college roommate for lunch. Twenty years ago you would have talked only of women, but today your friend is a little balder, a little paunchier, and a syndicator of tax shelters, and the conversation drifts to money. When you get stuck with the tab you hand the waiter a credit card and write "taxes" and your friend's name on your receipt.

On the way back to the office you buy this book. Keep the receipt: another deduction.

Back at the office your favorite charity calls, the one that somehow values your frayed suits like haute couture. That's why it's your favorite charity: the valuations for the old clothes you gave them have saved you enough on taxes to buy a new suit even at today's prices.

When you get home, your older daughter's private-school tuition bill is in the mail. Her tuition isn't deductible. But interest on the tuition (and on most loans) is. If a loan is taken out in her name, the deduction for the interest isn't worth anything, since she's got no income to offset the deduction against. So you take out the loan yourself, in your own name, and get to deduct the interest against your own considerable income. That helps reduce the tuition a bit, and every bit helps. She'll want a car when she's off to college. She may offer to pay for it herself, by borrowing. Same result though: the interest deduction on the loan isn't tax-beneficial to her, so you wind up taking out the loan in your name.

Then you open up the other bills: for the new insulation that now lines your attic, the new burglar-alarm system, the skylight you just put in, the down payment for the new kitchen. Each of these bills has tax consequences. Even if you aren't eligible to deduct a portion of those bills on this year's return (which you may be eligible for, as we'll later explain) your payments for all of these "capital improvements" increase the basis of your house (that is, the cost of the house to you) and therefore result in a lower profit (and a lower tax) when you ultimately sell the house. Then you pay the phone bill—and it seems as though you spend half the time using the phone to talk business with someone. A fair proportion of your phone bill allocable to business purposes is also deductible. Finally, you pay your monthly bill to the friendly bank that holds a mortgage on your home—your payment includes interest and local taxes, both deductible. In fact, those deductions over the years now total more than the original cost of your home.

Like it or not, you're in the tax business. Today the Internal Revenue Code is with you in all the old familiar places. You can ignore this reality year-round at your peril and try to do your best on the night of next April 14, wading through your disorganized collection of papers (or dumping them on an accountant's desk and paying him to do the wading). Or you can recognize the unhappy fact that the tax laws have something to say about too much of your life for you to ignore their consequences all year long. The fact is, the Internal Revenue Code and its accompanying regulations—thousands upon thousands of rules, several times longer than the complete works of Shakespeare and for the most part less comprehensible— have made a business out of life. Face it: The government has made everyday living into big business.

The reason most people work is for money. Think of how many clients or customers you have to service, or sales you have to make, to earn the money you give away by overpaying your taxes—and you'll realize that running your tax-life is like running a business, and Uncle Sam should be treated like an important client.

On the other hand, you can overlive the tax-life: spending only on deductible items, organizing a social and family life centered around tax consequences, constantly writing contemporaneous notes and memoranda of your activities to establish a record that will later support your tax position, and enjoying life only to the extent it helps you reduce your taxes.

Of course, there is a happy medium. Being generally aware of those tax laws likeliest to affect you is a start. Being aware that there are other tax laws you don't know about that may affect you is the next step.

In the next chapter we'll be translating into English the gobbledygook of tax laws you should know about. As you will learn there, the basic tax-minimization techniques involve lowering your income (by such techniques as splitting income among family members to get it taxed at lower rates, receiving income in different years rather than in one year to accomplish the same result, or making investments that produce nontaxable yields or capital gains), or increasing your deductions (by structuring your affairs to receive tax benefits from varying expenses).

To understand the significance of these techniques, you must understand the concept of the "graduated income tax." That's the kind of tax structure that exists in the United States. If you are in the 50-percent bracket, that does not mean that all of your income is taxed at a 50-percent rate. It means that all of your income over a certain amount is taxed at that rate; the rest is taxed at lower rates. A married couple whose total taxable income is $20,200 pays a total tax of $2,497, which is an effective overall percentage of 12.36 percent, but their last $4,200 has been taxed at a tax rate of 18 percent. If that same couple had instead earned $200,000, the total tax they would pay on the first $20,200 of taxable income is the same $2,497. Their next $4,400 is taxed at a rate of 22 percent. Their next $5,300 is taxed at 25 percent. And so on—until their taxable income reaches $162,400, at which point the excess is taxed at 50 percent. In other words, the higher rates only apply to dollars in excess of particular amounts. A million-dollar earner pays the same taxes on his first $10,000 of income as a peon.

Thus, in reducing your taxable income, you are reducing the taxes paid on your highest-taxed dollars. In other words, you are eliminating those dollars that are taxed at the highest rates. For example, if you can reduce your taxable income from $100,000 to $90,000, you are eliminating from the IRS's grasp taxes that would otherwise be paid on your highest-bracket $10,000 of income. Any reduction of income comes "off the top"—your lower bracket dollars are unaffected and remain taxed at the lower rate.

Before we get to a plain-English description of the specific tax laws that are most likely to help you reduce your taxes, bear in mind that these laws are written by lawyers and bureaucrats whose drafting techniques qualify them as killers of your native tongue and literary sadists of the first degree. These draftsmen have an uncanny ability to string together words in the English language in such a manner as to make them barely comprehensible. Their "English" requires translation into English.

The fact that these laws require translation should put you on notice that you need a qualified translator's help to properly prepare your tax return. If you do it yourself, odds are high you pay more in taxes than you should. But if you leave everything to your hired expert, you will also overpay. Your accountant knows the tax laws better than you do, but you know your past year's activities better than he does. Preparing your tax return to make sure you pay as little in taxes as the law allows requires a combination of your own efforts and those of a skilled professional. You should make the maximum use of both yourself and your preparer.

There are three interrelated steps in minimizing your

taxes: (1) preparing to prepare your return, (2) preparing the return, and (3) justifying the numbers on the return if you are audited.

You don't have to walk around all year long with a pocket dictator, continually memorializing every breath you take. It does make sense, though, to maintain a diary and periodically jot down what you've been up to. Chances are, some of it is tax-related. Not only does this make sense generally, but it's also required by the IRS if you're going to deduct such items as travel and entertainment expenses.

The more complete your diary, the more likely your dollars won't slip through the tax cracks. Consider your day-in-the-life, described a few pages ago. Your cash outlays that day—several taxis during the day, parking, this book, entertainment—totaled about $100. Those are all deductible dollars, which means that "losing" one of those expenses, or all of them, costs you money. If you kept no record of that day's activities, next year when you get around to preparing your tax return you've lost $100 in deductible cash expenses. In the 50-percent bracket, that cost you $50 in real after-tax dollars. You have to earn $100 in taxable income to make it up. In the 50-percent bracket, an extra $100 in taxable income isn't worth a penny more than an extra $100 deduction: they're both worth $50 in after-tax dollars. How long will you have to work to make that $100—longer than it would have taken to jot down those expenses at the end of the day?

You should have your return prepared by a professional preparer—a certified public accountant or someone with similar qualifications is preferable. The preparer's fee is deductible. His knowledge of the tax laws is presumably more extensive than yours (the cost of one slipup can more than exceed a professional preparer's fee). And his signature as "preparer" on the return may influence the

IRS not to audit if the computer kicks out your return for review toward a possible audit.

Just as odds are you should not prepare your own return, you should not leave everything to the preparer. Before visiting him, you should do pre-preparation yourself. Don't walk into his office with a disorganized batch of papers and hope for the best. If you do, he'll just spend his time, and your money, sorting them out—if he's conscientious. If he's not, your tax dollars will simply fly out the proverbial window, and you will have made an unknowing voluntary contribution to Uncle Sam. Such contributions, by the way, are not deductible.

You can give your accountant valuable assistance yourself. Spoon-feed him the information in a manner that will minimize the cost to you and maximize the help he is trained to give you.

Start with your checks. Don't think you can simply remember at the end of the year what deductible items you spent money on during the year. You should be saving all your monthly bank statements, deposit slips, and canceled checks.

Gather all your checks together, and spend a deductible dollar on a pad of columnar accounting paper. At the top of the columns, hand-write out the various categories of conceivably deductible expenses that your checks generally fall into. In column 1, write out the payee and date of each check (checks to the supermarket and butcher needn't be included, unless they were for a dinner party you gave for business associates). Then write the amount under the corresponding heading. There may be other categories of deductible expenses particularly applicable to you, and some of those listed above may not apply to you, but you get the point.

Your schedule may look like this:

1985 CHECKS

PAYEE AND DATE OF CHECK		RENT*	CON EDISON	PHONE†	AUTO/INSURANCE/MAINTENANCE†	OFFICE SUPPLIES	DUES & SUBSCRIPTIONS
American Express	1/27						
John's Stationers	1/16					49 27	
Con Edison	1/18		237 94				
N.Y. Telephone	1/26			197 24			
American Heart Assn.	1/19						
Sopher Management	1/27	1 440 –					
Cash	1/10						
Graphic Art Gallery	1/14						
Joe's Exxon	1/20				147 26		
Wall St. Journal	1/22						47 25
Interesting Travel Co.	1/10						
Sloane's	1/9						
IRS	1/15						
N.Y.S Income Tax	1/15						
ETC.							

* DEDUCT APPLICABLE % IF YOU ARE ENTITLED TO HOME OFFICE EXPENSE.

† DEDUCT APPLICABLE %.

CHARITIES	TRAVEL & ENTERTAINMENT APPLICABLE TO BUSINESS	OFFICE FURNITURE (DEPRECIATE)	FARES & TRAVEL APPLICABLE TO BUSINESS	CHECKS TO CASH	TAXES FEDERAL	TAXES STATE & LOCAL	MISC.
								1
								2
								3
								4
	84236							5
								6
								7
								8
250 -								9
								10
				300 -				11
							450 -	12
								13
								14
			56211					15
		125 -						16
					5000 -			17
						1250 -		18
								19
								20

Itemizing your year's checks will consume several pages —you'll be amazed at how many dollars you spend on these items each year. You should also separately list all large-dollar checks that don't fit into any of these categories even if they don't seem to have any tax impact— just so you will remember to ask your preparer about them. He'll either confirm that you're not entitled to any tax benefit, or pleasantly surprise you. For example, you may have bought a new car this year and not be entitled to any automobile deduction, but the sales tax you pay on an extraordinary item such as a car, motorcycle, motor home, or boat is separately deductible even if you use the general sales tax deduction permitted to you under the IRS's sales-tax tables. So it's a good idea to create a separate list of all large-dollar items just to run them past your preparer.

And speaking of sales taxes: You needn't limit the amount of your deduction to the figure in the IRS's tables. *All* sales taxes you pay are deductible, and those government tables generally show a lesser total of sales taxes than you actually pay during the year. Try saving all of your receipts one year, and add up the sales taxes shown on those receipts. They probably exceed the applicable figure for you in the IRS's table. You're entitled to the larger figure.

Also make separate listings of all tax payments you made during the year, to all government agencies, including the IRS. Taxes you paid last year to state and local governments are deductible on your federal return, and you get credit for them on your state return if the payments were allocable to last year's taxes. Even a tax deficiency you paid to the state government last year relating to a return several years old is deductible on your federal return, and if you paid interest on that deficiency, the interest is also deductible. And of course don't forget to credit yourself with any estimates you paid on your federal return.

You should then go through your diary and itemize all cash spent for business purposes. Take a separate page from the accounting pad and caption it "Travel and Entertainment"; caption another page "Taxis," and another one with any other applicable heading—office expenses, parking, investments or tax-related publications, and so on.Then go through your diary page-by-page. List each date on the applicable accounting page, and next to it the dollars spent that day.

If your diary has been maintained on a reasonably current basis, it's easy to do. If not you'll have to try to reconstruct the dollars from the events recited in the diary. By "reconstruct" we do not mean fictionalize; try to reasonably approximate the correct amounts based on your present ability to do so. But bear in mind that IRS regulations require that in most instances diary entries should be made contemporaneously, so even a later reconstruction may result in a disallowance, though if reasonably accurate it may be better than nothing. If your diary pages are blank, just try remembering where you were a year ago, with whom, for what purpose, and how much you spent —it's close to impossible. Odds are high you'll wind up paying more than you owe. That's why preparation of your 1986 return should begin in January 1986, not April 1987.

If you're making $50,000 or $100,000 or more a year, you may think these $5 and $25 and $50 items aren't worth the tedium of this exercise; but try it one year, add up the numbers, and you'll do it for life.

By the way, just to make sure you don't get carried away with the liberality of your cash business-related or other deductible expenditures during the past year, it's also a good idea, when you're scheduling out your checks, to

allocate a column for checks payable to "cash" or to yourself, which you cashed. If your deductible cash expenditures are substantially more than the total of these checks,
be sure you can explain where you got all that cash to
spend.

Now it's time to go through those old receipts, bills, and
miscellaneous chits you've been saving all year long. Many
of them will duplicate the other information you've already organized, such as bills paid by checks. Save these.
They will further substantiate your payments in the event
you are later audited. Others will be for additional deductible items you didn't pay by check or note in your diary.
All of these should be separately scheduled out on a separate sheet of paper.

You've now done a thorough job of preparing a complete picture of your last year's expenses to present to your
accountant. You've scheduled out all conceivably deductible checks, and all of your deductible cash expenditures.
You've separately listed all items you're not sure about,
which you can run past your preparer. Rest assured, the
numbers are far more comprehensive than he would've
done if you simply had dumped your records on his desk
and wished him good luck.

Organizing your income figures is usually a simpler job.
Employees receive W-2 Forms reflecting their salaries.
Professionals or other self-employed people are required
to keep books and records reflecting income, which a
bookkeeper or accountant usually maintains and periodically calculates. Partnerships issue K-1 Forms reflecting
net income (or loss) of each partner. Banks, other financial
institutions, corporations that pay dividends, and a multitude of other payers are required by law to issue forms
telling you how much taxable income you received and
reporting that figure to the IRS. The IRS has substantially
enhanced computer matching capabilities designed to cor-

relate those information returns with the sources and amounts you report on your own tax return, based on your social security number or taxpayer identification number. You should also go through your year's deposit slips to see whether they reflect other income not reported on these forms.

Another good idea before meeting with your preparer is to take a look at last year's return. It may remind you of some other deductions you've missed: the fee for your bank vault (if you safeguard taxable securities there, for example, but not if you keep only personal items or tax-exempt bonds), or professional or investment journals you regularly purchase but never log into your diary (*The Wall Street Journal* or *Barrons*, for example). It may also remind you that on last year's return you applied an overpayment of taxes as a credit against this year's return, instead of asking for a refund. Of course, it may also remind you that you received dividends from a corporation whose stock you still own but which didn't send you a 1099 Form this year. If that happens, you'd better add such dividends to your income, either by calculating the amount of dividends from your deposit slips or by contacting the corporation directly, since omitting income is a bad idea. The odds on this one are fairly high that you'll get caught, and a penalty—for substantial understatement of income, negligence, fraud, or worse—may be imposed.

You are now ready to meet with your preparer. You weren't before. Your accountant simply doesn't know your life the way you do. He doesn't know that the luncheon conversation you had with your own college buddy quickly turned from exaggerated former love conquests to the tax shelters he tried to sell you, or that the typewriter you bought was used primarily for business. It makes no practical sense for your accountant to thumb through your credit-card receipts and diary—the names and places don't tell him which were personal and which were business, or mainly business. He doesn't have the time, inclination, or patience to go through each of those credit-card bills to itemize the interest charges, or to pick up the myriad little items that mount up over the course of a year. That's not his job, it's yours. They're small numbers to him, but important real after-tax dollars to you. One area of your unequaled expertise is you: knowing what you did last year, with whom, and for what purpose.

You can't avoid the work by telling your accountant to simply estimate a number. First of all, estimates are frequently not permitted by law. Second, even where permitted, they may not stand up at audit. Sure, the odds of being audited are low, but those low odds aren't comforting when your number comes up.

Some of the information you've assembled may turn out to be irrelevant to your taxes. Chances are those twelve monthly checks you wrote out to the utility company for heating and lighting your home are purely personal items. But if your home office qualifies for a tax deduction (and we'll soon explain why it may), your accountant will tell you that the cost of heat and light allocable to the home office is deductible as a business expense. That translates into dollars in your pocket. If you use one room out of five in your house or apartment as a qualified "home office," then one fifth (if your rooms are of equal size) of your year's utilities bill becomes deductible. In dollar language, at an average of $200 per month you pay $2,400 annually for utilities; deducting one fifth results in after-tax savings to you of $240 in the 50-percent tax bracket—$2,400 × $\frac{1}{5}$ × 50% = $240.

You may think that's an unfair deduction even if it works in your favor—after all, you would have had to turn the heat on anyway during those cold winter nights. (Of course, it's more likely that if you don't qualify for the home-office expense you'll think *that's* unfair.) But fairness has nothing to do with the Internal Revenue Code. It is a mishmash of related and unrelated laws that have evolved over decades, fueled by numerous special interest groups, political and social considerations, and shifting legislative and bureaucratic assessments of what ought to be the law. The tax laws are not a code of equity but a system of forced financial sacrifices. If there's a lawful crevice you can properly slip through, do it. "Loopholes" don't exist only for Exxon and IBM, they're there for you as well.

When you provide your preparer with all the financial information you've assembled, you have prepared him to prepare your return. Discuss with him all of the information you've assembled. Make sure he knows of all the large expenditures you've made during the year. As to each of them, ask him whether there is any tax benefit for you. Don't be shy about sounding foolish; the worst he can say is, "Sorry, those are after-tax dollars you paid with." But he may be able, creatively and within the law, to suggest a basis for writing off all or part of that expense, which you hadn't even thought of, based on a law you've never heard of. After all, that's his job. You don't want to pay accounting fees for a glorified paper shuffler.

If you think you've got an item that warrants a deduction but he disagrees, don't docilely take No for an answer. First press him a bit and make him explain to you in plain English why you're wrong. After all, the tax laws may sometimes sound as if they're written in Greek, but accountants are trained to translate them into understandable English for you. Ultimately, you should have enough faith in your preparer to accept his opinion; if you don't, find someone else.

In fact, if you've done a thorough enough job to give him an overview of your financial affairs, he should be able not only to prepare your return but to offer helpful suggestions on your overall financial planning so you'll be in an even more advantageous position next April 15.

To do all this most effectively, you should have some basic knowledge of the tax laws that may apply to you. Now that sounds like an awfully complicated subject to master. In fact, though, for most of us the tax principles that can save us the most money are straightforward and simple. Here's what they are.

CHAPTER 9

Tax-Reduction Techniques That Work (and They're Legal)

The tax laws are full of loopholes just for you. All you've got to do is look for them, or hire someone who knows where they are.

Split Your Income

Because of the "graduated" tax rates, one method of reducing your taxes is to shift high-bracket dollars to lower brackets. Suppose you're single and your taxable income is $85,000. You're paying different percentages on different parts of that income, and the percentages increase as the dollars increase. The tax bites are in these amounts:

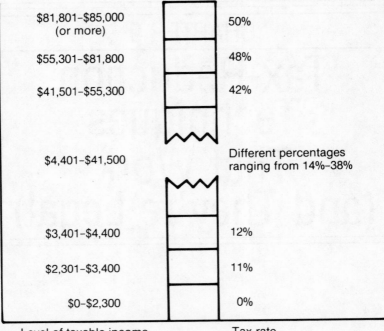

Level of taxable income   Tax rate

If you only could take some of this income—let's say $5,000—

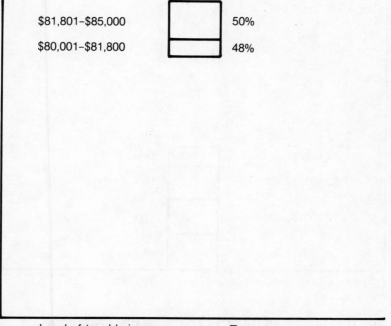

and move it here—

(turn page)

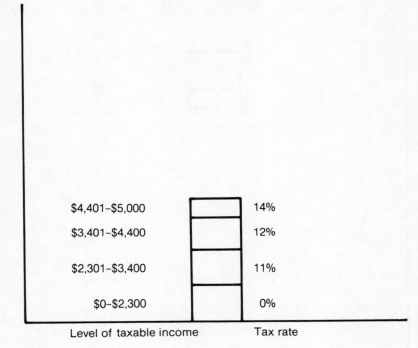

you'd save a lot of money ($2,139 in this example).

And you can.

There are various ways to split your income, shifting top-bracket dollars to the bottom brackets. Splitting your income among corporations, family members, trusts, and tax periods is one of the easiest and most effective tax planning techniques—and perfectly legal. These are some of the ways, and some of the pitfalls.

USE OF A CORPORATION

The tax law considers a corporation to be a taxable entity separate from its shareholders. Income earned by a corporation is taxed at rates far below the individual rates.

For example, a corporation with taxable income of $50,000 is taxed at a rate of 15 percent on its first $25,000 of taxable income and at 18 percent on its next $25,000, for a total tax of $8,250. An unmarried individual with that income pays $13,889 in taxes, an overall rate of nearly 28 percent.

Only when a corporation's net taxable income exceeds $100,000 does the rate climb to its maximum figure of 46 percent. Obviously, significant savings can be obtained by incorporating your small business and permitting some of your profits to accumulate in the corporation, to be taken out and taxed later.

As with all good plans, this one has certain limitations. A corporation can safely accumulate only up to $250,000 of undistributed profits without any possibility of a penalty. If the accumulations exceed that amount, the IRS may assert an "accumulated-earnings" penalty if it considers that the accumulations were made for the purpose of avoiding income taxes rather than for the reasonable needs of the business. But reasonable needs of the business include not only current needs, but also those reasonably anticipated for the future. Accumulations can be justified if you have definite and feasible future plans requiring the use of capital.

Of course, this use of a corporation results in the corporation paying a separate tax, even at these low rates. But the corporate tax can be avoided by setting up a type of corporation described in a subsection of the Internal Revenue Code designated Subchapter S. In the imaginative wit of tax practitioners, such a corporation is dubbed a "Subchapter S corporation."

A Subchapter S corporation is for taxpayers who want to have their cake and eat it too. Such a corporation does not pay taxes. Its income is considered to pass directly through to its stockholders, just like the income received by a partnership (which is also not a separately taxed entity). We'll shortly show how use of a Subchapter S corporation could have saved a typical taxpayer bundles of money and gallons of grief.

Corporations are also useful in avoiding estate taxes. For example, if you're starting a business, you can set up your corporation with two classes of stock, one voting and one nonvoting. The nonvoting class of stock can be structured so that nearly all the equity or dollar value of the corporation is attributed to those shares. Those shares can be given to your children. It's a new business, so the shares presumably have a low value and the gift is therefore not taxable. You retain the voting shares. With this setup you are able to keep full control of your corporation throughout your lifetime. You receive a salary from the corporation in the amount you choose, as long as the amount is reasonable in relation to the services you render. And the future growth of the company will inure to the benefit of the nonvoting shares held in your children's names. As your company grows, that growth will belong to your children, and you will have legally avoided all estate taxes on that growth.

USE OF FAMILY MEMBERS

Speaking of children, let's not forget how expensive they can be. The high costs of a college education can be made more bearable if the earnings on your savings are not eaten away by taxes. How can this be done?

Most simply, you can give that extra bank account or brokerage account to your children either pursuant to your state's Uniform Gift to Minors Act or by creating a trust for your children. There is a $10,000 ($20,000 if the gift is made jointly with your spouse) annual exclusion per recipient from both gift taxes and the requirement that you file a gift-tax return. If you are fortunate enough to be able to afford a gift-giving program over a period of years, you can give your children a sizable tax-free legacy during your lifetime, while removing from your income the interest earned on the principal given. You're also reducing your estate taxes in the process.

But let's say that you are not one of those fortunate few who can part with a large sum of money. Still, you don't like paying high tax rates on the interest your savings earn. You'd prefer that income to be tax-free or tax-low, but you want to keep the principal for either a rainy day or retirement. You can accomplish both results—retention of your investment and relatively tax-free income—by forming what is called a "Clifford trust," the name originating from a decision of the United States Supreme Court in a case involving a family surnamed Clifford.

Pursuant to the Clifford decision, you can place property in trust and have that property revert to you any time after ten years. During that ten-year-and-a-day (or more) period when the trust is in existence, all income earned by the trust is taxable to the trust. For tax purposes, the trust is considered a separate entity with its own tax rates, exemptions, exclusions, and deductions. The arithmetic is simple: If you are earning $1,000 per year on your investments, you are paying $500 of that in taxes (in the 50-percent bracket), whereas if the trust earns $1,000 and has no other income, the $1,000 is tax-free.

Another way to reduce your taxes while helping your children is a transfer to your children by sale or gift, coupled with a leaseback. In essence, you are shifting the tax away from your own high tax bracket to the low tax bracket of your children or a trust formed for your children. For example, if you are a physician with an office building, a stockbroker with computers, or a shoemaker with sewing equipment, you can sell or give the building, computer, or equipment to your children and then rent it from them for a fair rental fee. The rent that you pay your children will be taxable to them, presumably at a much lower tax bracket than yours. At the same time, your rental payments are deductible to you, and the deduction may exceed the depreciation and other expenses you could have taken had you kept ownership of the property.

Similar tax planning is often available with other close family members, and often overlooked. For example, think about your parents now retired in Florida, comfortably residing in their condominium by the sea. Probably the major portion of their monthly maintenance payment for their apartment consists of interest on their mortgage and local property taxes. Those sums are deductible on your parents' income-tax return. But they are now retired and in a relatively low tax bracket. Those thousands of dollars in deductions may only be generating a tax savings of 15 percent or 20 percent, whereas you are presently in your peak earning years, perhaps paying taxes at the 50-percent rate.

The remedy is simple. Your parents can either give or sell their apartment to you, and you lease it back to them for a rental cost equal to what their maintenance had been. The rent will be income taxable to you. However, you will now be paying the maintenance on the apartment, including the interest on the mortgage and local property taxes. Those sums, together with a depreciation deduction on what is now income-producing property, are deductible by you so that you get the full 50-percent in-pocket value of every dollar deducted. If you live in a state with a high local income tax, that savings is even more. And your parents aren't paying a dime more than they had been paying. Furthermore, as the value of the property increases, the transfer also avoids subjecting the increase to estate taxes.

The concept of splitting income has its limits. One of these is the "assignment-of-income" doctrine. Basically, all that means is that he who earns the money is taxed on it. You cannot avoid taxation at your high income tax bracket by merely telling your boss or your customer to pay your child for the services you have rendered. In order to achieve a transfer of taxation, you must first transfer the income-producing property before the income itself is earned. For example, a transfer of a bond after interest has already accrued, but before it is paid, will not achieve a shifting of the tax to the recipient. Interest accrued on bonds before the date of their transfer is the transferor's income. Similarly, if you happen to buy that state lottery ticket and transfer it to your child after the drawings show you won, the winnings will be taxed to you rather than your child. However, if you give the ticket to your child prior to the drawing, the winnings will be taxed to him.

Other limitations on splitting income can entail substantial risks if you get greedy. Take the case of John Fellini. John owned a trucking concern. The business was incorporated but paid little corporate income tax, since John reduced most of its profits through his salary and a substantial year-end bonus for himself. John was earning a hefty income and had entered the 50-percent bracket. To lower his taxes, John decided to place his two children, John, Jr. and Marie, on the corporate payroll. He put Marie down as a clerical worker and John, Jr. as a driver, and paid each a salary of $25,000. John, Jr.'s and Marie's tax rates were far lower than their father's, who was thereby able to reduce his own net taxable income by $50,000.

During the course of a routine audit of the business, a revenue agent, seeing the boss and two employees had the same last name, asked about the children. When he discovered their ages were six and four, he referred the case for criminal investigation.

If John Fellini had consulted with a tax adviser or had

some knowledge of basic tax planning, he could have legally accomplished his objective—splitting his income with his children. He could have elected to have his corporation taxed as a Subchapter S corporation, and placed shares of the corporation's stock in the names of his two children. He could have foregone his bonus or reduced his salary. The resulting corporate profits would have been income to the three shareholders in proportion to their stock ownership. John, Jr. and Marie's shares would have been taxed at a much lower tax bracket than their father's, and the Fellini family would have paid less in taxes to Uncle Sam.

Moral of the story: If you are armed with a knowledge of our tax laws, you may be able to accomplish legally what you think requires cheating.

USE OF TAX PERIODS

The splitting of income need not be only between people, but can also be between tax periods. Since taxation is an annually anchored event, shifting income and deductions to or from the current taxable period, as needed, can reduce the amount of taxes you will pay.

For example, when selling your business or other valuable asset at a substantial profit, you should consider making an "installment sale." As a general rule, the entire profit on a sale must be reported and is taxable in the year of the sale. However, if your contract is structured so that at least one payment is to be received after the close of the taxable year in which the sale occurred, you are eligible for "installment-sale treatment." (Caveat: A dealer who regularly sells personal property on an installment basis must affirmatively elect to use the installment method of reporting income before the IRS will permit him to do so.)

When a sale is reported to the IRS on the installment method, the amount of income from the installment sale that is taxed each year is determined by multiplying the amount received in that year by the percentage of gross profit realized on the sale. For example, if the sale price of your machinery is $1,000 payable in equal installments over two years, and your gross profit on the sale is $400 (i.e., 40 percent), you multiply the $500 received in the first year by 40 percent; that $200 is taxable in the first year. What you have accomplished is a shifting of the other $200 of profit to year two, even though the sale was consummated in year one.

This shifting or deferring of income can have two benefits. First, by dividing your large profit into two or more taxable years, each with its own graduated tax rate structure, you may find that your profits are taxed at a lower tax rate. Second, you have deferred your tax on a portion of the profit for an additional year or more. While a deferral of tax is certainly not as advantageous as its total elimination, it is the next best thing. Every year that a tax can be deferred gives you the use of money that otherwise would be in Uncle's hands, and with that money additional money can be generated.

A similar concept is a deferred-payment plan. You have probably read about sports superstars involved in such plans. Their compensation is structured so that a portion of their salary is payable over a long period of time, perhaps ten or more years. While the contract has fixed the total benefits the athlete will receive, the receipt of that money is deferred, which also defers the tax. An additional benefit is that the athlete will receive the money after his most productive years, and with graduated tax rates the actual taxes eventually paid will probably be lower.

You don't have to be a superstar to profit from this method. If your employer is about to pay you a sizable Christmas bonus on December 24, it may be to your advantage to postpone its payment for two weeks, thereby postponing the tax on that payment for a full year.

Two warnings. First, if the company paying the bonus

is your own company and is on a cash basis, then your corporation cannot get a deduction for the bonus paid to you until the year of actual payment. Second, you must avoid the "constructive-receipt-of-income" doctrine. Under this doctrine, the IRS will tax you on money not received within the year if you had the right to receive that money within the year but choose not to. This doctrine creates a very subtle line that can easily be crossed. For example, if you and your customer agree that payments for goods delivered in December will not be due until January, or if you and your employer agree that your bonus will not be paid until January, you have accomplished a deferral of income. However, if you have an absolute right to that payment in December but you yourself choose not to accept the money until January, the IRS will claim that you had "constructive" receipt of that money in December and therefore it is taxable in year one.

Timing should not only be considered in connection with the possible deferral of income but also should be considered when paying deductible expenses and managing your investments. Generally, you should accelerate deductions into the current year to reduce taxes, but the reverse may, at times, also prove helpful. For example, if you are expecting a surge of income in the following year from a large sale or bonus, you may benefit by deferring the payment of deductible expenses until that year, when those deductions will be more valuable to you because of your higher tax bracket.

Your stocks, bonds, commodities, and other capital assets held for investment will be taxed at a maximum rate of 20 percent if held for more than six months (unless purchased prior to June 23, 1984, in which case the holding period is one year). If the holding period is six months or less, the income on the sale is taxed at ordinary rates. Although you can net capital losses against capital gains, long-term capital losses (that is, losses on capital assets held for more than six months) can only offset up to $3,000 of ordinary income in any one year, and then only at a ratio of $2 of capital loss to each $1 of ordinary income. It is therefore wise for you to attempt to time your sales so that your gains are long-term. However, if your gains are short-term, you should try to match those gains with capital net losses so that you are not liable for tax at the ordinary rate. If you have losses, you should attempt to make them short-term so that you can use them to offset ordinary income at a ratio of 1:1.

The Internal Revenue Code also has a relief provision to deal with unusually good years that otherwise would be taxed at those uncomfortably high rates. That provision is called "income averaging." It permits you to take the portion of this year's income that is in excess of the average income you earned in the preceding three years and tax it as though it had been received in equal installments over a four-year period (that is, the current year and the three preceding years). You can determine your eligibility for the benefits of income averaging by doing the calculations on a Schedule G of Form 1040 available at any Internal Revenue Office.

Pension Plans

Through pension plans, salary-reduction plans (often called 401(k) plans after the Internal Revenue Code section allowing them) and profit-sharing plans, the law permits you to sock away sizable amounts of money without paying taxes on that money, or on the income generated by that money, until your retirement or an earlier distribution from the plan. With the use of such plans, the taxes on the money placed into the plan, and on the money that money earns, are deferred for so long that they virtually eliminate the tax.

There are qualified corporate retirement plans under

which the corporation receives a current deduction for contributions to the plan for its employees, while the em-ployee does not report the income of the plan until it is distributed to him. This money, when actually distributed, may qualify for a ten-year-forward income-averaging computation. Similarly, under a salary reduction plan up to 25 percent of your salary (but not more than $30,000) may be deducted by your employer and invested by him into a pension plan for your benefit. Many corporations will partially match their employees' contributions; those matching sums are not taxable to you until the money is removed from the plan. These plans are highly regulated as to who may participate and the rights and benefits of the participants. For example, such plans may not discrim-inate in favor of high-level employees, corporate officers, or stockholders.

Even employees of their own closely held corporations can have a plan whereby the corporation contributes sub-stantial amounts for their retirement. Under a defined contribution plan, the corporation may contribute up to 25 percent of an employee's earned income if such contri-bution does not exceed $30,000 per year (to be adjusted for inflation). Under another type of plan called a "de-fined-benefit" plan, the corporation may make a contri-bution that at retirement will produce an annual benefit of as much as $90,000 (to be adjusted for inflation). Al-though the corporation is entitled to the tax benefit of a current deduction for these contributions, the employee's tax is deferred until retirement or earlier distribution. If the contributions to the plan were in the form of the em-ployer corporation's stock, the tax on the unrealized ap-preciation of that stock is deferred beyond the distribution date until the stock is actually sold. Moreover, depending upon the plan itself and within strict limitations, you may be able to borrow up to half your vested amount from the plan (but not over $50,000) for a residential mortgage loan for either you or a member of your immediate family or, if repaid within five years, for any other purpose, without tax or penalty.

Partnerships and self-employed individuals are eligible for the rough equivalent of these corporate plans by setting up a Keogh Plan. As with a corporate plan, a Keogh Plan permits contributions of up to $30,000 or 25 percent of income or contributions that at retirement will produce an annual benefit of as much as $90,000 (to be adjusted for inflation).

The complexities of these pension and profit-sharing plans, and of related fringe benefits these plans allow, require technical expertise. What is important for you to know is that such plans do exist and are available to you and your company, and if you don't seek out advice to implement such plans, you are going to be overpaying your taxes. It's a no-loss proposition, so take advantage of it.

In addition, all working individuals, whether self-employed or employees and whether or not participants in another plan, may set up their own individual retirement account (IRA) and contribute into that account $2,000 of their earned income (for divorced people, alimony is deemed to be earned income for purposes of IRA contributions). That contribution is permitted as a deduction on the individual's income-tax return and is not reportable as income until it is distributed. An additional contribution of $250 can be made for your nonworking spouse. If possible, however, it may be wise for you to hire your spouse as a part-time consultant or independent contractor and pay your spouse $2,000 during the year. That sum could then be placed into another IRA, thereby creating a $4,000 deduction on your joint return instead of only $2,250.

If distributions are made from the plan before you reach the age of fifty-nine and a half, there is a 10-percent penalty on that distributed amount. But once you have deferred the taxes on the principal and income earned in your IRA account for approximately five years, those tax benefits will outweigh the 10-percent penalty even if you make an early withdrawal.

These plans are worth a lot of money to you. Imagine a rich uncle giving you money every year, free, for you to invest—tax-free. Suppose your idea of investing is simply to deposit the money into a bank account, and it earns 10 percent compounded daily. If the rich uncle gives you $1,000 on January 1, you've earned $105.20 in interest by December 31. And by the end of the second year, you've earned 10 percent on that $1,105.20—your $1,105.20 has generated another $116.26 in interest (including interest on the $105.20 interest generated in the first year—that's the magic of compound interest). The account has grown to $1,221.46. By the end of year ten, the $1,000 gift has grown to $2,718.95—and it's still earning tax-free interest.

And if that rich uncle had given you another $1,000 at the beginning of year two, and you invested it the same way—and another $1,000 every year—then by the end of year ten those ten $1,000 gifts would have grown to $18,059.04.

Uncle Sam offers just such a gift to you every year. If you're in the 50-percent bracket, setting up a $2,000 IRA gives you a $2,000 tax deduction, which saves you $1,000 in hard cash tax dollars you'd otherwise pay to Uncle Sam (the benefits of a Keogh Plan are even greater). If you're in a lower bracket, the gift is smaller, but the principle's the same. Whoever you are, the probability is enormously high that you should accept the gift.

By the way, contributions to your individual retirement plans can be made up until April 15 of the following tax year. As to qualified pension and Keogh Plans, contributions can be made after the April 15 deadline up until your return is filed, as long as your return is timely filed under extension and the plan itself was established before the end of the year for which you claim your deduction. If you don't have the money to place into your plan but can get that money through a tax refund, you can file your tax return early, claim a deduction for a contribution not yet made, and thereby generate a tax refund you then use to make the contribution.

Tax Shelters

In recent years, tax shelters have developed a bad name, since all sorts of sham transactions have been marketed by disreputable promoters as investments that magically erase all your tax obligations. The IRS has mustered its might to combat such abusive shelters. If you should purchase one, the chances of your getting caught and punished are exceedingly high.

The forms of these shelters are numerous. Real estate, oil and gas, equipment leasing, movies, et cetera, and some more et cetera. Beware! Don't go into a shelter merely for its tax consequences. Ask yourself: If not for the touted tax benefits, would you otherwise invest in this Grade-C Turkish-made, English-dubbed Western musical? Do you really think it's going to be a profitable movie? As the law is presently developing, so-called shelters are becoming a riskier and riskier business. Before entering one, consult with a trusted tax adviser.

With all these caveats in mind, however, you may find that there is a proper investment for you that can legally and significantly reduce your income taxes. That shelter most likely exists in real estate, whose tax advantages have been least affected by the stringent rules recently enacted to combat abusive shelters.

There are many legitimate investments with significant

tax incentives that can help shelter you from tax. These investments would be less attractive without their tax advantages, but they are in themselves economically realistic transactions with attractive earnings potential, even without their tax-sheltering features.

The key to most tax shelters is "leverage," simply a fancy term for borrowing. For example, with only $10,000 of your own, you may be able to purchase a building for $110,000 by borrowing $100,000. All your expenses incurred for that building (except capital improvements) and the interest on your mortgage are currently deductible. But what makes the investment a shelter is depreciation deductions and the "investment-tax" credit.

The building itself is depreciable. Assuming a typical depreciable life of eighteen years, you are entitled to an additional deduction of $6,111 per year on that $110,000 building—even though the building will still be standing and producing income long after eighteen years. There is also the investment-tax credit, which permits an immediate one-time credit of 10 percent of your entire investment (including borrowed money) in tangible personal property. Although such credits are not generally allowed for real estate or buildings, there is a rehabilitation investment credit ranging from 15 percent to 25 percent for all qualified rehabilitation expenditures. Remember, these are not merely deductions, but one-to-one write-offs against actual tax dollars.

Moreover, if the building's value is appreciating through the years, you are earning future dollars not only on your investment but also on the borrowed money.

Using Your Home as a Tax Advantage

As every homeowner knows, your home generates important tax savings. The interest on your mortgage, including the "points" paid to the bank to obtain the mortgage, is deductible; so are your state and local school and property taxes.

Practically all your home improvements can provide tax advantages. That new central air-conditioning system and new kitchen are considered capital improvements, and the costs of all capital improvements are added dollar-for-dollar to the "basis" or cost of your home, thereby reducing any taxable gain reportable by you when you sell it. But make sure you keep all bills and checks to prove the costs of those improvements. The language of the bills should be sufficiently descriptive to identify the work as capital improvements. This is important because mere repairs, which are defined as work that does not increase the value or prolong the life of the home, do not increase your basis. Remember, at the time of an audit the burden will be on you to establish your basis in your home. Bills and canceled checks should be kept for a period of at least six years after your home is sold (and still longer if you have a carryover basis into a new home).

Immediate tax credits are available to either an owner or a tenant for certain home improvements. A credit is more advantageous than either a deduction or basis increment: A credit is a direct and immediate dollar-for-dollar reduction against your taxes rather than a reduction in income upon which tax is computed. Credits are available for expenditures you make for certain materials and equipment that save energy or exploit new sources of energy. The energy-conservation credit is limited to 15 percent of the expenditure, with a maximum credit of $300. Thus, if you have insulated a wall, added storm windows, or made the fireplace flue more efficient, at a cost of $1,500, you can subtract $225 from your tax bill. There is also a 40 percent credit (to a maximum credit of $4,000) for conversions to alternative energy sources such as the installation of a solar heating system.

If your home is used also for business, numerous tax

advantages can follow. These include everything from amortizing a portion of the cost of the home and all of the furnishings for the portion used as an office, to annually deducting an allocable portion of monthly expenses, such as heat, electricity, and cleaning bills.

To qualify for a home-office deduction, a portion of your home must be used exclusively on a regular basis (a) as your principal place of business for any trade or business, or (b) as a place of business used by your patients, clients, or customers, and (c) if you are an employee, for the convenience of your employer and not of yourself. This test is quite restrictive; yet there are gaps to slip through. Thus, while the courts have denied the home-office deduction to teachers who use a home study to prepare their lesson plans or grade exams, they have granted the deduction to college professors who spend most of their working hours at home doing research and writing. The home-office deduction has also been allowed to musicians who, while earning their income by performing in concert halls, used a room at home for rehearsing. In both these examples where the deduction has been allowed, the employer—the college or the symphonic company—did not provide employees with suitable space for engaging in the necessary practice or research.

While your home has to be your principal place of business, that business doesn't have to be your principal business. So if you're earning extra money selling magazine subscriptions from your home, you may significantly reduce your tax on both that income and your major source of income through a home-office deduction if your motive in selling those magazines is to make a profit.

The Internal Revenue Code has several provisions to reduce the tax impact when you sell your home. If you are fifty-five years of age or older and sell or exchange the home that you have owned or used as your principal residence for three or more years of the past five-year period, you can elect, one time only, to exclude from your gross income up to $125,000 of gain on the sale of your home. Thus, if you're in your early fifties and thinking of selling your home, astute tax planning may call for postponing the sale.

Even if you haven't reached fifty-five there are deferral provisions available to everyone on the sale of a principal residence. To qualify, you must sell your principal residence and buy and use another within two years from the original sale. If you do, the gain on the sale of the first residence will not be subject to tax so long as the cost of the new residence equals or exceeds the selling price of the old. If the cost of your new home is less than the selling price of the old, gain is taxable to the extent of the difference. The basis of your new home, however, will be reduced by the amount of gain not recognized on the sale of your old home.

But what if you are about to sell a vacation home—not your primary residence—that does not qualify for any of these relief provisions? For example, Al and Francine Silver owned a seaside cottage on Cape Cod that had grown tremendously in value over the years. Their children were older, and the Silvers no longer needed a vacation home. They decided to sell the cottage and invest the proceeds in high-yield income-producing real estate, and then use that income for travel or other vacation plans. But they wanted to avoid the significant tax bite that Uncle Sam was about to take from their proceeds of the sale.

Their method was simple. They falsely described their Cape Cod home as their primary residence, thereby qualifying it under the exclusion-and-deferral provisions of the Code, as previously discussed. Unfortunately, the Silvers' return was chosen for audit and the examining agent quickly realized what had been done. He imposed a tax and negligence penalty—and the Silvers were relieved that a fraud penalty was not imposed.

With skilled planning the Silvers could have legally avoided all taxation. Step 1: By renting the cottage for a season or merely offering it for rental, the Silvers would have converted it into investment-type property for income-tax purposes. Step 2: They then should have located the income-producing property they wished to buy—let's say a commercial rental unit in Boston. Step 3: Then they should have found a buyer for their cottage. Step 4: That buyer could have purchased the Boston property and then exchanged that property with them for their vacation cottage.

If the properties had the same sale price, or if the cottage cost less than the Boston property (and the Silvers paid their buyer the difference), the transaction would have been tax-free. If the cottage cost more and they therefore received the difference in money from the buyer, they would have been taxed only on that difference, and even that amount would receive capital-gains treatment.

Under the Internal Revenue Code the Silvers would have been treated as if they had exchanged their original property for a property of "like kind," and such like kind exchanges are not taxable. Their basis in the cottage would have been carried over into the new property and the gain deferred until they sold the new property. By selling their cottage for cash and investing that cash in the Boston rental unit, the economic realities were the same, but they were taxed on the gain from the sale of their cottage. These taxes, in turn, left them with considerably less money to reinvest in the new property.

Deductions You May Have Overlooked

The Internal Revenue Code is a maze of deductions and credits, many relating to your employment and many relating to your personal life. Although you probably are familiar with most of the general categories, you still may be missing out on valuable deductions. Many of your expenditures which at first blush may not appear to you to be deductible may be deducted in the proper circumstances.

ORDINARY AND NECESSARY BUSINESS EXPENSES

The Internal Revenue Code permits you to deduct all of the ordinary and necessary expenses incurred in carrying on a trade or business. The breadth of this definition is readily apparent. Its limitations are few.

First you need a "trade or business." A trade or business is defined as any activity carried on for profit or potential profit. The activity is presumed to be carried on for profit if it shows a profit in any two out of five consecutive years (two out of seven if you're in horsebreeding). This does not mean that if you don't show a profit for at least two of five years the expenses will be disallowed. Rather, it means that the burden then will be on you to prove that your activities were carried on for profit even though you lost money: that you were not merely engaged in a hobby.

If your activities were only a hobby, you may deduct your ordinary and necessary business expenses only to the extent of the income earned from the hobby plus such items as interest expenses and state and local taxes. The IRS often attempts to apply the hobby-loss limitation in situations where your expense deductions are incurred in a secondary pursuit such as painting, writing, farming, or animal breeding, and you are attempting to use those expenses as deductions against your primary source of income. However, if you can convince the Service that despite your inability to obtain two profitable years, you actually and reasonably believe that your endeavors will ultimately prove profitable, your deductions for all ordinary and necessary business expenses should be allowed.

The term "ordinary" means an accepted practice in your field of business. Some courts, however, have given a less restrictive definition of "ordinary," defining it simply as a current expense as opposed to one that must be capitalized. The term "necessary" means merely helpful or appropriate in carrying on your trade or business. It does not mean indispensable or essential. Inherent in the definitions of both "ordinary" and "necessary" is the concept of reasonableness as to amount.

There are useful deductions available to you in connection with travel and entertainment expenses you incur in business. The transportation costs for a domestic trip are completely deductible if the trip is "primarily" for business, even if the trip is combined with a personal vacation. If foreign travel is done primarily for business but you do some personal vacationing while there, you may allocate your expenses between business and personal on a time basis. In fact, you are permitted under the tax laws to deduct all your travel expenses if you establish one of the following factors: (1) the trip does not exceed one week; (2) the personal portion of the trip was less than 25 percent of the total travel time; (3) you did not have control over your travel (this is presumed if you are not a managing executive of your employer or are unrelated to your employer); or (4) a personal vacation was not a major consideration in determining to make the trip. You may even deduct your spouse's expenses on the trip if you were encouraged by your employer to develop personal contacts through your spouse's attendance at business-related social functions.

Entertainment expenses are deductible if "directly related" to your trade or business. You are not required to show that business income actually resulted from the entertainment. So if you take a customer to a sporting event and try but fail to sell your product to him, the costs of those tickets and any related expenses are deductible. It is not even necessary for you to make your sales pitch at the event. Expenses that are "associated" with your business are deductible if the entertainment takes place directly before or after a substantial and bona fide business discussion.

The rules are even less strict for business meals. If a business discussion did not take place before, after, or at the meal, it is still deductible as long as there is a business purpose for the meal and the surroundings are conducive to a business discussion. You may even deduct your spouse's and customer's spouse's meals if their presence was useful to the business purpose of your getting together with your customer. Remember, however, when it comes to travel and entertainment expenses the Service has strict rules requiring substantiation as to amount, time, place, business purpose, and the identity of the person(s) entertained.

The IRS regulations include numerous examples of deductible business expenses: management expenses; commissions; labor; supplies; incidental repairs; operating expenses of automobiles used in the trade or business; traveling expenses while away from home solely in the pursuit of a trade or business; advertising and other selling expenses; insurance premiums against fire, storm, theft, or accidents; business lawsuits; rental of business property; and many others. The permissible scope is extremely broad, and many of the deductions available to you as business expenses will not be found in any textbook but are unique to your particular business. You know your business better than anyone, and you are best able to explain your expenses to your tax preparer, particularly to explain why those expenses are ordinary and necessary and therefore deductible.

Certain expenditures that may not seem deductible when viewed in isolation are in fact ordinary and necessary in their business context. For example, Abby Deutsch is a jewelry dealer with a booth in one of New York City's jewelry exchanges. Everything she sells is a unique item of beauty and great worth, and its proper presentation and display is essential to the sale of the item. She will personally wear a piece of jewelry for a customer to demonstrate its true beauty. Ms. Deutsch receives weekly manicures so that her hands are beautifully kept, thereby elegantly displaying the rings she shows. In the context of Ms. Deutsch's business, those manicures are ordinary and necessary and properly deductible by her.

As a general rule, the payment of a bribe or kickback is not deductible. The rationale is that to permit such deductions would encourage and underwrite payments that are against public policy. But again, in the proper context, even a kickback can be an ordinary and necessary business expense deductible to the payer. Ray Bart had a trucking company that did subcontracting work at a construction site for a large shopping mall in Akron, Ohio. When Bart's company obtained the subcontract, it was on condition that he pay regular kickbacks to the prime contractor's site supervisor. In 1983, Bart paid that supervisor over $50,000 in kickbacks. Bart felt that this was an ordinary and necessary expense of his business and deducted those payments.

The IRS challenged that expense and disallowed the deduction. Bart brought the issue to Tax Court, which agreed with the IRS. But Bart persevered and took his case to the United States Court of Appeals. The appellate court agreed with him that such payments were not of an abnormal nature, and were deductible as ordinary and necessary business expenses. The court held that all costs of doing business are deductible and that the kickbacks Bart had to pay were no less deductible than any other expense of doing business.

Bart's case is somewhat aberrant, because most states have commercial bribery laws that make such kickbacks illegal and their deduction against public policy. But in the state of Ohio no such law exists; the kickbacks were thus legal and deductible.

What if you don't have your own corporate business and are not self-employed? If you as an employee incur expenses for your employer, can you deduct those expenses? Yes. An employee who has business expenses in excess of the reimbursement he receives from his employer can deduct that expense on his income-tax return.

EXPENSES FOR THE PRODUCTION OF INCOME

The Internal Revenue Code also permits you to deduct all ordinary and necessary expenses incurred for the production or collection of income, or for the management, conservation, or maintenance of property held for the production of income or in connection with the determination, collection, or refund of any tax. As with business expenses, this catchall definition permits you to deduct a wide variety of expenses relating to your investment activities, such as subscription costs of investment books and periodicals, brokerage, accounting, and legal advice dealing with investments and taxes, safe-deposit box fees for the storage of taxable securities, payments for clerical help used in maintaining your investments, and incidental travel expenses incurred while visiting your broker, attorney, or even the investment itself. If your investment is in the form of real estate, you may deduct the cost of such expenses as management fees, repairs, depreciation, and insurance, even though the real estate is not a trade or business.

Even your nonbusiness legal expenses are deductible if the lawyering was rendered in connection with a tax question or the production, maintenance, or collection of income. For example, if you pay your attorney a fee to recover damages to a piece of property that produces income, those fees are deductible. Similarly, although legal fees for a divorce are deemed personal and therefore nondeductible, any portion of the fee attributable to advice relating to the protection or collection of income—such as alimony payments—is deductible. Thus, as with business expenses, "personal" expenses that appear nondeductible on their surface may in fact be deductible when viewed in the context in which the expenditures were incurred.

MOVING EXPENSES

Employees and self-employed individuals can deduct moving expenses incurred to obtain work in a new location. These expenses include the cost of moving your household goods and personal effects, travel costs (including meals and lodging) after obtaining employment to search for a new home, your family's travel costs (including meals and lodging) to your new home, temporary living expenses at your new location for a period of up to thirty days, and the costs incurred for the purchase or lease and sale of your new and old homes. The deduction for house hunting and temporary living expenses is limited to $1,500, while the deduction for the expenses incurred in the sale, purchase, or lease of your home is limited to $3,000 minus any amount deducted for house hunting or temporary living expenses.

In order to qualify for the moving-expense deduction, the requirements become somewhat technical. Your new place of work must be at least thirty-five miles farther from your prior home than was your old place of work or, if you had no former place of work, at least thirty-five miles from your former residence. You also must be employed full-time at your new place of work for at least thirty-nine weeks during the twelve-month period immediately following your arrival, or you must be a full-time employee or perform services as a self-employed individual on a full-time basis for at least seventy-eight weeks during the twenty-four month period immediately following your arrival in your new location, of which not fewer than thirty-nine weeks are during the initial twelve-month period. See how complicated they make a simple idea?

EXPENSES FOR HOUSEHOLD AND DEPENDENT CARE SERVICES

Housekeeping and babysitting expenses may also be deductible for you. If you and your spouse are employed and must therefore hire household or dependent care services for a dependent under the age of fifteen or a dependent or spouse who is physically or mentally incapable of caring for himself, you are entitled to receive a credit against your tax of 20 percent to 30 percent of the costs incurred for such care. The maximum credit of 30 percent is reduced by 1 percent for every $2,000 of income you earn over $10,000, down to a credit of 20 percent. There is also a monetary ceiling on the credit of $2,400 for one qualifying individual and $4,800 for two or more such individuals.

The costs of a babysitter, a maid, or even a cook qualify for this tax credit. In addition, there is a similar credit for expenses incurred at a dependent care center as long as the center complies with all applicable laws and regulations of the state and local government and as long as the dependent also spends at least eight hours a day at your home.

BAD DEBTS

Remember the time you lent your ex-friend Fred $1,000, which he never repaid? That bad debt may be deductible to you. You must show that Fred's debt is wholly or partially worthless—that is, that Fred is unable to repay you. His inability to repay can be proved either by his bankruptcy, lack of assets, disappearance, ill health, or death.

Such a bad debt, when deductible, is usually only a short-term capital loss. A short-term capital loss is not as valuable to you as an ordinary loss because it is only deductible against $3,000 of ordinary income per year for a limited number of years. But there may be a way to convert Fred's bad debt from a short-term capital loss to an ordinary loss. If the bad debt is a business debt, it is deemed ordinary and fully deductible to you. Debts owed to a corporation are always deemed business debts, but what about debts owed to an individual? If the debt arose from a loan made to a supplier, a customer, or similar-type business relation, the debt generally will be deemed business in nature. Even more clearly, if your loan was for Fred to repair the car he drove to bring supplies to you, the debt would be business in nature and deductible as an ordinary rather than short-term capital loss.

What if you lend money to your own corporation in order to help keep it afloat? Such debts are considered personal in nature, the theory being that they were made either as a personal investment or to protect a personal investment. However, you may be able to avoid that result if your dominant motive for the loan to your corporation was not to protect the corporation or your investment, but rather to protect your job with the corporation. If the purpose of the loan was to protect your job, the law considers the loan as having been made in connection with your personal trade or business as an employee of the corporation. It is therefore of a business nature and deductible as an ordinary loss.

LOSSES

You are permitted to deduct all losses that are not insured if the loss was incurred in connection with (1) a trade or business, (2) a transaction entered into for profit, or (3) a fire, storm, shipwreck, or other casualty or theft. The loss is only deductible to the extent it exceeds $100. Casualty and theft losses are allowed only to the extent such losses exceed casualty gains plus the sum in excess of 10 percent of your adjusted gross income. A casualty gain is the recognized gain from an involuntary conversion of your property arising from a casualty or theft. For example, if you receive insurance proceeds of $1,500 for a stolen ring that originally cost $1,000, you have a casualty gain of $500.

This 10-percent rule severely limits the availability of casualty losses. But certain twists in its application may make this deduction useful to you. If a storm causes physical damage to trees on your property, the amount of your casualty loss deduction is not the original cost of those trees nor their replacement cost, but the lesser of your basis or cost in the property or the amount of your property's decline in value due to the loss of the trees. The loss of a beautiful shade tree can decrease the fair-market value of a home many times the value of the tree itself, and the deduction may be available to you despite the limitation of the loss to 10 percent of adjusted gross income.

A casualty-loss deduction that is due to a disaster is one of those rare deductions that may be claimed either in the year of its occurrence or, if you elect, in the year before its occurrence. A "disaster loss" must occur within an area proclaimed by the President of the United States as a federal disaster area qualifying for federal assistance. Should such a loss occur this year prior to your filing last year's return, you may elect to claim the loss on last year's return.

Another interesting application of the casualty/theft loss deduction occurs where the theft occurred by fraud. Let's say you invested in a tax shelter where the promoter fraudulently represented to you that the shelter was legitimate and that your investment was sound. Some time after you made the investment, you discovered that the "shelter" was an empty shell and that the IRS has disallowed your deduction because your investment had no economic reality. Nevertheless, you may deduct (subject to the 10-percent limitation) the amount of your investment as a theft loss based on the willful misrepresentations of the promoter.

MEDICAL EXPENSES

In light of medical reimbursement insurance and the restriction limiting your deduction to only those medical expenses exceeding 5 percent of your adjusted gross income, you may believe that medical-expense deductions are no longer useful to you. But the term "medical deduction" includes far more than merely doctor bills. It includes items such as false teeth, wigs, hair transplants, eyeglasses, cosmetic surgery, medically necessary home improvements, and all incidental travel. For example, if on your doctor's advice you install central air-conditioning in your home for your daughter's allergies, or you construct a swimming pool to treat your arthritic condition, you may deduct as a medical expense the amount you spend, to the extent that your cost exceeds the increase in value to your home resulting from the capital improvement.

You may deduct not only your own medical expenses but also those of your spouse and dependents. A dependent's medical expenses are deductible to you even if you are not entitled to claim that individual as a dependent exemption. For example, if you are providing more than half of the support of your child or parent and you pay his or her medical expenses, you may deduct those expenses even though he or she earns too much money to permit you to claim an additional exemption.

As the above examples show, the Internal Revenue Code, properly applied, offers you numerous avenues to legitimately reduce your taxable income. When reviewing your own tax picture with your return preparer, you should apprise him fully of the nature of your business, investments, and personal expenditures. The facts in your possession coupled with knowledgeable advice can be used handily and profitably to your advantage. The extra dollars spent seeking that knowledge will be returned to you manifold in tax-saved dollars.

CHAPTER 10
Some Friendly Advice

So you still think you can cut corners and get away with it, don't you?

Statistically, you're probably right. Most people who cheat on their taxes are never caught, especially if they're not piggish about it.

But there's another side to the equation, besides the low odds of getting caught: the devastatingly high price if the odds catch up to you. None of the people you've read about in this book expected to get caught.

John Doe sat down nervously opposite his newly retained lawyer. His nails, once finely manicured, were now thoroughly chewed. His face was sweaty. He loosened his tie. He was almost crying. Doe had just learned that the IRS's Criminal Investigation Division had begun investigating him.

"Why was I so stupid! I had everything I needed. It doesn't make sense. The dollars I tried to save wouldn't have changed my life-style one bit. Instead of dipping a couple of fingers into the cookie jar I dove head-first into the cake. Now I've ruined myself and my family!"

Fortunately for Doe, he had been not only greedy but ignorant as well. He had deliberately deducted phony expenses on his tax return, but had also overlooked a substantial deduction. After a year of investigation, the special agents pulled out of the case. Doe had mistakenly over-reported his taxes while trying to cheat.

Cheating the government is a crime. Cheating yourself is a shame.

If you ignore the sorry fact that the tax laws have infiltrated our daily lives, you will pay the consequences. You are under no obligation to make voluntary contributions to the IRS. If you don't become familiar with the tax laws, or if you don't hire someone who is, then you're overpaying.

Among those thousands of tax rules and regulations, within that indecipherable mass of verbiage, numerous tax benefits are there for you to take, legally. The law allows what the law allows, and it allows you many tax benefits. You don't have to cheat to get what you're entitled to, you just have to know what's yours.

You are legally entitled to put your toe right up to the line that separates the legal from the illegal. Do it. You only owe what you owe.

But do it knowledgeably, and don't cross the line. If you overstep, the sanctions are severe.

And if you do overstep, get help fast. How quickly you get help often determines whether you get nailed or get off.

APPENDIX

The Internal Revenue Manual of the IRS describes itself as being "the single official compilation of policies, procedures, instructions and guidelines relating to the organization, functions, administration and operations of the Service." For many years, the contents of the Manual were available only to IRS personnel. The IRS opposed disclosing the Manual to the public because "it would be a substantial aid to the fraudulent taxpayer wishing to avoid detection." Nevertheless, as a result of enactment of the Freedom of Information Act, the IRS was ordered to make its entire Manual available to the public.

Today, the Manual is available in nine enormous volumes containing tens of thousands of pages, most of which comprise minutiae of interest only to Service employees in specialized functions. However, the Manual also contains informational gems revealing basic operational policies and instructions for IRS agents to follow in their selection and audit of returns and in their collection of taxes.

The Appendix you are about to read contains carefully selected excerpts from three of the most important portions of the Manual: the "Classification Handbook," which describes the process by which returns are selected for audit; "Audit Guidelines for Examiners," which instructs agents on auditing techniques to be used in examining returns; and "Collection Activity," which describes the techniques agents should use to collect taxes.

Language is verbatim from the Manual. Section numbers are from the IRS's own internal numbering system.

Classification Handbook

Introduction

110
PURPOSE

This Handbook provides an overview of the classification process and contains instructions to assist classifiers/screeners.

120
SCOPE

(1) Due to limited resources, the Service can examine only a small percentage of the returns filed. The classifier's role is to ensure that these resources are used effectively. The classifier must decide which returns are most in need of examination and through examination will promote the highest degree of voluntary compliance.

(2) During classification details there are several important points a classifier should keep in mind:

    (a) Alertness to items that would result in potential overassessments as well as items that would result in potential deficiencies.

    (b) Any return given to a classifier when they have had personal transactions with the taxpayer and/or when the business or social relationship with the taxpayer is of a nature that might impair the impartiality or independence of the classifiers. These returns should be brought to the attention of the manager in charge of classification.

    (c) Any return where the type, the industry or the potential issue is unfamiliar to the classifier should be brought to the attention of the manager.

130
STANDARDS FOR CLASSIFICATION

(1) Discriminant Function (DIF) returns are selected for screening by computer. Each selected DIF return will be screened by an experienced examiner to eliminate those returns not worthy of examination.

(2) Non-DIF returns will be manually classified by experienced examiners to select returns that contain significant issues.

(3) All returns will be identified for assignment to a revenue agent, tax auditor, or tax examiner based on the complexity of the issues involved and the degree of accounting and auditing skills required to conduct a quality examination.

(4) During the classification process, the scope of the examination will be determined for all tax auditor and tax examiner returns except for pre-contact analysis returns and for designated revenue agent returns.

Administrative

220
Sorting of Classified/Screened Returns

(1) During the course of classification, returns should be separated as follows:

- (a) Selected returns for Office Examination—interview and precontact analysis.
- (b) Selected returns for Field Examination.
- (c) Selected returns for Service Center Correspondence Examination.
- (d) Returns that are unusual in nature. This would include the following items:
  1. Returns where charge-out documents are missing or do not match the return.
  2. Returns to be transferred.
  3. Returns where charge-out contains special messages; e.g., Information Report Available (if not in the case file), etc.
  4. Other returns as provided by local instructions.
  5. Special program returns (Tax Shelters, Tax Protesters, etc.).

Overview

310
Discriminant Function (DIF) System

(1) Most returns, both individual and corporate, that are examined each year are DIF returns. Therefore, the majority of the classifiers' work will be to screen DIF returns.

(2) For each examination class, different items on the return are scored. The score for an individual item is based on TCMP correlation analyses. The total DIF score for a return is the sum of the scores of

the individual items, and the higher the score, the greater the probability of tax change.

(3) It must be remembered that the DIF score indicates the overall tax change potential of the return as a whole. It should not be assumed that any single item on a return caused the return to receive a high DIF score. The absence of an item(s) may have been equally important in the scoring process. Items that you think attributed to the high score may not have been scored at all, either because there was no correlation between that item and tax change in the TCMP sample or because other items on the return which are correlated to that item were scored. In other words, the significant items you identify may or may not have been scored.

320
REVIEW OF ENTIRE RETURN

(1) Regardless of the type or class of return being classified/screened, the classifier/screener should first review the return in its entirety. This action is important in that it:

(a) Quickly gives a complete overview of the total return.
(b) Allows the establishment of thoughts on the interrelationship of the various income, expense, and credit items on the return.
(c) Puts you in a position to evaluate each item as to its significance.
(d) Provides an opportunity to quickly eliminate from consideration items or areas of the return with minimum or no examination potential.

330
SIGNIFICANT

(1) Invariably, the definition of significant will depend on the classifier's perception of the return as a whole and the separate items that comprise the return. There are several factors, however, that must be considered when determining whether an item is significant. These factors are:

(a) Comparative size of the item—A questionable expense item of $6,000 with total expenses of $30,000 would be significant; however, if total expenses are $300,000, ordinarily the item would not be significant.
(b) Inherent character of the item—Although the amount of an item

may be insignificant, the nature of the item may be significant; i.e., airplane expenses claimed on a plumber's Schedule C.

(c) Evidence of intent to mislead—This may include missing, misleading, or incomplete schedules, or incorrectly showing an item on the return.

(d) Beneficial effect of the manner in which an item is reported—Expenses claimed on a business schedule rather than claimed as an itemized deduction may be significant.

(e) Relationship to/with other item(s) on a return. Business expenses without corresponding income. Similarly, the lack of dividends reported when Schedule D shows sales of stocks.

Screening of Individual Returns

510
NON-BUSINESS INDIVIDUAL RETURNS

(1) Determination of Office/Field Examination.

(a) Once you determine that the return will not be accepted-as-filed, it must be decided if the examination should be conducted by a revenue agent or a tax auditor. In making this determination, you must give consideration to the type(s) of issue(s) identified for examination.

(b) You should not exclude substantial issues to convert what would be a revenue agent examination to a tax auditor examination. Nor do the number of issues, standing alone, determine whether or not the return is to be examined by a revenue agent or a tax auditor.

(2) Provided below are examples of items which generally cause the return to be identified for field examination:

(a) Issues which require onsite inspection of the taxpayer's books, records or assets.

(b) Complex Schedule D transactions.

(c) Returns with unusually complex rental income and expenses.

(d) Tax shelter returns.

(e) Donations of real property which would involve an engineering specialist.

(f) Alimony, if it appears there is a property settlement involving business property (i.e., accounts receivable, inventory).

(3) Training Returns—Selected returns meeting training criteria will be identified during each classification detail, unless advised by the district that no training will be conducted.

(4) Correspondence Examination

(a) Enumerated below are considerations which should cause a return to be selected for correspondence examination. Under centralized classification, returns selected with these criteria should be flagged for the correspondence unit in the service center.

1. All the questioned items are susceptible to direct verification from records that could be easily submitted by mail. You should not exclude substantial items from the checksheet to convert what might be an interview examination to a correspondence examination.

2. Inspection of the previous or subsequent year return is not necessary.

3. Some examples of issues which can be verified by correspondence are:
   —Simple itemized deductions (exclusive of office-in-the-home, and education expense)
   —Information Returns Selection System/Information Returns Program for Wages, Interest, or Dividends
   —Payments to an IRA/Keogh Plan
   —Interest penalty on early withdrawal of savings
   —Child care credit
   —Credit for the elderly
   —Residential energy credit
   —Self employment tax

(b) Single issues should generally not be examined, as experience has shown that such examinations frequently result in insignificant or no tax change when other questionable items are not present on the return.

(c) Certain issues do not lend themselves to a correspondence examination. The following issues are inappropriate for correspondence examination:

1. Exemptions.

2. Income from tips, pensions and annuities, rents and royalties, and income not subject to tax withholding.

3. Determination of whether income reported constitutes capital gain or ordinary income.

4. Deductions for travel and entertainment.

5. Deductions for bad debts.
6. Determinations of basis of property.
7. Complex miscellaneous itemized deductions such as casualty and theft losses where determination of a fair market value is required.
8. Returns in which the classifier feels an office interview is needed to ensure the taxpayer's rights under the law, or the appearance of the return (writing, grammar, neatness, etc.) indicates that the taxpayer may not be able to communicate effectively in writing.

(5) Regular Interview Examination—Returns selected for office interview examinations should contain issues which lend themselves to an analytical approach and require individual judgment, in addition to direct verification.

(6) Pre-Contact Analysis

(a) Returns may contain issues which, based on the classifier's judgment and experience, require examination planning and analysis by a tax auditor before contacting the taxpayer. Local instructions (as provided by the districts) will be followed in selecting a return for pre-contact analysis. These returns must be kept to a minimum to utilize Centralized Files and Scheduling efficiently.

(b) Examples of types of returns which may be subject to pre-contact analysis are:

1. Returns with complex issues requiring research before contacting the taxpayer for examination.
2. Returns with income low in relation to the taxpayer's financial responsibilities and the audit technique may involve a net worth statement, gross profit reconstruction, or statement of application of funds (indirect methods).
3. Returns exhibiting factors which indicate a need for visual inspection of the taxpayer's place of business or residence.
4. Any return (business or non-business) selected for 13 or more issues.
5. Any return selected for examination having an indication that a Power-of-Attorney is on file.
6. Business returns that contain more than one business schedule, either C or F, and both schedules should be examined in depth.
7. Any return selected for district or service center examination identified as an employee return.

520
ISSUE IDENTIFICATION

Discussed below are suggested guidelines to assist in the identification of significant issues on individual nonbusiness returns. In identifying issues on the classification checksheet, you should be specific.

530
EXEMPTIONS AND ITEMIZED DEDUCTIONS

531
GENERAL

(1) Important! Look first at overall potential based on the amount of excess itemized deductions above the zero bracket amount.

(2) Verify that itemized deductions are not claimed elsewhere on the return when the standard deduction has been elected (i.e., personal real estate taxes and mortgage interest deducted on rental schedule).

532
EXEMPTIONS

(1) Exemptions claimed by the noncustodial parent have proven to have high potential for adjustment.

(2) When married persons file separately, both taxpayers may not have made the same election for standard or itemized deductions. If dependent children are claimed, the other spouse may also be claiming them.

533
MEDICAL EXPENSES

High medical expenses for large families, deceased taxpayers, or older taxpayers are usually not productive.

534
TAXES

(1) Real Estate Taxes—Consider changes in address.

(2) Sales Tax—Consider significant amounts above table allowance or nonqualifying items.

535
INTEREST EXPENSE

(1) Interest is generally not productive when questioning all the small items that might be listed or combined.

(2) Productive issues could come from payments to individuals, and closing costs on real estate transactions.

(3) Home mortgage interest usually is unproductive.

536
CONTRIBUTIONS

(1) Check to see if contributions exceed 50 percent of Adjusted Gross Income (AGI).

(2) Check large donations made to questionable miscellaneous charities.

(3) Check for payments which may represent tuition.

(4) Check for large donations of property, other than cash.

537
CASUALTY OR THEFT LOSSES

Watch for business assets, valuation methods, and limitations.

538
MISCELLANEOUS DEDUCTIONS

Scrutinize large, unusual, or questionable items.

540
INCOME

541
CAPITAL TRANSACTIONS

(1) Gains on sales of rental and other depreciable property, where the taxpayer has been using an accelerated method of depreciation or ACRS [Accelerated Cost Recovery System], should be questioned since the taxpayer may have to report ordinary income.

(2) Loss on the sale of rental property, recently converted from a personal residence, is usually productive.

(3) Current year installment sales and exchanges of property should be carefully scrutinized as taxpayers frequently make errors in computing the recognized gain.

(4) Check to see if the gain on a sale is large enough to require the alternative minimum tax computation.

542
PENSION AND/OR ANNUITY

(1) Verify if distribution qualifies under the three-year rule.

(2) Check whether distribution qualifies as a lump sum distribution.

543
RENTAL PROPERTIES

(1) Consider fair rental value.

(2) If the rental property is located at the same address as the taxpayer's residence, consider whether the allocation is proper between the rental portion and the portion used personally by the taxpayer.

(3) Repairs may be capital improvements.

(4) Consider whether the cost of land is included in the basis.

(5) The rental of vacation/resort homes should be scrutinized.

544
SALES OF RESIDENCE

Check to be sure that the taxpayer purchases a more expensive residence to qualify for deferral of the gain.

545
UNREPORTED INCOME

(1) Is the income sufficient to support the exemptions claimed?

(2) Installment sale of property but no interest reported.

(3) Does the taxpayer show interest and real estate tax deductions for two residences but no rental income?

(4) If a taxpayer lists his/her occupation as waiter, cab driver, porter, beautician, etc., tip income is a productive issue.

(5) Are there substantial interest expenses with no apparent source of funds to repay the loans?

(6) Does the taxpayer claim business expenses for an activity that shows no income on the return (i.e., beautician supplies, but no Form 1099 or W-2 for that occupation)?

546
COPY OF SCHEDULE K-1

(1) Returns containing office examination type issues will be selected for office examination without regard to distributive type income from Forms 1065, 1120S, and 1041. However, if the Schedule K-1 requires inspection, the entity's name and year of Schedule K-1 should be listed on the classification checksheet.

(2) Items of self-employment income shown on Schedule K-1 should be matched to Schedule SE to ensure that the amounts are properly included in the self-employment tax computation.

550
ADJUSTMENTS TO INCOME

551
MOVING EXPENSES

Review W-2's for address and other compensation. Also, consider sale of residence.

552
EMPLOYEE BUSINESS EXPENSES

(1) Amounts should be reasonable when compared to the taxpayer's occupation and income level.

(2) Avoid auto expenses as an issue where the standard mileage computation is used and the mileage shown does not appear excessive.

(3) Transportation expenses for construction workers, carpenters, etc., who appear to have several different employers at different locations, have not proven to be productive. However, be alert for expenses claimed for travel to a remote job site(s).

(4) Expenses for clubs, yachts, airplanes, etc., must meet the facilities requirements of IRC 274 [relating to disallowance of certain travel and entertainment expenses] and therefore are usually productive issues.

560
TAXPAYER'S PREVIOUS/SUBSEQUENT YEAR RETURN

(1) Determine whether the previous/subsequent year return should be inspected. If so, you must note the checksheet. Situations where inspection may be warranted are:

(a) Probable carryover adjustments (i.e., capital loss carryover, substantial depreciation changes).
(b) Items which, if disallowed in the selected year, may be allowable in the following year.

570
BUSINESS INDIVIDUAL RETURNS

(1) Determination of Office/Field Examinations—One of the key contributions to the success or failure of our Examination Program in the business categories is the selection of the proper function to conduct the examination. If we are to meet our Program objectives, it is essential that we input those returns that are most adaptable for office interview to Office Examination and those requiring the skills of a revenue agent to Field Examination. This decision is very important from several aspects:

(a) The planned time of an examination of a business return in Office Examination is about half of that planned for Field Examination. However, substantial issues should not be excluded as identified issues to convert what would be a Revenue Agent assignment to a Tax Auditor assignment.
(b) Office examinations usually do not involve a visitation to the taxpayer's place of business. Field examination returns should require a more in-depth knowledge of accounting principles.

(2) Generally, business returns should be selected for Field Examination when the following conditions occur:

(a) Voluminous records.
(b) Complex accounting method.
(c) Extensive timeframe required to complete the examination.
(d) Advisability of on-site inspection of business.
(e) Inventories are substantial and material.
(f) Termination of business before the end of the taxable year.
(g) Unusual issues that appear to be complex and time consuming to develop. For example:

1. Nontaxable transfers.
2. Complex oil or mineral explorations.
3. Sale of IRC 1231 assets [property used in trade or business and involuntary conversions].
4. Unstated interest (IRC 483 [interest on certain deferred payments]).

(h) The size of a business is also an indicator of what may be involved when an actual examination is made of the books and records of any particular taxpayer.

(i) The businesses listed below would normally not be adaptable to Office Examination:

1. Contractors
2. Manufacturers
3. Auto dealers
4. Funeral parlors

(3) The areas discussed above are meant to operate only as a guide. In addition to considering these items, heavy reliance must be placed on judgment and experience.

571
NET PROFIT

(1) Is the taxpayer engaged in the type of business or profession normally considered to be more profitable than reflected on the return?

(2) Is the zero bracket amount used with high gross income and low net profit shown on the business schedule? Experience has shown that the incidence of fraud is greater on low business returns when the return reflects large receipts ($100,000 or more), a sizeable investment, and the standard deduction is used.

(3) Does the address, real estate taxes and/or mortgage interest indicate a higher mode of living than justified by the reported income?

(4) Does the return reveal large amounts of interest/dividend income not commensurate with current sources of income?

572
COST OF GOODS SOLD

(1) Check for the possibility of withdrawal of items for personal use.

(2) Is the ending inventory inclusive of all costs, direct and indirect?

573
Bad Debt Deduction

(1) Is it a cash business?

(2) Is it disproportionate for the indicated value of sales?

574
Depreciation

(1) Does the schedule contain an adequate description of the asset?

(2) Are personal assets being depreciated?

(3) Consider investment credit aspects and sales of property simultaneously with depreciation issues.

575
Sale of Assets

(1) Is there a sale of business assets during the year without investment credit or depreciation recapture?

(2) Is the gain large enough to require the alternative minimum tax computation?

576
Farm Returns

In the analysis of a Schedule F, you should keep in mind the usual features of a farm return. The farmer may be engaged in a specialized area of dairy cattle, beef cattle, grain, swine, vegetables, poultry, or a multiple of these items. The operation may vary from that of a few acres to several thousand acres. The operator of the farm may rent all the land farmed or may own all or a portion of it. Consider whether the farm is an actual business operation or a hobby.

581
Self-Employment Tax

(1) All returns should be screened for self-employment tax issues, including returns with Schedule SE attached. Look for income such as director's fees, janitorial services, miscellaneous income, partnership income, etc., which may be subject to self-employment tax.

(2) Some items of income earned by independent contractors may be reported as wages or other income. Where the income appears to be

personal service income, it must be considered for Social Security Tax purposes.

Classifying/Screening Corporate Returns

621
GENERAL

(1) Classifying/screening of the corporation return must include the balance sheet and Schedule M items. Substantial change in accounts receivable, reserve for bad debts, loans to or from stockholders, accounts payable, treasury stock, capital stock, or retained earnings would indicate an examination of these items may be warranted. In addition, such potential issues as a "Thin Corporation," IRC 531 [accumulated earnings tax], substantial changes in accruals, and decreases in assets which are not accounted for on Schedule D of the return may be identified from an inspection of the balance sheet.

(2) All Schedule M items should be scrutinized to determine the difference between income shown on the books, and taxable income shown on the tax return.

(3) The following general items must also be considered during the classifying/screening process:

(a) Overall composition of the return. Is the return complete, containing all necessary information and schedules? Who prepared the return?

(b) Data reported on the return compared to the norms and standards of the business or industry of the taxpayer. Refer to Techniques Handbook for Specialized Industries for additional information.

(c) Location of the business. This could have a bearing on the volume of business.

(d) Prior examination results.

(e) The existence of controlled groups, interest in foreign corporations, deductions for facilities, or convention expenses.

(f) Experience has shown that the following characteristics result in potentially productive features:

1. International features.
2. Copy of a National Office approved Technical Ruling attached, but all conditions as set forth in the Ruling have not been met.

3. New corporation, which incorporated a going business and reflects goodwill, other boot, or accelerated depreciation.
4. Liquidation under IRC 331, 332, 333, or 337. These generally trigger recapture under the provisions of IRC 47, 1245, and 1250.
5. A consolidated return, especially one that does not contain schedules showing each member's respective share of income, expenses, assets, liabilities, and capital.
6. A short period return.
7. Credits and/or losses that have been carried forward when information on the return indicates the item(s) should have been carried back.
8. A member of a controlled group, claiming the full amount of the surtax exemption, etc., and not including a properly executed election.
9. Last-In, First-Out (LIFO) inventory method being used for the first time.
10. Manufacturing concern not using the required Full-Absorption accounting method to value inventory.
11. Substantial passive income may indicate a Personal Holding Company.
12. A low asset return, reflecting a net operating loss, may be a productive return.
13. Returns with Minimum Tax issues.
14. Foreign Tax Credit present on the return.

622
PROFIT AND LOSS METHOD

(1) After considering the general guidelines above, you should begin a more detailed review of the return utilizing both the profit and loss and balance sheet approaches. Some of the items to be considered under the profit and loss approach are:

(a) Large or unusual changes in inventories, or no inventory reflected for nonservice type business.
(b) Sales of assets without a Schedule D or Supplemental Schedule of Gains and Losses (Form 4797) attached.
(c) No amount claimed as amortization on a newly formed corporation.
(d) Amounts claimed as Other Deductions without supporting schedules attached.

(e) Questionable bad debt, either under the Specific Write-off or Reserve Method.

(f) Expenses which may be high or unusual for the type of business.

623
BALANCE SHEET METHOD

(1) A balance sheet approach, paying particular attention to substantial changes between opening and closing balances, can disclose a number of potential issues:

(a) Cash:

1. Large ending balance—possible accumulated earnings tax.
2. Negative balance—improper accruals.

(b) Trade Notes and Accounts Receivable:

1. Change in accounting method.
2. Premature write-offs.
3. Excessive deduction for bad debts.
4. Interest income unreported.

(c) Inventories:

1. Change in method of valuation.
2. Change in nature of business.
3. Possible write-down.

(d) Investments:

1. Interest income and dividend income understated or omitted.
2. Expense(s) of tax-free income deducted. Unreported sales, erroneous basis, installment election.
3. Stockholder loans buried.
4. Related issue.

(e) Other current assets—deferred expenses.

(f) Loans to stockholders—dividend issue.

(g) Building and other depreciable assets:

1. Unreported sales.
2. Investment credit recapture.
3. Incorrect basis.

(h) Intangible assets:

1. Goodwill has been written-off.
2. Sale of license or patent.
3. IRC 351 [transfer to corporation controlled by transferor].

(i) Loans from stockholders:

1. Thin corporation.
2. Interest deduction vs. dividend.

(j) Other liabilities:

1. Improper accruals.
2. Deferred income accounts.
3. Reserve for contingencies.

(k) Capital accounts:

1. Unreported sale.
2. Stock issued for services.
3. Thin corporation.

(l) Paid-in surplus:

1. Diversion of earned income.
2. Accumulated earnings tax.

(m) Retained earnings—accumulated earnings tax.

(n) Treasury Stock:

1. Potential dividend to stockholder.
2. Bargain purchase by a stockholder.

(o) Schedules M-1 and M-2—All items should be reviewed for proper tax treatment.

Classifying/Screening Partnership Returns

711
GENERAL

Partnership returns are identified by three categories: DIF, non-DIF, and Automatics. Returns with 10 partners or less, which do not meet automatic criteria, are scored under the DIF system. Returns with 11 or more partners and returns which meet automatic criteria, regardless of size, are not computer classified.

712
SELECTION FEATURES

(1) The general instructions for individual and corporate returns apply equally to partnership returns. The returns must be scrutinized both as to line items and the return as a whole in selecting returns with the highest examination potential.

(2) Initial and first year returns are often productive. Common issues are:

(a) Contributions to capital for possible recognition of gain or loss at the partners' levels.

(b) Partners with no contributed capital where services may have been performed in exchange for the partnership interest.

(c) Large loss claimed on returns commencing business late in the year.

(d) Large loss claimed in relation to investment.

(e) Loss claimed in excess of investment through nonrecourse financing. Loan and prepaid interest costs should be amortized over the life of the loan.

(f) Large depreciation deduction where property may not have been placed in service during the year.

(g) Pre-opening expense (management fee, license fees, etc.) which should be capitalized.

(3) Other areas applicable to partnerships:

(a) Additional contributions by a partner which could constitute a sale or exchange.

(b) Disproportionate allocation of losses or specific deductions to partners—However, review Schedule K-1 to determine the date of entry of new partners.

(c) Withdrawal by partners may include "phantom gain" through assumption of liabilities by others.

(d) The sale or exchange of partnership assets may result in recapture of ordinary income.

(e) Component or other depreciation method resulting in shorter than guideline lives.

713
PARTNERSHIP DISTRIBUTIONS

In general, errors are common in final year partnership returns. Basis and recognition vs. nonrecognition of gain or loss are productive areas.

Audit Guidelines for Examiners

230
INITIAL INTERVIEW

(1) The initial interview is the most important part of the examination process. The first few minutes should be spent making the taxpayer comfortable and explaining the examination process and appeal rights. This would also be a good time to ask the taxpayer if he/she has any questions.

(2) Sufficient information should be developed to reach informed judgments as to:

    (a) financial history and standard of living;

    (b) the nature of employment to determine relationship with other entities and the existence of expense allowances, etc.; this could include the exchange of merchandise or services (bartering);

    (c) any money or property received which was determined to be tax exempt and/or nontaxable income; and

    (d) the potential for moonlighting income.

(3) If warranted by issues on the return or responses to previous questions, the following information should be developed:

    (a) the real and personal property owned, including bank accounts, stocks and bonds, real estate, automobiles, etc., in this country and abroad.

    (b) any purchases, sales, transfers, contributions or exchanges of personal assets during the period; and

    (c) the correctness of exemptions and dependents claimed.

(4) Remember, the taxpayer is being examined and not just the return. Therefore, develop all information to the fullest extent possible.

330
STANDARDS FOR EXAMINING RETURNS

(1) The scope of the examination should be limited or expanded to the point that the significant items necessary for a correct determination of tax liability have been considered.

(a) *Explanation—Tax Auditors*

1. The scope of the examination on nonbusiness returns not requiring pre-contact analysis will be set by classification. The classification checksheet should list significant items that warrant examination. However, the Tax Auditor may expand the examination when significant issues arise as a result of information secured during the examination. Also, instances may arise where, in the judgment of the Auditor, a significant item was not identified during classification. In the latter instance approval of the group manager is necessary, when possible, before the scope may be expanded.

(b) *Explanation—Revenue Agent*

1. The scope of the examination will be set by the revenue agent. For non-DIF returns, significant items will be identified by the classifier on the classification checksheet. However, the examiner is not precluded from extending the scope of the examination beyond the identified items or from eliminating certain items if circumstances warrant. For DIF returns, classification will not identify significant items, and the revenue agent will have sole responsibility for determining the scope of the examination.

(2) Adequate evidence should be obtained through inspection, inquiry, and analysis of supporting documents to ensure full development of relevant facts concerning issues of merit.

(a) *Explanation*

1. Evidence is the sum total of all information presented by the taxpayer, representative, or third parties regarding an issue. Evidence can include the taxpayer's books and records, the taxpayer's oral statements, statements of the taxpayer's representative, statements of third parties, or documentation submitted by or obtained from third parties. If the issue involves specific recordkeeping required by law, then documentation should be presented as evidence. However, where the issue does not normally involve formal documentation, oral statements may be adequate evidence. Adequate evidence, therefore, does not require complete documentation.
2. Inspection is the critical examination of evidence presented to determine its applicability to the issue questioned and whether it is adequate substantiation for the issue under examination.

Based upon the professional judgment of the examiner, it may be necessary not only to inspect the taxpayer's documents or books and records, but also to inspect the taxpayer's place of business, review his/her standard of living, and evaluate third party information.

3. Inquiry is the technique of asking a question or a logical sequence of questions, written or oral, that will secure information regarding the issue being examined or that will determine the relevance of evidence presented. The examiner may pose questions to the taxpayer(s), their representative, and, when appropriate, third parties.

4. Analysis refers to the process of arranging, sorting or scheduling the evidence presented in a logical manner to facilitate reaching conclusions regarding the issue under examination.

(3) Examination results will reflect technically correct conclusions based on consideration of all relevant facts and the proper application and interpretation of the tax laws.

(a) *Explanation*

1. When an examination is pursued to the proper depth, all relevant facts will have been accumulated. To reach technically correct conclusions, the examiner must apply the appropriate tax laws to the facts. The conclusions reached should be based on an objective interpretation of the law, whether it is in the taxpayer's or government's favor.

2. An examiner has various research materials available that will aid in arriving at technically correct conclusions:
   a. IRC;
   b. Regulations;
   c. Commercial Tax Services;
   d. Published decisions;
   e. Rulings; and
   f. Actions on decisions.

3. If the examiner is still unable to reach a conclusion, the group manager should be consulted. Formal requests for technical advice should be made if appropriate.

510
INDIVIDUAL RETURNS

520
INCOME

521
INTRODUCTION

Examiners must be alert to detect the possibilities of omitted income. Some indications of possible unreported income may be apparent on the face of the return. If income reported appears insufficient to meet the cost of living and other disbursements including those claimed on the return and substantiated during the examination, examiners should ask questions designed to uncover potential sources of income not reported on the return. Two sources are moonlighting income and income from bartering. The reasons for failure to report the income should be developed and the file documented accordingly.

522
INCOME—WAGES AND SALARIES, UNEMPLOYMENT BENEFITS, ETC.

(1) Review compensation arrangement to determine special privileges (paid vacations, use of company car, etc.).

(2) Particular consideration should be given to the source of taxpayer's income as certain occupations and trades are more susceptible than others to omitted income. Some examples are:

(a) Members of certain trades usually work for contractors from whom they receive a W-2. Due to the nature of their work, they may do part-time work for homeowners and others who may not file W-2's. They should be directly questioned as to the possible existence of such income.

(b) Itinerants, such as fruit-pickers and seasonal workers, may have income from other sources during the off-season.

(c) Practical nurses may be employed by individuals as well as by hospitals or rest homes and the wages received from individuals may not be covered by a Form W-2.

(d) Returns of taxpayers reporting income from occupations where tips are commonly received should be carefully reviewed to determine if this income was reported. Taxpayers who receive tip income may not maintain complete and accurate records. The examiner should test check to determine the accuracy of the amounts reported.

(3) Low income of one spouse may indicate the other spouse received income and possibly did not receive a Form W-2 or 1099. The possibility of unreported income is increased if the amount of income reported seems inadequate in view of the reported exemptions and deductions. In these circumstances, the examiner should ask specific questions to determine if additional income was received.

(4) For taxable years beginning after December 31, 1978, unemployment compensation may be taxable. Examiners should be alert to unemployment benefits which may not have been reported.

(5) Be alert to outside employment, prizes, tips, etc.

(6) Development of information verifying reported deductions or income may reveal facts indicating the taxpayer is the beneficiary of an estate or trust and should have reported distributable income from that source.

523
INCOME FROM BARTERING

(1) When verifying income, the examiner should be alert to the possibility of "bartering" or "swapping" techniques or schemes. Such non-cash exchanges may be done directly; however, the greater volume of these exchanges is handled through reciprocal trade agencies. Both services and inventory may be exchanged for "credits." These "credits" can then be used to obtain other goods or services. Bartering does result in taxable income and should be reported as such.

(2) Some areas of possible tax abuse are as follows:

   (a) Nonrecognition of current income.
   (b) The trading of services or inventory for capital assets (which would convert ordinary income to capital gain) or for fixed assets (which should be depreciated over the useful life of the assets).
   (c) The exchange of inventory or services for personal goods and services, such as vacations, houseboats, luxury cars, use of vacation home or condominium, or payment of personal or stockholder debts.

(3) In addition, examiners should be alert for the following:

   (a) Deductions and/or payments for credit liability insurance or insurance guaranteeing lines of credit.
   (b) Deductions and/or payments for membership fees, annual dues, or service charges to specialized reciprocal trading companies.

(c) The write-off or mark-down of inventory, especially for excess or supposedly obsolete inventory.

(d) The factoring or sale of accounts or notes receivable to specialized reciprocal trading firms.

524
DIVIDEND INCOME

(1) The examination of dividend income reported by the taxpayer should not be limited to the information documents attached to the return. If more than $100 is excluded, the ownership of securities by both husband and wife should be ascertained.

(2) The method used by the taxpayer in determining dividend income should be secured. Understanding the method used may suggest the most appropriate way to check for accuracy. A list of securities owned at the beginning of the taxable year, used in conjunction with subsequent sales and acquisitions, will afford the most exact results.

(3) If the taxpayer merely records dividends when received and also keeps some securities in the broker's custody, the broker's monthly statements should be checked for dividends credited to the account. Most taxpayers who have security trades during the year retain their monthly statements. These statements should be checked when verifying dividend income.

(4) The examiner should verify the accuracy of claims that dividend income is either fully or partially tax-exempt, or nontaxable, such as distributions representing partial return of capital.

(5) Be aware of duplication of credits such as foreign dividends received and recorded net of foreign tax paid, and a further credit being taken on the return.

(6) Be alert for stock splits which increase the number of shares upon which the taxpayer would receive dividend income.

525
INTEREST INCOME

(1) Be alert to income from interest on income tax refunds and savings accounts which may not appear on the tax return or taxpayer's records

(2) Interest earned on "qualified tax-exempt savings certificates" may be excluded from a taxpayer's return. Verify that certificates qualify and that the amount of the exclusion claimed is proper.

(3) Verify claims that interest from state or municipal bonds is either fully or partially tax-exempt.

(4) Taxpayers should be asked whether they have cashed or transferred any Government bonds, held any matured Government bonds, or had any savings accounts during the taxable year. When ownership of Series E Bonds is transferred, interest income earned must be reported in the year of transfer.

(5) The verification of interest income should also be made in conjunction with the examination of capital transactions. Interest bearing securities sold during the year should be compared to interest reported. The interest accrued to date of sale is sometimes reported as part of the proceeds, rather than as interest income.

(6) Verify that savings and loan interest, as well as credit union interest, though commonly called dividends, has been treated as interest income for tax purposes.

(7) Verify that other interest income items such as interest on paid up insurance policies, interest on prior year tax refunds, interest on G.I. insurance dividends on deposit with the Veterans Administration, and interest on insurance dividends on deposit with an insurance company which are withdrawable upon demand have been reported.

(8) If property was sold in prior or current years and a purchase money mortgage or second mortgage constituted part payment, interest income should be reflected in the return. Verify that mortgage collections have been allocated to principal and interest.

526
STATE TAX REFUNDS

Verify that state income tax refunds which caused a decrease in tax in prior years have been included in income in the year refunded.

570
SCHEDULE A—DEDUCTIONS

In verifying deductions claimed by a taxpayer, examiners should also be alert to the possibility of unclaimed deductions. If one examination reveals such unclaimed items, they should be allowed in the examination report.

571
MEDICAL EXPENSES

(1) Verify amounts claimed and determine that the deduction is claimed in the proper year.

   (a) Determine whether medical expenditures of a capital nature increase the value of the property.

   (b) Determine that costs of transportation do not include amounts spent for board and lodging.

(2) Ascertain whether any insurance reimbursement has been made or is expected.

(3) Determine that the expense was incurred primarily for the diagnosis, cure, mitigation, treatment or prevention of disease, or for the purpose of affecting any structure or function of the body (including transportation and medical insurance).

(4) Medicines should be separated so that the proper limitation can be applied.

(5) Determine that the percentage limitation, the maximum amount limitation and the dependency qualification have been correctly applied.

(6) Be aware that amounts allowed as child care expense cannot also be claimed as medical expense.

572
TAXES

(1) Verify amounts claimed and determine that the deduction has been taken in the proper year.

(2) Determine whether the tax is of the type deductible in accordance with the rules and regulations.

(3) Ascertain that no foreign income taxes have been claimed as a deduction where election has been made to claim the foreign tax credit.

(4) Examiners should verify that the taxpayer has not claimed duplicate deductions for taxes, i.e., itemized deduction and rental expense.

573
INTEREST

(1) Verify amount claimed and determine that the deduction has been taken in the proper year.

(2) Determine whether the payments are for interest or for other items, such as discounts, finance charges or principal. Finance charges on revolving charge accounts are considered to be interest and are deductible.

(3) Ascertain whether the interest payments are made on a valid, existing debt owed by the taxpayer. If there is a joint and several liability, the entire amount of interest is deductible by the payor. Interest paid as a guarantor does not constitute an interest deduction.

(4) Ascertain whether the debt was incurred to carry or purchase [an asset] the income from which is tax-exempt, or was incurred to purchase a single premium life insurance, endowment or annuity contract after March 1, 1954.

(5) Loans from related individuals should be analyzed to determine that the interest rate paid does not exceed the normal rate for available money.

(6) When verifying an interest deduction, the examiner should inspect the instruments of indebtedness, such as mortgage statements, loan contract, etc. Cancelled checks are not usually evidence of the liability or payment of interest, and generally, should be supported by documentation.

(7) If the taxpayer maintains brokerage accounts, the statements should be analyzed. Interest charged on margin accounts should not be netted against interest or dividend income. It must be claimed as an itemized deduction.

(8) Examiners should verify that the same interest deduction is not claimed twice, i.e., Itemized Deductions and Rental Expense.

(9) Examiners should be alert for situations where taxpayers have claimed deductions for accrued interest on existing liabilities and foreclosure proceedings have subsequently occurred. Verify the taxpayer has included the difference between the liability per the books and the liability which was relieved by the foreclosure as income.

(10) If the taxpayer moved during the year under examination, the examiner should check the allocation of interest on the closing statement.

(11) If the taxpayer assumed a mortgage during the year under examination, the examiner must make a proper allocation between the buyer and the seller since the lender will normally issue a statement on total interest paid during the year for that mortgage.

574
CONTRIBUTIONS

(1) Verify amounts claimed and determine that the deduction has been taken in the proper year.

(2) Determine whether the payments were made to qualified organizations. An individual may claim a charitable contribution deduction to a church that has not been recognized by the Service as tax exempt. Such deduction is not barred merely because the church has never applied for recognition of exempt status. Similarly, when an organization has applied but has not provided the Service with sufficient information upon which to make a favorable determination of exempt status, a charitable deduction is not automatically barred.

(3) Determine that percentage limitation is correctly computed, has not been exceeded, and that any contribution carryover is correct.

(4) Determine if contributions claimed are nondeductible personal expenses and ascertain if donor received benefits or consideration in return.

(5) Where a taxpayer claims out of pocket expenses in rendering donated services to a qualified organization, the examiner should determine whether there was reimbursement by the organization.

(6) In a case where property is contributed, ascertain:

   (a) whether ordinary income property, capital gain property, or a combination are involved,
   (b) cost and fair market value at time of gift, and
   (c) whether donor retains any control over the property. If inventory or stock in trade is involved, be alert to double deductions.

(7) When examining unsubstantiated cash contributions, examiners should ask themselves this question: Is the total amount of contributions claimed reasonable in relation to the amount available out of which contributions could have been made? Such available cash must take into consideration the amount of gross income less the other deductions claimed on the return, personal living expenses, income tax withheld and any estimated tax payments.

575
CASUALTY AND THEFT LOSSES

(1) Ascertain that a loss has actually been incurred. Property may have been fully depreciated, nonexistent, sold, previously expensed, lost, etc.

It may be necessary to verify the adjusted basis of the property. In such a case, the taxpayer should be required to submit evidence as to the original cost, subsequent improvements, and the amount of depreciation claimed in prior years.

(2) Be alert to the possibility that cash stolen may not have been included in income.

(3) Trace handling of losses involving inventory or stock in trade to ascertain that a double deduction is not claimed.

(4) Ascertain that the loss is claimed in the proper year—casualty losses generally in the year incurred—theft or embezzlement in the year discovered.

(5) Determine if gains from involuntary conversion are reported which would change the tax treatment of the casualty and theft losses.

(6) Determine that the amount claimed is equal to the difference in value before and after the loss (limited by cost or other basis), and that the taxpayer was the owner of the property. If a personal residence is involved in the loss deduction, the examiner should ensure that the basis of the property has been reduced for all gains previously unrecognized.

(7) Ascertain that insurance proceeds or claims, salvage proceeds, or salvage value have been properly taken into account.

(8) Casualty losses affecting items incidental to real property, such as trees or shrubbery, must be verified as a loss of a minor portion of the asset. The shrinkage in market value, limited to adjusted basis, which forms the allowable deduction, must be determined by reference to the property as a whole, both as to fair market value and adjusted basis.

(9) Be alert to the possibility that the taxpayer may be engaged in arson-for-profit activities.

   (a) Indicators of possible arson schemes with potential tax consequences are:

      1. Failure to report insurance proceeds which exceed the basis of the property destroyed by fire.

      2. Failure to report the correct adjusted basis of the property destroyed.

      3. Failure to reduce a casualty loss claimed on a return by the insurance proceeds received.

      4. Reducing insurance proceeds by payoffs to "torches"—individuals starting the fires.

(b) Examiners should consider using in-depth examination techniques in cases where the taxpayer is suspected of being engaged in arson-for-profit activities.

576
EDUCATIONAL EXPENSES

(1) Determine if the expenses were primarily incurred for the purpose of maintaining or improving skills or meeting express requirements for retention of status.

(2) Examiners should be alert to the special situation of school teachers. Often the requirements of a local board are different than those of a State Board of Education. A teacher may be incurring educational expenses in order to meet the minimum requirements of one of the boards.

(3) If the educational expense involves overseas travel, the tour folio, registration receipt, and transcript of studies from the overseas educational institution should be reviewed. Consideration should be given to the amount of time devoted to educational pursuits.

(4) Verify amounts claimed and determine that the deduction is claimed in the proper year.

(5) Ascertain whether any reimbursement has been received from an employer, governmental agency, or other third party.

580
BUSINESS RETURNS

581.2
BASIS OF ACCOUNTING

(1) Examiners must determine at the beginning of an examination the basis of accounting, that is, whether cash or accrual, and in the course of the examination must see that whatever basis is used is consistently maintained as to all accounts.

(2) Unusual items of income and deductions which tend to distort a taxpayer's income should in every case receive special attention and comment.

(3) Items of income and expense deductions which occur in each taxable period should be scrutinized for any inconsistency in the manner of handling.

581.3
EXAMINATION OF EMPLOYER'S ACCOUNTING PROCEDURES FOR EMPLOYEES' EXPENSES

Examination of an employer's return may disclose allowances or reimbursements made by the employer for travel, entertainment, and other such business expenses incurred by employees, including officers of a corporation. Unless the total amount of allowances or reimbursements is insignificant, the examiner will ascertain during each such examination whether the taxpayer uses acceptable accounting procedures in requiring an accounting of business expenses incurred by employees.

582
GROSS RECEIPTS OR SALES

(1) In the initial testing of the sales account the following techniques may be considered:

   (a) Test methods of handling cash to see if all receipts are included in income. Scan daily cash reconciliations and related book entries and bank deposits. Note any undeposited cash receipts on hand at the end of the year.

   (b) Test reported gross receipts by the gross profit ratio method.

   (c) Note items unusual in origin, nature, or amount in the books of original entry and test them by reference to original sales slips, contracts, job record book, bank deposits, etc. Also, check selected entries made at different times of the year, including some at the beginning of the year. Test check footings and postings to the general ledger.

   (d) Review bank statements and deposit slips for unusual items. Test check deposits by comparing selected items to cash receipts and income entries on the books. Determine the net increase or decrease in the bank balances at the beginning and end of the year. If a taxpayer has not reconciled the bank statements, the examiner must do so for this analysis. Compare the ending balance to the balance per books.

   (e) Scan the sales account in the ledger for unusual entries. Test entries from the general journal and sales journal. Compare total receipts to total business income bank deposits and reconcile any differences.

   (f) Be alert to the possibility of income which may be taxable even though not appearing on the books (constructive receipt, income from foreign sources, etc.).

(2) If the results of these initial tests compare favorably with gross receipts reported, further verification would generally be based on the particular circumstances of the case. For example, a high percentage of cash receipts which are not regularly deposited or properly accounted for would be a basis for further testing.

(3) If further verification is necessary, the following techniques should be considered.

(a) If original receipts and records are not too numerous, match up invoices, contracts or similar documents with any records kept by job or contract and reconcile any differences. If receipts and records are numerous, test check at various intervals and also look for unusual items. If possible, make test of quantities of the principal product sold in comparison with production or purchases (automobile dealers, builders, etc.).

(b) Check the receipts to the sales or general journal and reconcile any differences.

(c) Question any unusual sales discounts or allowances.

(d) Determine the extent to which receipts were used to pay operating expenses, liabilities, personal expenses, etc. At this phase of the examination, consideration should be given to test checking cash register tapes or other records of receipts to see that all are included in income.

(e) Determine the method and adequacy of accounting for merchandise withdrawn for personal use. Withdrawals should be accounted for as the merchandise is withdrawn and not on an estimated basis. Normally, purchases will be reduced by the cost of such merchandise; however, the amount may be credited to sales.

(f) If the taxpayer reports on the accrual basis, determine if all receivables are included in income.

(g) Scan sales agreements, contracts, and related correspondence for leads to unrecorded bonuses, awards, kickbacks, etc.

(h) If the records indicate that contracts or sales may have been completed but corresponding income not reported, further inquiry should be made about the sales. If practicable, check journal entries and bank deposits for the first few weeks of the following year to see if the amounts were taken into income at that time.

(i) Review workpapers made for tax return purposes and make sure that adjustments are appropriate. Reconcile receipts per books with receipts reported. Resolve any differences.

(j) It may be necessary during the examination to secure additional records, documents, or other clarifying evidence. If such additional data will resolve matters, advise taxpayers of what is in question and the information needed. They should then be given an opportunity to furnish the information.

(k) Be alert to indications of:

1. Capital gains treatment of items which may constitute ordinary income. For example, capital gain on the sale of lots held for resale by a real estate dealer in the regular course of business.

2. Sales made or services rendered in exchange for other goods and services which were not included in income.

3. Unreported commissions or rentals from activities operated on the taxpayer's business premises. In some cases, there may be arrangement for operating concessions or businesses such as cafes, bars, candy counters, vending machines, and newsstands.

584
GROSS PROFIT RATIO TEST

(1) In cases where inventories are a material income producing factor the gross profit test serves as a guide for the reasonableness of gross receipts, inventories, purchases, and business net profit.

(2) The term gross profit ratio refers to the ratio of gross profit realized on sales to gross receipts from the sales. It is expressed as a percentage of the selling price.

(3) Expressed in another manner it is the margin between the cost of sales and gross receipts expressed in terms of a percentage of sales.

(4) The selling price is always 100 percent because it is the total amount of money expected from the sale.

(5) *Margin* is always figured on the selling price. It is a *percentage of sales.* Example: Suppose an article is purchased for $1.20 and sold for $1.60. The margin would be 40 cents, which is ¼ or 25 percent of the selling price. Therefore, the margin or gross profit ratio on this article would be 25 percent.

(6) A related term sometimes used is *markup.* Markup can be computed either as a *percentage of cost or of selling price.* Although many consider

markup a percentage of the selling price, figuring markup on the cost price is easier and less confusing. The examiner may wish to compute markup on the cost of goods to determine the correct sales. Bear in mind that the percentages of margin and markup on cost are not the same. Margin and markup in dollars are identical; however, the percentages are different. Both represent the differences between the cost of merchandise and selling price.

(7) . . .

(8) The important thing to keep in mind is that when markup is figured on the selling price, a different markup percentage must be used than when figuring the markup on the cost price. Otherwise, the anticipated margin will not be attained. Example: Suppose an article is purchased for $1.20 by the seller who then marks it up 25 percent. What must the selling price be? The markup of 25 percent times the cost, $1.20, equals 30 cents. Add 30 cents to the cost price of $1.20 and we have a selling price of $1.50 with a margin of 30 cents or 20 percent gross profit ratio. However, if we want to markup the article so that we have a 25 percent margin we must first determine the percentage that will yield the desired margin when applied to the cost price. A 25 percent margin is equivalent to a 33⅓ percent markup on cost. Multiplying 33⅓ percent times the cost, $1.20, equals 40 cents. Adding 40 cents to the cost price gives us a selling price of $1.60, and a margin of 40 cents, or 25 percent.

(9) But, a *markup on cost* of 25 percent gives a selling price of $1.50. Therefore, if it were necessary to have a margin of 25 percent to cover the cost of operation and net profit, the taxpayer would be losing money by pricing merchandise on the basis of a 25 percent markup on cost. To realize a 25 percent margin, the taxpayer would have to use a markup of 33⅓ percent on the cost price.

(10) The following example illustrates the application of the gross profit ratio as a percentage of sales:

Example:

Gross Sales	$50,000
Cost of Sales	40,000
Gross Profit (Margin)	$10,000

(a) Here, the gross profit ratio is 20 percent. In other words, 20 percent of $50,000 sales gives the margin of $10,000.

(b) From the markup table it is found that a 20 percent gross profit ratio (margin) is the equivalent of a 25 percent markup based on cost. In other words the cost of sales in the amount of $40,000 must be increased by 25 percent or $10,000, to give the $50,000 gross sales.

(11) A change in the gross sales results in a change in the gross profit ratio and the markup:

Example

Gross Sales	$60,000
Cost of Sales	40,000
Gross Profit (Margin)	$20,000

(12) There has been an increase in gross sales of $10,000 ($50,000 to $60,000) or a 20 percent increase in gross sales. This has resulted in a gross profit ratio now of 33⅓ percent. The markup (on cost) formerly 25 percent is now 50 percent.

(13) After the ratio for the business under examination has been determined compare with prior years' ratios of the same business and with the ratio for businesses engaged in similar activities. In making the comparison with the ratio of similar businesses remember that the ratio will vary according to the size, sales, volume, and location. For example a neighborhood grocery market with sales of $10,000 to $50,000 would have a different gross profit ratio than a supermarket in a shopping center with sales in excess of $100,000.

(14) Average figures on gross profit ratios for different sizes and types of businesses are available in various publications prepared by private concerns. These may be suitable for testing purposes.

(15) If the comparison indicates that there is a probable error in the reported gross profit figure, consider the items included in the following list as possible reasons for the error.

(a) *Gross Receipts*

1. Possible inclusion of extraneous items not subject to the gross profit ratio, such as rents, interest, dividends, etc.
2. All accounts receivable not reported when accrual basis of accounting is used.
3. All collections of accounts receivable not reported when cash basis of accounting is used.
4. Income constructively received not reported.
5. Installment sales incorrectly reported.

6. Sale of ending inventory not included in gross receipts when business is sold.
7. Theft of inventory items by employees.
8. Unreported gross receipts from bartering.

(b) *Inventory*

1. Inventory improperly valued or incorrect amount carried over from the prior year.
2. Figures are estimated.
3. Inventories not used even though they are a material income producing factor.
4. Ending inventory understated.

(c) *Purchases*

1. Items included which are not properly a part of cost of sales.
2. Personal withdrawals not properly accounted for.
3. Purchases not reduced for returned merchandise.
4. Purchase discounts not properly reflected.

5(10) (16)0
TRAVEL AND ENTERTAINMENT

(1) Many T and E items are not identified as such on returns filed by taxpayers, being earmarked instead under the functional activities which generate the expense, for example, "advertising," "promotion," "selling," "miscellaneous," etc., expense.

(2) Examiners should be alert for such items as company-owned or rented automobiles, hunting lodges, fishing camps, resort property, pleasure boats or yachts, airplanes, apartments and hotel suites; families at conventions or business meetings; and expense-paid vacations of owners and employees, or members of their families, not reported on Form W-2.

(3) Cash expenditures and checks payable to owners and employees closely related by blood or marriage to the owners, should be closely examined as to the actual payment of the expenditures and the business purpose.

Fraud

911
INTRODUCTION

(1) The fraud investigation is one of the most important phases in the administration and enforcement of our Internal Revenue laws. The

importance of fraud work can best be measured in terms of its effect on our voluntary compliance system. Fraud or indications of fraud are usually discovered during the course of an examination. It is essential to be able to recognize them in order to promptly report these findings as outlined by the Internal Revenue Manual.

(2) Recommending the fraud penalty is a serious matter which demands careful consideration of all the facts and circumstances in each case.

(3) The purpose of this Chapter is to provide information and guidelines to aid the examiner in understanding what fraud is and to recognize the indications of fraud. It is not intended that the examiner conduct every examination in the same manner as a potential fraud case.

912
DEFINITION OF FRAUD

(1) Actual fraud is defined in *Corpus Juris* as follows: "Actual fraud is intentional fraud; it consists of deception intentionally practiced to induce another to part with property or surrender some legal right and which accomplishes the end designed." More simply, it is obtaining something of value from someone else through deceit.

(2) Fraud sometimes involves false documents or returns, statements, and includes attempted evasion, conspiracy to defraud, aiding, abetting, or counseling fraud and willful failure to file income, estate, gift, and excise tax returns.

913
AVOIDANCE DISTINGUISHED FROM EVASION

(1) Avoidance of tax is not a criminal offense. All taxpayers have the right to reduce, avoid, or minimize their taxes by legitimate means. The distinction between avoidance and evasion is fine, yet definite. One who avoids tax does not conceal or misrepresent, but shapes and preplans events to reduce or eliminate tax liability, then reports the transactions.

Evasion, on the other hand, involves deceit, subterfuge, camouflage, concealment, some attempt to color or obscure events, or making things seem other than they are.

   (a) Example: Mr. Maple purchased stock in the Oak Corporation on January 2, 1978. Mr. Maple decided on December 3, 1978 to sell the stock which would have resulted in a substantial recognized short-term capital gain.

(b) Upon realizing the benefits to be derived from the long-term capital gain provisions of the IRC, Mr. Maple waited until February 1979 to sell the stock. This is an act of tax avoidance. If Mr. Maple did not realize the benefits which could be gained from the long-term capital gain treatment until after the stock was sold in December 1978, and he then altered the date on the purchase statement and reported the sale as a long-term capital gain with a purchase date of November 1977, his acts would be tax evasion.

921
CIVIL AND CRIMINAL FRAUD DISTINGUISHED

(1) Civil fraud cases are remedial actions taken by the government to assess the correct tax and to impose civil penalties as an addition to the tax. Criminal fraud cases are punitive actions with penalties consisting of fines and/or imprisonment. Civil penalties are assessed and collected administratively as part of the tax. Criminal penalties are enforced only by prosecution and are provided to punish the taxpayer for wrong-doings, and serve as a deterrent to other taxpayers. One offense may result in both civil and criminal penalties.

(2) The normal three year statute of limitations does not apply in civil fraud cases. The tax and penalties may be assessed at any time regardless of the years involved. However, the statute of limitations for prosecution purposes (usually six years) runs from the time the offense was committed (usually the due date of the return). It is not necessary that criminal prosecution be sought in order to assess the civil fraud penalty.

(3) The major difference between civil and criminal fraud cases is the degree of proof required. In criminal cases, the Government must present sufficient evidence to prove guilt beyond a reasonable doubt. A lesser degree of proof is required in civil fraud cases. The evidence relating to the adjustment may not be sufficient to prove criminal fraud, but may be adequate for civil fraud.

(4) In a civil fraud case, the tax liability and penalty is assessed against the taxpayer whose return is involved. In a criminal case, action may be taken against all participants in the fraud, even though their own

returns are not involved. An accountant or bookkeeper may be charged with evading a client's or employer's taxes when aiding or abetting in the preparation of false returns. Corporate officers may be charged with evading the corporation's taxes, etc.

931
BASIC FACTS TO BE PROVED

(1) In order to establish fraud, two basic facts must be proved:

  (a) that the tax liability was understated; and
  (b) that the understatement was due to deliberate intent to evade tax.

932
UNDERSTATEMENT OF TAX LIABILITY

(1) The first basic fact to be proved is that the taxpayer failed to report the correct tax liability, i.e., that there was taxable income which was understated, or that the taxpayer had income subject to tax but failed to file a return and report this tax liability. Proof may be obtained by direct evidence of specific items not properly reported on the return or indirectly by use of income reconstruction methods to show that the tax on the return is an understatement of the correct tax liability.

(2) In specific item cases, the examiner will show that certain items were not completely or accurately reflected on the return resulting in an understatement of income. For example, failure to report interest income or improper deduction of personal living expenses. By contrast, the examiner may resort to indirect measures to prove the inaccuracy of the return. These measures include, but are not limited to, the net worth, source and application of funds, and bank deposit methods of reconstruction of income. With these methods, the examiner shows that in the final result the income reported on the return is understated. The courts have approved the use of these methods in civil and criminal fraud cases.

(3) Tax evasion schemes used by taxpayers to reduce their tax liability will fall into one of the following categories:

  (a) understatement or omission of income;
  (b) claiming fictitious or improper deductions;

(c) false allocation of income;

(d) improper claims for credit or exemption.

933
INTENT TO EVADE TAX

(1) The second basic fact which the Government must prove to establish fraud is that the understatement of tax liability was due to deliberate intent to evade tax. The fact that income was understated does not, standing alone, prove that such understatement was intentional. A failure to report the correct income may be due to mistake, inadvertence, reliance on professional advice, honest difference of opinion, negligence, or carelessness, none of which constitutes deliberate intent to defraud.

(2) Intent to evade tax occurs when a taxpayer knows that the misrepresentation is false. Intent is a mental process, a state of mind. It is necessary to judge a taxpayer's intent by actions. The things that a person says or does are assumed to be the natural consequences of the person's intention.

940
BADGES OF FRAUD

(1) The taxpayer who knowingly understates income leaves evidence in the form of identifying earmarks, or so-called "badges" of fraud. Some of the more common "badges" of fraud are as follows.

(a) *Understatement of Income*

1. An understatement of income attributable to specific transactions, and denial by the taxpayer of the receipt of the income or inability to provide a satisfactory explanation for its omission.
   a. Omissions of specific items where similar items are included. Example: Not reporting $1,000 dividend from Company A, while reporting $50 dividend from Company B.
   b. Omissions of entire sources of income. Example: not reporting tip income.
2. An unexplained failure to report substantial amounts of income determined to have been received. This differs from the omission of specific items in that the understatement is deter-

mined by use of an income reconstruction method (net worth, bank deposits, personal expenditures, etc.).

    a. Substantial unexplained increases in net worth, especially over a period of years.

    b. Substantial excess of personal expenditures over available resources.

    c. Bank deposits from unexplained sources substantially exceeding reported income.

3. Concealment of bank accounts, brokerage accounts, and other property.

4. Inadequate explanation for dealing in large sums of currency, or the unexplained expenditure of currency.

5. Consistent concealment of unexplained currency, especially when in a business not calling for large amounts of cash.

6. Failure to deposit receipts to business account, contrary to normal practices.

7. Failure to file a return, especially for a period of several years although substantial amounts of taxable income were received. Examiners should not solicit delinquent returns where the taxpayer has willfully failed to file. A referral report should be submitted.

8. Covering up sources of receipts of income by false description of source of disclosed income.

(b) *Claiming Fictitious or Improper Deductions*

1. Substantial overstatement of deductions. For example, deducting $5,000 as travel expense when actually the expense was only $1,000.

2. Substantial amounts of personal expenditure deducted as business expenses. For example, deducting rent paid for personal residence as business rent.

3. Inclusion of obviously unallowable items in unrelated accounts. For example, including political contributions in Purchases.

4. Claiming completely fictitious deductions. For example, claiming a deduction for interest when no interest was paid or incurred.

5. Dependency exemption claimed for nonexistent, deceased, or self-supporting persons.

(c) *Accounting irregularities*

1. Keeping two sets of books or no books.

2. False entries or alterations made on the books and records,

backdated or post dated documents, false invoices or statements, other false documents.

3. Failure to keep adequate records, especially if put on notice
by the Service as a result of a prior examination; concealment
of records, or refusal to make certain records available.

4. Variance between treatment of questionable items on the return as compared with books.

5. Intentional under- or over-footing of columns in journal or
ledger.

6. Amounts on return not in agreement with amounts in books.

7. Amounts posted to ledger accounts not in agreement with
source books or records.

8. Journalizing of questionable items out of correct account. For
example: From the Drawing account to an expense account.

(d) *Allocation of income*

1. Distribution of profits to fictitious partners.

2. Inclusion of income or deductions in the return of a related
taxpayer, when difference in tax rates is a factor.

(e) *Acts and Conduct of the Taxpayer*

1. False statement, especially if made under oath, about a material fact involved in the examination. For example, taxpayer
submits an affidavit stating that a claimed dependent lived in
his household when in fact the individual did not.

2. Attempts to hinder the examination. For example, failure to
answer pertinent questions or repeated cancellations of appointments.

3. The taxpayer's knowledge of taxes and business practice
where numerous questionable items appear on the returns.

4. Testimony of employees concerning irregular business practices by the taxpayer.

5. Destruction of books and records, especially if just after examination was started.

6. Transfer of assets for purposes of concealment.

(f) *Other Items*

1. Pattern of consistent failure over several years to report income fully.

2. Proof that the return was incorrect to such an extent and in
respect to items of such character and magnitude as to compel
the conclusion that the falsity was known and deliberate.

(2) The following actions by the taxpayer, standing alone, are usually not sufficient to establish fraud. However, these actions with some of the "badges" listed above, may be indicative of a willful intent to evade tax:

   (a) Refusal to make specific records available. (Examiner should note time and place records were requested.)

   (b) Diversion of portion of business income into personal bank account.

   (c) File return in different district. (This is weak but should be noted.)

   (d) Lack of cooperation by taxpayer. Examiner should cite specific episodes, threats, etc.

(3) The presence of one or more of these "badges" of fraud does not necessarily mean that the return is fraudulent. However, it should alert the examiner to this possibility and invite further and more probing inquiry.

951
REQUIREMENTS OF PROOF

(1) The examiner must be familiar with the following legal terms in order to understand the requirements of proof.

   (a) *Evidence* is all the means by which an alleged matter of fact, the truth of which is submitted to investigation, is established or disproved. Investigators obtain facts which by inference tend to prove and disprove the ultimate, main, or principal fact. *Evidence is distinguished from proof* in that the latter is the result or effect of evidence.

   (b) A *presumption* (of law) is a rule of law that courts and judges shall draw a particular inference from a particular fact, or from particular evidence, unless and until the truth of such inference is disproved.

   (c) An *inference* is a logical conclusion from given facts.

   (d) *Preponderance of evidence* is evidence that will incline an impartial mind to one side rather than the other so as to remove the cause from the realm of speculation. It does not relate merely to the quantity of evidence. It means that the evidence offered produces the stronger impressions upon the mind and is more convincing when weighed against the evidence offered in opposition.

   (e) *Clear and convincing evidence* is that which need not be beyond a reasonable doubt but must be stronger than a mere preponderance of evidence.

(f) *Reasonable doubt*

1. A reasonable doubt is a doubt founded upon a consideration of all the evidence and must be based on reason. Beyond a reasonable doubt does not mean to a moral certainty or beyond a mere possible doubt or an imaginary doubt. It is such a doubt as would deter a reasonably prudent man or woman from acting or deciding in the more important matters involved in his or her own affairs.

2. An understanding of the requirements of proof is essential in establishing fraud. It is necessary to prove actual fraud in a return in order to assert the civil fraud penalty. In those cases in which the statute of limitations would bar an assessment of a deficiency, fraud must be proved in order to make the assessment.

952
BURDEN OF PROOF

Burden of proof is the obligation of the party alleging the affirmative of an issue to prove it. As a general rule, the burden is on the taxpayer to overcome the presumption that the Commissioner's determination is correct. However, in a fraud case, the burden is on the Government to prove the taxpayer intended to evade the tax.

953
DEGREE OF PROOF

(1) The degree of proof required in civil cases is the preponderance of evidence, except where fraud is alleged. In civil fraud cases, "clear and convincing evidence" is necessary in order to prevail on the fraud issue. In civil fraud cases, it is not necessary to prove that the entire deficiency was based on fraud, but only that some part of the deficiency was due to fraud.

(2) In a criminal prosecution case, proof beyond a reasonable doubt is necessary for a conviction. The Criminal Investigation function is responsible for sufficiency of the evidence in all criminal cases.

960
TECHNIQUES OF EXAMINATION

961
GENERAL

(1) The discovery and development of fraud cases is a normal result of effective examinations. Auditing techniques employed by examiners, if they are to be effective, should be designed to disclose not only errors in accounting and application of tax law, but also irregularities that indicate the possibility of fraud. The percentage of returns in which fraud is involved is small. However, examiners should remain alert to recognize the indications of fraud, if they exist. In doubtful situations, consult with the group manager.

(2) Fraud, as defined earlier, involves misrepresentation and concealment. Therefore, fraud will not ordinarily be discovered when examiners readily accept the completeness and accuracy of the records presented and the explanation offered by the taxpayer. To discover fraud, it is oftentimes necessary to go behind the books and to probe beneath the surface. Just when and to what extent an examiner should use these techniques and how far to extend the examination will depend on the examiner's judgment in a particular case. The examination should be extended to the point that the examiner is satisfied that the income reported is substantially correct.

(3) Most fraud cases involve business and professional taxpayers operating as individuals, partnerships or corporations. The reason for this is that these taxpayers have a greater opportunity to understate their income or overstate their deductions than do taxpayers whose primary source of income is from salaries or wages. However, fraud can be and is present in all types of returns.

(4) It is the unusual, inconsistent, or incongruous items which alert examiners to the possibility of fraud, and the need for further investigation.

962
ATTITUDE AND CONDUCT OF THE TAXPAYER

(1) The first symptom alerting the examiner to the possibility of fraud will frequently be provided by the taxpayer. Conduct during the examination and method of doing business may be indicative of the filing

of improper returns. The examiner should be alert to the following actions.

(a) repeated procrastination on the part of the taxpayer in making and keeping appointments for the examination;

(b) uncooperative attitude displayed by not complying with requests for records and not furnishing adequate explanations for discrepancies or questionable items;

(c) failing to keep proper books and records, especially if previously advised to do so;

(d) disregard for books and records;

(e) destroying books and records without a plausible explanation;

(f) making false, misleading, and inconsistent statements;

(g) submitting false documents or affidavits to substantiate items on the return;

(h) altering records;

(i) using currency instead of bank accounts;

(j) engaging in illegal activities;

(k) failing to deposit all receipts; and

(l) quick agreement to adjustments and undue concern about immediate closing of the case may indicate a more thorough examination is needed.

Collection Activity

5223
ANALYSIS OF TAXPAYER'S FINANCIAL CONDITION

(1) The analysis of the taxpayer's financial condition provides the interviewer with a basis to make one or more of the following decisions:

    (a) require payment from available assets;

    (b) secure a short-term agreement or a longer installment agreement;

    (c) report the account currently not collectible;

    (d) recommend or initiate enforcement action (this would also be based on the results of the interview);

    (e) file a Notice of Federal Tax Lien; and/or

    (f) explain the offer in compromise provisions of the Code to the taxpayer.

(2) In all steps that follow, information on the financial statement will be compared with other financial information provided by the taxpayer, particularly the copy of the taxpayer's latest Form 1040. If there are significant discrepancies, they should be discussed with the taxpayer. In the event further documentation is needed, it will be the taxpayer's responsibility to provide it. Discrepancies and their resolution will be noted in the case file history.

(3) Analyze assets to determine ways of liquidating the account:

    (a) if the taxpayer has cash equal to the tax liability, demand immediate payment;

    (b) otherwise, review other assets which may be pledged or readily converted to cash (such as stocks and bonds, loan value of life insurance policies, etc.);

    (c) if necessary, review any unencumbered assets, equity in encumbered assets, interests in estates and trusts, lines of credit (including available credit on bank charge cards), etc., from which money may be secured to make payment. In addition, consider the taxpayer's ability to make an unsecured loan. If the taxpayer belongs to a credit union, the taxpayer will be asked to borrow from that source. Upon identification of potential sources of loans, establish a date that the taxpayer is expected to make payment; and

(d) if there appears to be no borrowing ability, attempt to get the taxpayer to defer payment of other debts in order to pay the tax first.

(4) When analysis of the taxpayer's assets has given no obvious solution for liquidating the liability, the income and expenses should be analyzed.

(a) When deciding what is an allowable expense item, the employee may allow:

1. expenses which are necessary for the taxpayer's production of income (for example, dues for a trade union or professional organization; child care payments which allow a taxpayer to work);

2. expenses which provide for the health and welfare of the taxpayer and family. The expense must be reasonable for the size of the family and the geographic location, as well as any unique individual circumstances. An expense will not be allowed if it serves to provide an elevated standard of living, as opposed to basic necessities. Also, an expense will not be allowed if the taxpayer has a proven record of not making the payment. Expenses allowable under this category are:
   a. rent or mortgage for place of residence;
   b. food;
   c. clothing;
   d. necessary transportation expense (auto insurance, car payment, bus fare, etc.);
   e. home maintenance expense (utilities, home-owner insurance, home-owner dues, etc.);
   f. medical expenses; health insurance;
   g. current tax payments (including federal, state and local);
   h. life insurance, but not if it is excessive to the point of being construed as an investment;
   i. alimony, child support or other court-ordered payment.

3. Minimum payments on secured or legally perfected debts (car payments, judgments, etc.) will normally be allowed. However, if the encumbered asset represents an item which would not be considered a necessary living expense (e.g., a boat, recreational vehicle, etc.), the taxpayer should be advised that the debt payment will not be included as an allowable expense.

4. Payments on unsecured debts (credit cards, personal loans, etc.) may not be allowed if omitting them would permit the

taxpayer to pay in full within 90 days. However, if the tax-payer cannot fully pay within that time, minimum payments may be allowed if failure to make them would ultimately impair the taxpayer's ability to pay the tax. The taxpayer should be advised that since all necessary living expenses have been allowed, no additional charge debts should be incurred. Generally, payments to friends or relatives will not be allowed. Dates for final payments on loans or installment purchases, as well as final payments on revolving credit arrangements after allowing minimum required payments, will be noted so the additional funds will be applied to the liability when they become available. If permitting the taxpayer to pay unsecured debts results in inability to pay or in only having a small amount left for payment of the tax, the taxpayer should be advised that a portion of the money available for payment of debts will be used for payment of the taxes and that arrangements must be made with other creditors accordingly.

(b) As a general rule, expenses not specified in (a) above will be disallowed. However, an otherwise disallowable expense may be included if the employee believes an exception should be made based on the circumstances of the individual case. For instance, if the taxpayer advises that an educational expense or church contribution is a necessity, the individual circumstances must be considered. If an exception is made, document the case history to explain the basis for the exception.

(c) The taxpayer will be required to verify and support any expense which appears excessive based on the income and circumstances of that taxpayer. However, proof of payment does not automatically make an item allowable. The criteria in (4) (a) apply.

(d) In some cases, expense items or payments will not be due in even monthly increments. For instance, personal property tax may be due once a year. Unless the taxpayer substantiates that money is being set aside on a monthly basis, the expense will be allowed in total in the month due and the payment agreement adjusted accordingly for that month. Expense items with varying monthly payments should be averaged over a twelve-month period unless the variation will be excessive. In such instances, exclude the irregular months from the average. For example, if a utility bill will be excessive during the three winter months, average the other nine months.

(e) In arriving at available net income, analyze the taxpayer's deductions to ensure that they are reasonable and allowable. The only automatically allowable deductions from gross pay or income are federal, state and local taxes (including FICA or other mandatory retirement program).

    1. Other deductions from gross pay or income will be treated and listed as expenses, but only to the extent they meet the criteria in (4) (a) above.

    2. To avoid affording the taxpayer a double deduction for one expense, ensure that such amounts remain in the total net pay figure and are also entered on the expense side of the income and expense analysis.

    3. If the exemptions on the W-4 are going to be decreased, make the appropriate adjustments in the net income figures.

(f) To reach an average monthly take-home pay for taxpayers paid on a weekly basis, multiply the weekly pay times 52 weeks divided by 12 months (or multiply amount times 4.3 weeks). If the taxpayer is paid biweekly, multiply pay times 26 weeks divided by 12 months (or multiply amount times $2\frac{1}{6}$). If the taxpayer is paid semimonthly, multiply pay times 2.

(g) The amount to be paid monthly on an installment agreement payment will be at least the difference between the taxpayer's net income and allowable expenses. If the taxpayer will not consent to the proposed installment agreement, he/she should be advised that enforced collection action may be taken. The taxpayer should also be advised that an appeal of the matter may be made to the immediate manager.

(5) When an analysis of the taxpayer's financial condition shows that liquidation of assets and payments from present and future income will not result in full payment, consider the collection potential of an offer in compromise.

5225
VERIFICATION OF TAXPAYER'S FINANCIAL CONDITION

(1) In some cases it will be necessary or desirable to obtain additional information about the taxpayer's financial condition. The extent of the investigation will depend upon the circumstances in each case.

(2) If items appear to be over- or understated, or out of the ordinary, the taxpayer should be asked to explain and substantiate if necessary. The explanation will be documented in the case history. If the expla-

nation is unsatisfactory or cannot be substantiated, the amount should be revised appropriate to the documentation available.

5231.1
GENERAL INSTALLMENT AGREEMENT GUIDELINES

(1) When taxpayers state inability to pay the full amount of their taxes, installment agreements are to be considered.

(2) Future compliance with the tax laws will be addressed and any returns and/or tax due within the period of the agreement must be filed and paid timely.

(3) Levy source information, including complete addresses and ZIP codes, will be secured.

(4) Equal monthly installment payments should be requested. Payment amounts may be increased or decreased as necessary.

(5) Once the determination is made that the taxpayer has the capability to make a regular installment payment, that agreement will be monitored through routine provisions unless the payment amount is less than $10 (in which case the account should be reported currently not collectible). The major benefits of this approach are issuance of reminder and default notices (if the account is system-monitored) and enforcement action if the agreement is not kept.

(6) . . .

(7) The taxpayer should be allowed to select the payment due date(s). But if there is no preference, the date when the taxpayer would generally be in the best financial position to make the payment(s) should be chosen.

(8), (9) . . .

(10) If the interviewer and the taxpayer cannot agree on the amount of installments, the taxpayer should be advised that an appeal may be made to the immediate manager.

(11) An installment agreement which lasts more than two years must be reviewed at the mid-point of the agreement, but in no event less than every two years.

Levy and Sale

5311
INTRODUCTION AND GENERAL CONCEPTS

(1) Under the Internal Revenue Code, levy is defined as the power to collect taxes by distraint or seizure of the taxpayer's assets. Through

levy, we can attach property in the possession of third parties or the taxpayer. Generally, a notice of levy is used to attach funds due the taxpayer from third parties. Levy on property in possession of the taxpayer is accomplished by seizure and public sale of the property. There is no statutory requirement as to the sequence to be followed in levying, but it is generally less burdensome and time consuming to levy on funds in possession of third parties.

(2) Levy authority is far reaching. It permits a continuous attachment of the non-exempt portion of the wage or salary payments due the taxpayer, and the seizure and sale of all the taxpayer's assets except certain property that is specifically exempt by law. Prior to levying on any property belonging to a taxpayer, the Service must notify the taxpayer in writing of the Service's intention to levy. The statute does not require a judgment or other court order before levy action is taken. The Supreme Court decision in the matter of *G.M. Leasing Corporation* v. *United States,* 429 U.S. 338 (1977), held that an entry without a warrant and search of private areas of both residential and business premises for the purpose of seizing and inventorying property pursuant to Internal Revenue Code section 6331 is in violation of the Fourth Amendment. Prior to seizure of property on private premises, a consent to enter for the purpose of seizing or writ of entry from the local courts must be secured.

(3) Procedures are designed (except in jeopardy cases) to give taxpayers a reasonable chance to settle their tax liabilities voluntarily before the more drastic enforcement actions are started. At least one final notice must be issued before service of a notice of levy.

(4) . . .

(5) Under the self-assessment system, a taxpayer is entitled to a reasonable opportunity to voluntarily comply with the revenue laws. This concept should also be followed in connection with levy action. This does not mean that there should be a reluctance to levy if the circumstances justify that action. However, before levy or seizure is taken on an account, the taxpayer must be informed, except in jeopardy situations, that levy or seizure will be the next action taken and given a reasonable opportunity to pay voluntarily. Once the taxpayer has been advised and neglects to make satisfactory arrangements, levy action should be taken expeditiously, but not less than 10 days after notice.

(6) Notification prior to levy must be given in accordance with (2) above. It should be specific that levy action will be the next action taken.

In the event the service center has not sent the taxpayer the 4th notice which includes notice of intention to levy at least 10 days before the levy, the revenue officer must provide the notice to the taxpayer as indicated in (2) above.

(7), (8) . . .

(9) A notice of levy should be served only when there is evidence or reasonable expectation that the third party has property or rights to property of the taxpayer. This concept is of particular significance, since processing of notices of levy is time consuming and often becomes a sensitive matter if it appears the levy action was merely a "fishing expedition."

5312
STATUTORY AUTHORITY TO LEVY

(1) IRC 6331 provides that if any person liable to pay any tax neglects or refuses to pay the tax within 10 days after notice and demand, the tax may be collected by levy upon any property or rights to property belonging to the taxpayer or on which there is a lien.

(2) IRC 6331 also provides that if the Secretary determines that the collection of tax is in jeopardy, immediate notice and demand for payment may be made and, upon the taxpayer's failure to pay the tax, collection may be made by levy without regard to the 10-day period. However, if a sale is required, a public notice of sale may not be issued within the 10-day period unless IRC 6336 (relating to sale of perishable goods) is applicable.

(3) Under the IRC, the term "property" includes all property or rights to property, whether real or personal, tangible or intangible. The term "tax" includes any interest, additional amount, addition to tax, or assessable penalty, together with any cost that may accrue.

(4) Generally, property subject to a Federal tax lien which has been sold or otherwise transferred by the taxpayer, may be levied upon in the hands of the transferee or any subsequent transferee. However, there are exceptions for securities, motor vehicles and certain retail and casual sales.

(5) Levy may be made on any person in possession of, or obligated with respect to, property or rights to property subject to levy. These include, but are not necessarily limited to, receivables, bank accounts,

evidences of debt, securities and accrued salaries, wages, commissions, and other compensation.

(6) The IRC does not require that property be seized in any particular sequence. Therefore, property may be levied upon regardless of whether it is real or personal, tangible or intangible, and regardless of which type of property is levied upon first.

(7) Whenever the proceeds from the levy on any property or rights to property are not sufficient to satisfy the tax liability, additional levies may be made upon the same property, or source of income or any other property or rights to property subject to levy, until the account is fully paid. However, further levies should be timed to avoid hardship to the taxpayer or his/her family.

5314.1
PROPERTY EXEMPT FROM LEVY

(1) IRC 6334 enumerates the categories of property exempt from levy as follows.

   (a) *Wearing apparel and school books necessary for the taxpayer or for members of his family*—No specific value limitation is placed on these items since the intent is to prevent seizing the ordinary clothing of the taxpayer or members of the family. Expensive items of wearing apparel, such as furs, are luxuries and are not exempt from levy.

   (b) *Fuel, provisions and personal effects*—This exemption is applicable only in the case of the head of a family and applies only to so much of the fuel, provisions, furniture, and personal effects of the household and of arms for personal use, livestock, and poultry as does not exceed $1,500 in value.

   (c) *Books and tools of a trade, business or profession*—This exemption is for so many of the books and tools necessary for the trade, business, or profession of the taxpayer as do not exceed in the aggregate $1,000 in value.

   (d) *Unemployment benefits*—This applies to any amount payable to an individual for unemployment (including any portion payable to dependents) under an unemployment compensation law of the United States, any state, the District of Columbia or the Commonwealth of Puerto Rico.

   (e) *Undelivered mail*—Addressed mail which has not been delivered to the addressee.

(f) *Certain annuity and pension payments.*

(g) *Workmen's compensation*—Any amount payable to an individual as workmen's compensation (including any portion payable to dependents) under a workmen's compensation law of the United States, any state, the District of Columbia, or the Commonwealth of Puerto Rico.

(h) *Judgment for support of minor children*—If the taxpayer is required by judgment of a court of competent jurisdiction, entered prior to the date of levy, to contribute to the support of his/her minor children, so much of his/her salary, wages, or other income as is necessary to comply with such judgment.

(i) *Minimum Exemption from Levy on Wages, Salary and Other Income*— IRC 6334(a) (9) limits the effect of levy on wages, salary and other income, by an amount of $75 per week for the taxpayer and an additional $25 a week for the spouse and each dependent claimed by the taxpayer. Income not paid or received on a weekly basis will, for the purpose of computing exemptions, be apportioned as if received on a weekly basis.

(2) In addition, Public Law 89–538 exempts deposits to the special Treasury fund made by servicemen and servicewomen (including officers) and Public Health Service employees on permanent duty assignment outside the United States or its possessions.

(3) Except for the exemptions in (1) and (2) above, no other property or rights to property are exempt from levy. No provision of state law can exempt property or rights to property from levy for the collection of federal taxes. The fact that property is exempt from execution under state personal or homestead exemption laws does not exempt the property from federal levy.

(4) The revenue officer seizing property of the type described in (1) (a), (b), and (c) above should appraise and set aside to the owner the amount of property to be exempted.

538(10)
RECORDS OF ATTORNEYS, PHYSICIANS, AND ACCOUNTANTS

(1) Records maintained by attorneys, physicians, and accountants concerning professional services performed for clients are usually of little intrinsic value and possess minimum sale value. Questions of confidential or privileged information contained in these records may cause complications if the records are seized. Additionally, the case files of

the professional person frequently either are, or contain, property of the client, and therefore to this extent are not subject to seizure. Accordingly, it is not believed desirable to seize case files or records for payment of the taxpayer's tax liabilities.

(2) When office facilities or office equipment of attorneys, physicians, or public accountants are seized for payment of taxes, case files and related files in seized office facilities or office equipment of such persons will not be personally examined by the revenue officer even though information concerning accounts receivable may be contained in the files. When storage facilities (filing cabinets, etc.) are seized, the taxpayer should be requested to remove all case files promptly.

538(11)
SAFE DEPOSIT BOXES

538(11).1
GENERAL

(1) The procedures outlined below should be followed in an attempt to secure the opening of a taxpayer's safe deposit box in instances in which the taxpayer's consent to or cooperation in opening the box cannot be obtained.

(2) Ordinarily two keys are used to open a safe deposit box: a master key held by the bank or trust company which owns the box and an individual key in the possession of the person who rents the box.

(3) Irrespective of the possession of the necessary equipment to do so, it is not to be expected that a bank or trust company will open a safe deposit box without the consent of the lessee of the box unless protected by a court order. Under these circumstances the government must prevent the taxpayer from having access to the box, or obtain a court order directing that the box be opened, by force if necessary.

(4) At the time that a safety deposit is secured, Publication 787, Seal for Securing Safety Deposit Boxes, will be signed by the revenue officer and affixed over the locks for security while the box remains under seizure. When the box is eventually opened, all residue from the seal should be removed by the revenue officer, or the bank official in the revenue officer's presence, with isopropyl alcohol or a similar solvent. To avoid damage to the safety deposit box, no sharp implement or abrasive substance should be used. The seal will dissolve when saturated with alcohol and rubbed with a cloth.

538(11).2
PREVENTING ACCESS TO SAFE DEPOSIT BOX

(1) A notice of lien should be filed prior to seizure since assets other than cash may be in the safe deposit box.

(2) A notice of levy, Form 668-A, with a copy of the notice of lien attached, should be served on an officer of the bank or trust company and request made for surrender of the contents of the box.

(3) . . .

(4) The official may advise that the institution does not have the necessary key to open the safe deposit box or that the institution does not have the authority to open it. He/she may also suggest that the lessee's (taxpayer's) consent be secured, or that a court order be obtained to open the box.

(5) Under these circumstances, the revenue officer should not insist that the box be opened and no attempt should be made to have the box opened by force. The box should be sealed by affixing a seizure notice, Publication 787, Seal for Securing Safety Deposit Boxes. It should be placed over the locks in such a manner so that the box cannot be opened without removing, tearing or destroying the affixed seal. The bank or trust company should then be advised not to permit the box to be opened except in the presence of a revenue officer.

(6), (7) . . .

(8) Usually, taxpayers who have been reluctant to cooperate will eventually find it necessary to open their boxes, and will only be able to do so in the presence of a revenue officer. At that time, the revenue officer, with Form 668-B in his/her possession, will be in a position to seize any property in the box.

(9) When the rental period of the safe deposit box expires and is not renewed, a bank or trust company usually has the right and power to open the box. The revenue officer should attempt to ascertain the true situation in any given case, and if the right and power exists, should try to take advantage of this opportunity to seize the contents of the box.

538(11).3
OBTAINING COURT ORDER TO OPEN

(1) Occasionally, the procedure outlined in IRM 538(11).2 will not be satisfactory and immediate action may be desirable or necessary. For instance, the statute of limitations may be about to expire, the taxpayer

may have disappeared or be in concealment, or the taxpayer or bank officials may refuse cooperation and deny access to a safe deposit box.

(2) Under these circumstances a Summons should be prepared and served on the taxpayer-boxholder in an attempt to secure information as to the contents of the box and to gain access. If this action does not accomplish the desired results, a writ of entry should be sought or a suit requested to open the safe deposit box.

Currently Not Collectible Accounts

5610
DETERMINATION OF CURRENTLY NOT COLLECTIBLE TAXES

5611
GENERAL

(1) A Collection employee may determine that the accounts are currently not collectible.

(2) Reporting an account currently not collectible does not abate the assessment. It only stops current efforts to collect it. Collection can start again any time before the statutory period for collection expires.

5632
UNABLE-TO-PAY CASES—HARDSHIP

5632.1
GENERAL

(1) If collection of the liability would prevent the taxpayer from meeting necessary living expenses, it may be reported currently not collectible under a hardship closing code. Sometimes accounts should be reported currently not collectible even though the Collection Information Statement (CIS) shows assets or sources of income subject to levy.

(a) [The Manual] provides guidelines for analyzing the taxpayer's financial condition.
(b) Since each taxpayer's circumstances are unique, other factors such as age and health must be considered as appropriate.
(c) Document and verify the taxpayer's financial condition.
(d) Consider the collection potential of an offer in compromise.

(2) Consider an installment agreement before reporting an account currently not collectible as hardship.

Offers in Compromise

5712
GROUNDS FOR COMPROMISE

5712.1
GENERAL GUIDELINES

The compromise of a tax liability can only rest upon doubt as to liability, doubt as to collectibility, or doubt as to both liability and collectibility. IRC 7122 does not confer authority to compromise tax, interest, or penalty where the liability is clear and there is no doubt as to the ability of the Government to collect. To compromise there must be room for mutual concessions involving either or both doubt as to liability or doubt as to ability to pay. This rules out, as grounds for compromise, equity or public policy considerations peculiar to a particular case, individual hardships, and similar matters which do not have a direct bearing on liability or ability to pay.

5713.2
ADVISING TAXPAYERS OF OFFER PROVISIONS

(1) When criminal proceedings are not contemplated and an analysis of taxpayer's assets, liabilities, income and expenses shows that a liability cannot realistically be paid in full in the foreseeable future, the collection potential of an offer in compromise should be considered. While it is difficult to outline the exact circumstances when an offer would be the appropriate collection tool, the existence of any of the following should govern offer consideration.

(a) Liquidation of assets and payments from present and future income will not result in full payment of tax liability.

(b) A non-liable spouse has property which he/she may be interested in utilizing to secure a compromise of spouse's tax debt.

(c) The taxpayer has an interest in assets against which collection action cannot be taken. For example, the taxpayer who owes a separate liability, has an interest in property held in "tenancy by the entirety" which cannot be reached or subjected to the Notice of Federal Tax Lien because of the provisions of state law. Under the compromise procedures, the taxpayer's interest is included in the total assets available in arriving at an acceptable offer in compromise.

(d) The taxpayer has relatives or friends who may be willing to lend or give the taxpayer funds for the sole purpose of reaching a compromise with the Service.

5721
GENERAL

The offer in compromise is the taxpayer's written proposal to the Government and, if accepted, is an agreement enforceable by either party under the law of contracts. Therefore, it must be definite in its terms and conditions, since it directly affects the satisfaction of the tax liability.

5723.1
PRESCRIBED FORM

A taxpayer seeking to compromise a tax liability based on doubt as to collectibility must submit Form 433, Statement of Financial Condition and Other Information. This form includes questions geared to develop a full and complete description of the taxpayer's financial situation.

5723.3
REFUSAL TO SUBMIT FINANCIAL STATEMENT

If a taxpayer professing inability to pay refuses to submit the required Form 433, the offer will be immediately rejected since the Service cannot determine whether the amount offered is also the maximum amount collectible.

5725.1
LIABILITY OF HUSBAND AND WIFE

(1) Under IRC 6013(d)(3), the liability for income tax on a joint return by husband and wife is expressly made "joint and several." Either or both of the spouses are liable for the entire amount of the tax shown on a joint return. When the liability of both parties is sought to be compromised, the offer should be submitted in the names of and signed by both spouses in order to make the waiver and other provisions of the offer form effective against both parties.

(2) An "innocent spouse" may be relieved of liability in certain cases under IRC 6013(e) and IRC 6653(b). In the event that one of the jointly

liable taxpayers claims to be an "innocent spouse," the question should be referred to the district Examination function for determination.

(a) Should the offer be acceptable, the report should not be prepared until after the district Examination function has made its determination. Since a favorable decision for the party claiming "innocent spouse" will change the amount of the liability sought to be compromised, any recommendation for acceptance must reflect the redetermined liability.

5740
INVESTIGATION OF OFFERS

5741.1
GENERAL

(1) Once an offer in compromise is received in Special Procedures function, a determination whether the offer merits further consideration must be made. SPf should use all information contained in the offer file and may consult with the revenue officer assigned the TDAs [tax deficiency assessments] to obtain additional financial information or verify existing information.

(2) Summary rejection in SPf can be made on the grounds that the offer is frivolous, was filed merely to delay collection, or where there is no basis for compromise. A desk review of the offer can result in this determination. Although not all-inclusive, the following list provides guidelines on the criteria for summary rejection most often encountered:

(a) Taxpayer has equity in assets subject to the Federal tax lien clearly in excess of the total liability sought to be compromised,

(b) The total liability is extremely large and the taxpayer has offered only a minimal sum well below his/her equity and earnings potential (e.g., offering $100 to compromise a $50,000 tax liability). Although the taxpayer could be persuaded to raise the offer, the fact that this initial amount offered was so low indicates bad faith and the desire to delay collection,

(c) The taxpayer is not current in his/her filing or payment requirements for periods not included in the offer,

(d) The taxpayer refuses to submit a complete financial statement (Form 433),

(e) Acceptance of the offer would adversely affect the image of the government,

(f) Taxpayer has submitted a subsequent offer which is not significantly different from a previously rejected offer and the taxpayer's financial condition has not changed,

(g) In cases involving doubt as to liability for the 100-percent penalty, the liability is clearly established and the taxpayer has offered no new evidence to cast doubt on its validity.

5741.2
PUBLIC POLICY

(1) An accepted offer, like any contract, is an agreement between two parties resulting from a "meeting of the minds". It is incumbent upon each party to negotiate the best terms possible. Normally, the offer and subsequent negotiations are of a private nature. However, when accepting an offer, the Service is in a unique position since it represents the government's interest in the negotiations and the accepted offer becomes part of public record. Therefore, public policy dictates that an offer can be rejected if public knowledge of the agreement is detrimental to the government's interest. The offer may be rejected even though it can be shown conclusively that the amounts offered are greater than could reasonably be collected in any other manner. Because the Government would be in the position of foregoing revenue, the circumstances in which public policy considerations could be used to reject the offer must be construed very strictly. The following may be used as a guideline for instances where public policy issues are most often encountered:

(a) Taxpayer's notoriety is such that acceptance of an offer will hamper future Service collection and/or compliance efforts. However, simply because the taxpayer is famous or well-known is not a basis in and of itself for rejecting the offer on public policy grounds.

(b) There is a possibility of establishing a precedent which might lead to numerous offers being submitted on liabilities incurred as a result of occupational drives to enforce tax compliance.

(c) Taxpayer has been recently convicted of tax related crimes. Again, the notoriety of the individual should be considered when making a public policy determination. The publicity surrounding the case, taxpayer's compliance since the case was concluded, or the taxpayer's position in the community should all be considered prior to rejecting an otherwise acceptable offer.

(d) Situations where it is suspected that the financial benefits of criminal activity are concealed or the criminal activity is continuing would normally preclude acceptance of the offer for public policy reasons. Criminal Investigation function should be contacted to coordinate the Government's action in these cases.

ABOUT THE AUTHORS

SANDOR FRANKEL is a trial lawyer in New York City. His law firm, Bender & Frankel, specializes in the defense of tax fraud cases during IRS investigations and at trial. Mr. Frankel has defended innumerable such cases and has written and lectured professionally on the subject. A former federal prosecutor, he has also served with President Johnson's White House Task Force on Crime and as counsel to the National Commission on Reform of Federal Criminal Laws. Mr. Frankel is a graduate of the Harvard Law School and a member of Phi Beta Kappa. His previous books have received wide critical acclaim, including *Beyond A Reasonable Doubt* which was awarded the Edgar Allan Poe Prize as the Best True Crime Book of the Year in America.

ROBERT S. FINK, a trial lawyer and partner in the nationally prominent New York law firm Kostelanetz & Ritholz, specializes in the civil and criminal defense of taxpayers. Mr. Fink is chairman of both the American Bar Association's Committee on Civil and Criminal Tax Penalties and the New York State Bar Association's Committee on Unreported Income and Compliance. He is a member of the Advisory Committee to the Tax Division of the United States Department of Justice. Mr. Fink has testified as an expert witness on the IRS's investigative powers before subcommittees of both houses of Congress. He is the author of the two-volume legal treatise entitled *Tax Fraud: Audits, Investigations, Prosecutions* as well as numerous articles, and is a frequent lecturer on those subjects to legal and accounting groups and to agents of the IRS. Mr. Fink holds J.D. and LL.M. degrees from New York University School of Law.

Robert Piper

AUTHOR

Little Red

TITLE

DATE DUE	BORROWER'S NAME	ROOM NUMBER
NOV 27	Jalisha M.	
DEC 24		
Jan 2		
14		

DEMCO 32-239

DATE DUE	BORROWER'S NAME	ROOM NUMBER